By the Same Author

WITH ENSIGNS FLYING
The Story of British Destroyers in World War II

SUBMARINE VICTORY
The Story of British Submarines in World War II

BATTLE OF THE JAVA SEA

CRETE 1941: THE BATTLE AT SEA
(Published in the USA as NAZI VICTORY)

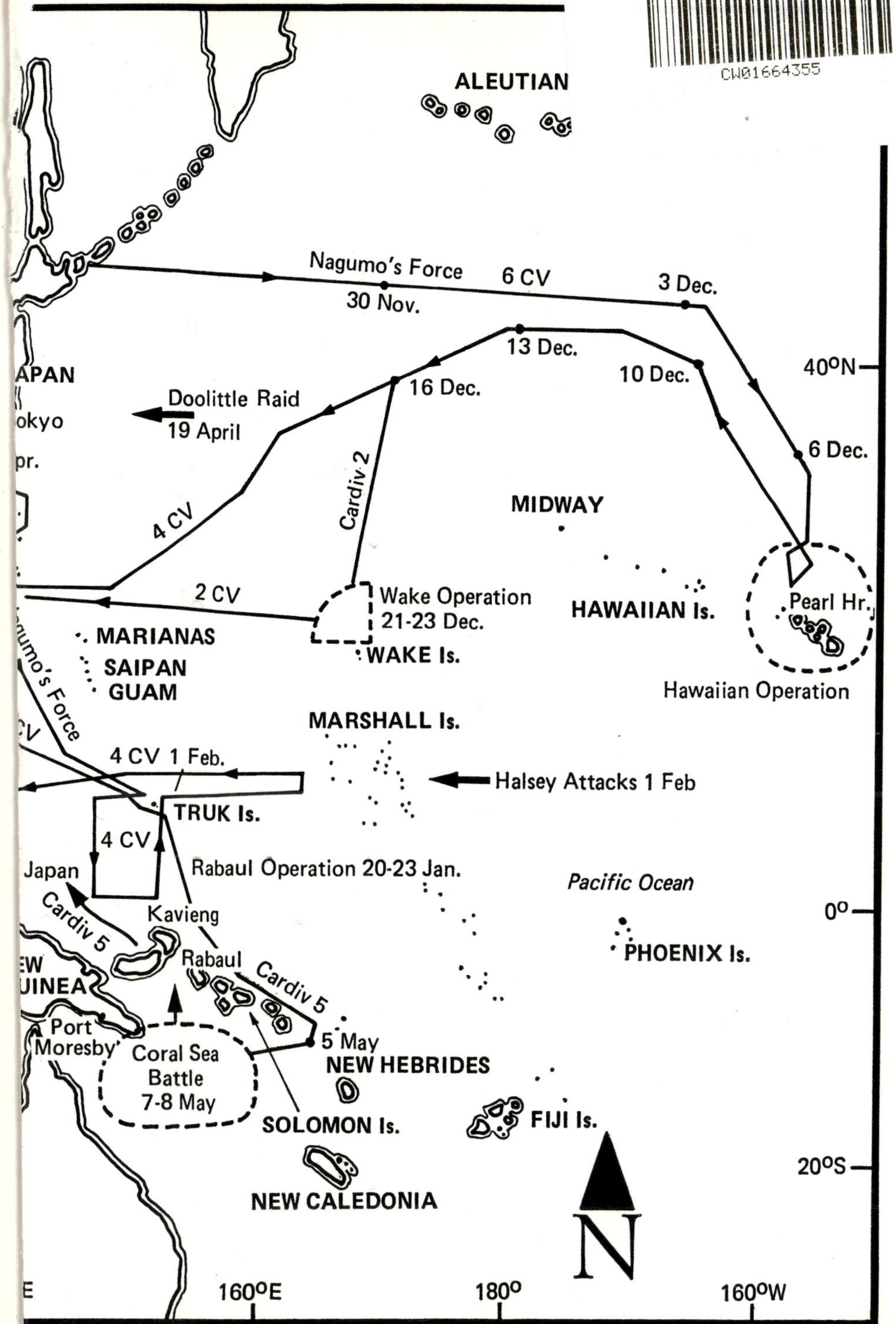

Japan's War at Sea

JAPAN'S WAR AT SEA

Pearl Harbor to the Coral Sea

David A. Thomas

ANDRE DEUTSCH

First published 1978 by
André Deutsch Limited
105 Great Russell Street London WC1

Printed in Great Britain by
Cox & Wyman Limited
London, Fakenham and Reading

ISBN 0 233 97011 8

'In less than two generations, with no background but the remote past the Japanese people advanced from the two-handed sword of the Samurai to the iron-clad ship, the rifled cannon, the torpedo and the Maxim gun . . . The transition of Japan under British and American guidance from the Middle Ages to modern times was swift and violent.'

WINSTON S. CHURCHILL
The Second World War
Vol III
The Grand Alliance

Contents

Appendices

List of Plates

List of Figures

Acknowledgments

I AM INDEBTED to a great number of people and organisations throughout the world for their generous help in the preparation of this book.

Foremost among the individuals who deserve mention is my naval historian friend Günter Schomaekers from Germany. He has been a constant source of encouragement and has helped immeasurably by suggesting new lines of research and by providing information. He kindly read the book in manuscript and corrected many errors. I gratefully acknowledge his kindness.

I am grateful to Lady C. Crace, widow of the late Admiral Sir John Crace, for her help and guidance and to J. A. F. Somerville, son of the late Admiral Sir James Somerville. Mr and Mrs S. H. Twyman generously provided photographs, newscuttings and mementoes of HMS *Cornwall*'s last commission.

Frank C. Kennerley, Borough Librarian of the London Borough of Redbridge, and his staff were unfailing in their help in obtaining books for my research including many obscure and foreign volumes.

Roderick Suddaby, Keeper of the Department of Documents at the Imperial War Museum kindly made available the papers of the late Captain A. W. S. Agar VC, of Admiral Sir John Crace and of Paymaster Commander E. F. McNeil-Smith.

R. E. Squires of the Imperial War Museum's Photographic Library, once again put at my disposal his profound knowledge of the naval photographic collection.

I acknowledge the help, too, of the Public Records Office and of the Naval Historical Branch of the Ministry of Defence.

The US Naval authorities extended their customary high standard of assistance and cooperation in the provision of photocopies of documents, reports, charts, photographs and a wealth of information. Dr D. C. Allard, Head, Operational Archives Branch, Department of the Navy, receives my grateful thanks as does Robert A.

Carlisle, Head, Still Photographic Branch, Office of Information, Department of the Navy. The Navy History Division, Office of the Chief of Naval Operations, the US Naval Photographic Center, the Office of Naval Intelligence, the Biographical Branch of the Department and the National Archives in Washington were all liberal with their help and earn my gratitude.

I am grateful, too, to the United States Naval Institute, Annapolis and to Professor Paul S. Dull, Oregon University, for his information on the *Tabular Record of Movements* of Japanese ships.

I am appreciative of the kind help provided by A. J. Sweeting, Acting Director of the Australian War Memorial, for providing me with much information and referring me to the Department of Defence (Navy Office), in the archival-historical section of which the late George H. Gill worked on primary source material for the Australian element of the naval operations recounted here.

The Chief of the War History Office of the Japanese Defence Agency in Tokyo kindly provided me with much information and I also acknowledge the help of Raita Ogawa, Vice President of Koku Shinbun Sha, of Captain H. Sato, Defence Attaché, Embassy of Japan in London and of Bernard Millot, the French naval historian.

I also wish to put on record the help given by L. L. von Münching of the Office of Naval History, The Hague, for providing valuable information from his forthcoming book on the history of the Dutch merchant navy in World War II which has formed the basis of Appendices C and D.

Many publishers and authors have kindly consented to my quoting from their works and my thanks are due to the following: *Midway: The Battle that Doomed Japan* by M. Fuchida and M. Okumiya, Hutchinson & Co; *Hitler's Table Talk 1941–1944: His Private Conversations*, Weidenfeld & Nicolson; *History of the United States Naval Operations in World War II*, Vol IV by Samuel Eliot Morison, Little Brown & Co Inc, in association with The Atlantic Monthly Press; *Australia in the War of 1939–1945*, Vol II by George H. Gill, Australian War Memorial; *Fighting Admiral* by Captain D. McIntyre, Evans Bros; *Queen of the FlatTops* by Stanley Johnson, Jarrolds (Publishers); *Zero!* by M. Okumiya, Cassell & Co; *The Second World War*, Vol III, by Sir Winston Churchill, Cassell & Co; *Darwin: Australia's Pearl Harbour* by Douglas Lockwood, Cassell, Australia.

ACKNOWLEDGMENTS

The Director of Publications and Her Majesty's Stationery Office have granted permission to quote from War Cabinet Minutes and Chief of Staff Memoranda in the Public Records Office, Captain Agar's *Report* and *Supplementary Report*, Admiral Sir John Crace's *Report*, *Letter* to Sir Guy Royle and *War Diary*, Admiral Sir Dudley Pound's *Minute* and Field Marshal Earl Wavell's *Despatch*, all identified in footnotes to the main text.

D.A.T.

Preface

THIS BOOK IS ABOUT battle at sea. Its prime objective is to chronicle the story of the Imperial Japanese Navy's aircraft carriers during the period immediately following their strike at Pearl Harbor and ending before their defeat at the Battle of Midway. The story reveals a chain of events, unprecedented in the long history of naval warfare. These events dominated the struggle for naval, military and aerial supremacy in the Indian and Pacific Oceans during the early and formative months of the war with Japan. The annals of war at sea present no more startling and dramatic scenes than the raid on Pearl Harbor, the annihilation of Force Z, the Battle of the Java Sea, the Indian Ocean strike, the Battle of the Coral Sea and the Battle of Midway. In all of them the role of airpower, relatively new and untried in naval warfare, played a large part. It also made the speed of action and twists of fortune fiercer than ever before.

It is not the purpose of this book to relate the story of Pearl Harbor nor of the Battle of Midway, for the documentation covering these is bulky and their stories have often been told. Indeed, these two events have so over-shadowed the complex struggle for naval ascendancy in the eastern theatre that the intervening battles and engagements, many of them of appreciable consequence, have been glossed over and almost lost to sight. These engagements are less well documented and less known, but they deserve recording so that they may take their place in the story of those few tempestuous months.

The months January to May 1942 saw the Japanese carrier strike at Rabaul, the vicious attack upon Darwin, the mopping-up operations in the seas to the south of Java, the foray into the Indian Ocean, the clash with units of the British Eastern Fleet, the attacks upon Colombo and Trincomalee, the curious operation against merchant shipping in the Bay of Bengal, the plan to invade Port Moresby and the ensuing Battle of the Coral Sea.

The Japanese admirals involved in these events were Vice

Admiral Chuichi Nagumo, Rear Admiral Tamon Yamaguchi, Vice Admiral Jisaburo Ozawa, Rear Admiral Takeo Takagi and Rear Admiral Chuichi Hara. Of these, Nagumo was outstandingly successful and earned a formidable reputation among both friend and foe: a reputation marred only by the treachery of the attack on Pearl Harbor and lost irrevocably in the Battle of Midway.

He and his Carrier Striking Force ranged almost unmolested over thousands of square miles of ocean, dominating a whole theatre of war. It is difficult to discover a parallel in naval history to the achievements and maraudings of Nagumo's Carrier Force, both for its wide-ranging scope and for the concentrated intensity of its attacks.

During a period of little more than four months, beginning with the outbreak of war in the Pacific, Nagumo's forces shattered the US Pacific Fleet, inflicted heavy losses upon the Royal Navy and put to flight Admiral Sir James Somerville's hastily assembled and oddly assorted Eastern Fleet, struck at merchant shipping, destroyed oil, dock and shore installations in places as far apart as Rabaul in New Britain, Tjilatjap in Java, Port Darwin in Australia's Northern Territory, the insignificant township of Amboina, Ceylon's capital of Colombo and the fleet base at Trincomalee. Other Japanese carriers – the new *Shokaku* and *Zuikaku* forming the 5th Carrier Squadron under the command of Rear Admiral Takagi – fought the Battle of the Coral Sea, heralded by both sides as a considerable victory. And it was yet another admiral who was responsible for the Bay of Bengal strike. Vice Admiral Ozawa commanded the Malaya Force which ranged throughout the Bay at will sinking an armada of merchantmen totalling over 93,000 tons.* This in itself was a curious venture. Hitherto the Imperial Japanese Navy had restricted its activities to attacking enemy warships. A mission specifically mounted to attack merchant shipping had not been undertaken before, nor was the operation ever to be repeated.

In these few months Nagumo's Force had operated through 120 degrees of longitude, marauding and plundering its way across one-third of the world's surface from Hawaii in the Pacific to faraway Ceylon in the Indian Ocean. During this period – up to the end of April – his Carrier Striking Force had sunk five battleships,† one

*See Appendix C for details.

†Two became a total loss, *Arizona* and *Oklahoma*: three others were sunk or beached but salvaged later, *West Virginia, California* and *Nevada.*

aircraft carrier, two heavy cruisers and seven destroyers: it had damaged several more capital ships and it had destroyed hundreds of Allied aircraft. Yet not a single ship of Nagumo's Force had been sunk or even damaged! Seldom sighted, it was never effectively attacked and the only sign of battle it bore was the blistered paintwork on its gun barrels. Judged by any standards Nagumo's ships had scored a series of staggering victories.

Now, with the passage of time, we can see these Japanese successes more clearly and it becomes apparent that of Nagumo's many ventures, two were crucial and deserve comment: the Indian Ocean sortie and the Battle of the Coral Sea. The time wasted on the former and the losses suffered in the latter were to have grave and far-reaching consequences for Japan's navy.

A claim, often repeated, that the Indian Ocean sortie was costly to the Japanese in terms of aircraft, and more importantly, of aircrews, is not supported by the record which suggests that they lost less than ten aircraft out of a force numbering about 400. The operation proved far costlier to the RAF.

What the Indian Ocean operation did cost the Japanese was time: and the few weeks – from 26 March 1942 when Nagumo's force left Staring Bay in the South Celebes until late in April when it arrived back in the homeland – gave the American Navy some respite, a desperately needed breather which they put to good use.

The more one considers this phase of Nagumo's career the more one hardens to the view that the Indian Ocean sortie, crowned though it was with the sinking of the carrier *Hermes*, and the cruisers *Dorsetshire* and *Cornwall*, was a serious blunder. If Admiral Yamamoto, the C-in-C Combined Fleet, had had the strategical wisdom not to embark on the venture, the Japanese forces could have been strengthened at the Battle of the Coral Sea in the following month: the denial of this additional strength allowed a US carrier to escape destruction; and one month later still, in June, the outcome of the Battle of Midway itself could have been affected.*

As for the losses suffered by the Japanese in the Coral Sea

*Described by so many historians as 'decisive' or more grandly as 'one of the most decisive battles of history'. And again as 'a true turning point in history'. But the battle's significance is summed up best by Captain S. W. Roskill: 'Just as Trafalgar did not of itself bring victory in the Napoleonic War, the Battle of Midway did not decide the struggle for the Pacific.' What it did achieve was a restoration in the balance of power.

engagements, the sinking of the light carrier *Shoho* and the damaging of the fleet carrier *Shokaku* cannot, of course, be judged serious in themselves. They were, in fact, outweighed by the losses inflicted upon the US task forces – especially the sinking of the majestic fleet carrier *Lexington* and the damaging of the carrier *Yorktown*. There were, however, other significant aspects of the Coral Sea battle such as its being the first in the annals of war at sea in which the opposing warships never came within sight of each other: the offensive activity between the contestants was effected almost exclusively by naval aircraft thus underlining the lessons of Taranto and Pearl Harbor that the aircraft carrier had superseded the battleship as the main arm of the navy. The battle was also the first of the Pacific war in which a Japanese invasion was thwarted. More importantly – for the Americans – the Coral Sea engagements blooded scores of pilots whose combat experience over these blue waters stood them in good stead at Midway in the following month.

CHAPTER I

Eruption in the East

FOR THE ALLIED navies 1942 began as badly in the Pacific as the convulsive year of 1941 had closed. Nor did the future seem any brighter in the European theatre. 1941 had been a year of mounting and calamitous losses for the Royal Navy in the Atlantic, the Mediterranean and latterly in the Gulf of Siam. Losses in the dying days of May, while the Battle of Crete swayed first one way then the other, mounted alarmingly. Admiral Sir Andrew Cunningham's Mediterranean Fleet endured determined and relentless *Luftwaffe* attacks losing one ship after another. Four cruisers were lost – the *Fiji*, the modern *Gloucester*, the 10,000 ton *York** and the little AA cruiser *Calcutta*. Six destroyers went down under the accuracy of the Stuka dive bombers' aim – *Juno, Greyhound, Kashmir, Kelly, Hereward* and *Imperial*. Two more destroyers, *Nubian* and *Kelvin*, would be out of the war for months with severe damage and another six suffered varying degrees of damage. Furthermore, two battleships, the carrier *Formidable* and five more cruisers were seriously damaged.

It was the same *Luftwaffe* that had launched countless attacks upon the carrier *Ark Royal*, but it was a U-boat's torpedo which finally put paid to her Mediterranean commission; she sank only a few miles from the sanctuary of Gibraltar's harbour.

Earlier, in May 1941, at the beginning of the epic chase of the mighty German battleship *Bismarck* during her sortie into the waters of the north Atlantic, the pride of the Royal Navy, the magnificent 42,000-ton battle-cruiser *Hood*, symbol of Imperial might and splendour, exploded in frightening testimony to the accuracy of *Bismarck*'s gunnery, leaving only three survivors from a ship's company of over 1400.

Equally spectacular was the end of the veteran battleship *Barham*

*Actually sunk by Italian charioteers in Suda Bay but still capable of being used as an AA bastion until bombed to become a total loss.

which blew up in a gigantic burst of flame and smoke as a result of three torpedoes from *U-331* off Sollum. She sank leaving a pall of dense smoke towering hundreds of feet aloft to mark the loss of more than 500 men.

After just two years of war against a powerful Germany the Royal Navy had suffered the loss of no less than thirty-one submarines and fifty-six destroyers in the Atlantic and Mediterranean. Each loss necessitated an Admiralty re-appraisal of ship dispositions and meant robbing one theatre as a calculated risk to meet the mounting peril in another. It was for this reason that the eastern theatre with its uneasy peace was depleted of warships, until the increasing Japanese threat necessitated a change of emphasis and the battle-cruiser *Repulse* and the battleship *Prince of Wales* were despatched as a deterrent by a reluctant Admiralty spurred on by the insistence of the Prime Minister.

But by 11 December 1941 the Japanese had assembled a powerful air fleet in the Gulf of Siam numbering 200 aircraft of modern design manned by crews who had gained experience and skill in aerial warfare above the towns and fields of China. The two British ships were sunk in a brief encounter with almost scornful ease. In a trice Japanese aircraft had upset months of careful British planning and long periods of politico-naval wrangling and had shifted the balance of naval power overnight.

Before the year of 1941 closed other losses were to be suffered by the Royal Navy in the Mediterranean. On the night of 18 December an audacious attack was launched upon the British battle fleet at anchor in Alexandria harbour. Italian saboteurs laid time-fused mines beneath the hulls of the battleships *Queen Elizabeth* and *Valiant*. Early in the morning of the nineteenth the mines detonated and opened up an eighty-foot hole in the bottom of *Valiant* and blasted another gash forty feet square beneath the boilers of *Queen Elizabeth*. Both battleships settled on the mud of the harbour and were useless burdens for many months.

Nor was this the end of Cunningham's misfortunes. The successful Force K which had ravaged Axis convoys across the Mediterranean supplying and fortifying the *Afrika Korps* was itself ravaged by a minefield. Approaching Tripoli the Force ran into a newly-laid minefield the first indication of which was when the cruiser *Neptune* struck a mine and suffered severe damage. The cruisers *Aurora* and *Penelope* were both damaged by explosions but they managed to extricate themselves from the field. The destroyer *Kandahar* made an attempt to approach the stricken *Neptune* but she herself was mined. She lay helpless in the water until she eventually drifted clear and her crew was taken off by a sister destroyer. The *Neptune*'s story ended less happily. She drifted helplessly, detonated two more mines and finally sank. Of her crew of 700 only one man survived.

Thus, by the end of 1941, Admiral Cunningham's Mediterranean Fleet had been reduced to a parlous state: he no longer had even one seaworthy battleship: his cruiser strength could be counted on the fingers of one hand and his destroyers numbered a mere handful. With the Battle of the Atlantic still being fiercely contested, with the Mediterranean Fleet at its lowest ebb, with the sinking of Force Z in the Gulf of Siam, the Royal Navy's strength had reached its nadir. The price of admiralty, in ships as well as blood, was high.

But by now even more menacing events had erupted in the east. Japan, in an act of infamy, had struck at Pearl Harbor. The US Pacific Fleet now joined the Royal Navy in tasting the bitterness of defeat and loss.

Japan had embarked upon a well prepared war plan. The strike at Pearl Harbor was a means of preventing the US Pacific Fleet from interfering with a complex, multi-pronged southward military thrust to seize the vital oil, rubber and tin supplies in the East Indies and Malaya. The plan then allowed for the establishment of a defensive perimeter of this 'Southern Resources Area' sweeping in a broad arc from the Andamans in the Bay of Bengal to the far away Bismarck Archipelago. The perimeter to the north and east – completing the limits of the new Japanese Empire – would follow a line running from the Kuriles through Wake Island and the Caroline and Marshall Islands. Phase II of the Japanese plan covered the consolidation and strengthening of this perimeter.

The primary Japanese objectives had been accomplished with almost contemptuous ease – with a few valiant exceptions – and this engendered a false sense of security and even invincibility among Japan's leaders. This is readily understandable.

Victory is often the harvest of careful and thoughtful planning. A key element in Japan's forward planning for the defence of her homeland had been the creation of 'unsinkable' carriers – the construction of airfields on the islands of the mandated Marianas,

Carolines and Marshalls together with the building of fast fleet carriers. All of this intense activity took place throughout the 1930s; and it seemed to have proved successful as a foundation for offence.

By 1 October 1941 Japan had created two important naval commands. The first was the Eleventh Air Fleet, a land-based command in the hands of Vice Admiral Nishizo Tsukahara. The other – and most vital – was the First Air Fleet, the command of which was given to Rear Admiral Chuichi Nagumo. It comprised the 1st Carrier Squadron comprising *Akagi* (36,500 tons) and *Kaga* (38,200 tons): the 2nd Carrier Squadron under the flag of Rear Admiral Tamon Yamaguchi in *Hiryu* (17,300 tons) with *Soryu* (15,900 tons): the 5th Carrier Squadron commanded by Rear Admiral Chuichi Hara aboard the newly commissioned *Zuikaku* with *Shokaku*, both of 25,675 tons: each squadron of carriers was screened by its own cruisers and destroyers.

Nagumo had as his Air Operations Officer Commander Minoru Genda, acknowledged to be the country's leading carrier tactician. Now that he held this key position, Commander Genda was able to influence plans and policies. The First Air Fleet adopted his far-sighted ideas. Fast carriers, for example, would now operate in a concentrated tactical formation for mutual defence, providing a greater volume of AA fire and necessitating fewer defensive aircraft. Destroyers would serve as screening vessels. Fuelling of carriers at sea was initiated. Carrier force manoeuvres and training were undertaken with fervour. Launching of aircraft and flying-on, combat tactics and bombing practice became rigorous. Attack became the order of the day. Defensive functions like reconnaissance and search patrolling were given over to land-based planes.

To Genda must go the credit for having created the first carrier task forces of World War II.

Exercising overall command of this élite force, as of the entire Imperial Japanese Navy, was the Commander-in-Chief of the Combined Fleet, Admiral Isoroku Yamamoto, architect of the Pearl Harbor attack and the strong man behind all the major naval decisions during his tenure of office. In December 1941 he was an alert, aggressive and dominating figure of fifty-seven. The son of a schoolmaster, he was blooded in 1905 at the age of twenty-one at Tsushima Strait in the first major fleet action of the twentieth century when Admiral Heimachoro Togo 'crossed the T' of

Admiral Rojdestvensky's Russian Fleet in classical fashion and annihilated the enemy.

The experience earned Yamamoto honourable scars: two fingers were blown from his left hand by a Russian shell. He grew to be an outwardly calm, diffident professional officer; athletic, muscular with a reputation as a clown and a story-teller. At Naval Staff College he graduated top of his class. Helped by the sponsorship of Prince Kuni, the Empress's father, he spent two years at Harvard where he specialised in the study of the manufacture of petroleum and aviation fuels. A few years later, bolstered by this knowledge, he was overseeing the planning of air development at the Staff College and this in turn led to his appointment to the command of the top secret air development station on the banks of Kasumiga-Ura, a misty lake north-east of Tokyo which gave rise to the name of the Misty Lagoon Air Development Station.

With young test pilot Prince Yamashina he developed naval torpedo bombing techniques, and he taught a generation of young test pilots to land on a simulated flight deck constructed out of wharves and barges. Thus he became an early and pioneering advocate of the naval use of aircraft. He returned to the USA as a naval attaché in Washington for a spell of duty which was regarded as a personal triumph, excelled only by his appointment a few years later as chief technical adviser to the Japanese delegation at the Naval Disarmament Conference in London.

Yamamoto returned to Tokyo to still further triumphs. In 1930, newly promoted to flag rank, the Rear Admiral's carrier-borne aircraft staged a spectacular 'victory' in the autumn fleet exercises by 'sinking' the battleships of the opposing fleet.

By now he was regarded in the west as a brilliant tactician whose inscrutability also served him well in his playing of bridge and of chess, at both of which he excelled and in both of which he endeavoured and cleverly succeeded in concealing the loss of his fingers. Although he neither smoked nor drank, cigarettes and a bottle of Johnny Walker whisky were always available in his cabin and office. He was formal to the point of aloofness with his subordinates.

He is regarded by some as the only undisputed genius – in terms of strategy and tactics – that Japan produced in World War II; a man whose grasp of naval strategy was unrivalled and who had the courage and capacity to translate revolutionary ideas into action.

But investigation fails to support these views. His strategy was suspect. US naval historian Samuel Morison refers to 'the strategic imbecility' of the Pearl Harbor Attack, claiming that it brought the US into instant unity,* silenced isolationism and rendered it improbable that the US would agree to a compromise peace, thereby making impossible of achievement a fundamental objective of Japan's Basic Plan for the Greater East Asia War. Yamamoto's greatest blunder was to fail to sink the US carriers in Pearl Harbor. It is ironic but true that the most praiseworthy strategic decision Yamamoto made – albeit too late – was to seek out and destroy them at Midway. The fact that he lost the battle only underlines his failure to have achieved the end earlier.

If Yamamoto, aloof, remote and never seen with his coat or tunic off, was the architect of the early victories in the naval war in the east, it was Vice Admiral Chuichi Nagumo who was the executor and judged by Japanese standards he was equal in all respects to the highest traditions of his Samurai ancestors.

He was an intelligent and capable officer who showed early promise of promotion to flag rank. He was short and stocky but like so many diminutive men displayed an urgency and zest in all he undertook as if to compensate for the physical size of his body. His naval career followed a normal enough course for officers who were clearly earmarked for promotion: he served on the Naval General Staff, on the staff of the Combined Fleet, as an instructor at the Naval War College. He belonged to what Japanese navy officers referred to as the 'Red Brick Group', a reference to his tour of duty at the red brick Navy Ministry.

By 1933, as a Captain, he commanded the new 11,350-ton cruiser *Takao* in the 4th Cruiser Squadron. This squadron exercised intensively in night engagements and torpedo attacks, a form of warfare in which Nagumo had specialised. He was thought of highly by his contemporaries and enjoyed a popularity with his subordinates.

Mitsuo Fuchida† who was a lieutenant at the time of Nagumo's captaincy states in his book: 'Every aspect of his leadership impressed me. His speeches at manoeuvre conferences were always logical and enlightening, and one could not help respecting his

*This can be compared with the unifying effect of the 'Dunkirk spirit' in Britain in 1940.

†*Midway: The Battle That Doomed Japan* by M. Fuchida and M. Okumiya, Hutchinson, 1957, page 127. This book is subsequently referred to simply as *Midway* by M. Fuchida.

extraordinary ability. Candid yet open-hearted and considerate . . . we held him in high esteem and placed complete confidence in him.'

Captain Nagumo strengthened his popularity among the younger naval officers by his active opposition to the 1935 Second London Naval Limitation Conference. Nagumo went so far as to submit a petition through Fleet Headquarters urging early abrogation of the Treaty. At a time when the attitude of the central authorities seemed weak-kneed, Nagumo's firm action attracted much support throughout the Fleet. The Japanese delegation, in fact, walked out of the Conference which enhanced Nagumo's reputation even further.

Promotion to Rear Admiral brought him command of the 1st Destroyer Flotilla and further advanced his professional reputation. By 1941 he was Vice Admiral and had won command of the First Air Fleet with his flag in *Akagi*. Strangely, on the threshold of matchless wartime victories, his reputation in the eyes of Fuchida – and others – began to wane. Strangely, too, he was now commanding an air arm, a post to which he was not by background and experience best fitted. His knowledge of naval air warfare was limited. He had to rely heavily upon his staff.

It was on this appointment that Fuchida who was now a wing leader in the Admiral's flagship resumed his acquaintanceship with Nagumo, but noted with disappointment that while he was as warm-hearted and sympathetic as ever his once vigorous fighting spirit seemed to have gone: he seemed rather average and appeared to have aged considerably. Yet in the months to come, on the brink of battle, he stood on the bridge of his flagship looking tough and fierce, the very embodiment of the Samurai spirit.

Commander Minoru Genda, Nagumo's Operations Officer, complained to Fuchida that the Admiral no longer seemed to take the initiative in directing operations: he simply rubber-stamped the recommendations of his staff. Genda summed up his views to Fuchida:*

Whenever I draft a plan it is approved almost without consideration. This might appear to make my job easier, but it doesn't. On the contrary, it is disquieting to see my own plans approved without check from above, and then issued as formal orders. I am self-confident, but not so self-confident

**Midway* by M. Fuchida, page 128.

that I don't realise that anyone can make mistakes. Often I am puzzled over how to resolve an important problem. When I consider that a stroke of my pen might sway the destiny of the nation, it almost paralyses me with fear. If I were serving under a commander like Admiral Onishi or Admiral Yamaguchi, my plans would be thoroughly studied from every possible angle and returned to me with comments and opinions. I would then feel more sure and more free to propose ideas that might be extreme.

These criticisms are supported in many ways by the oft-repeated statement that it was Nagumo's Chief of Staff, Rear Admiral Ryunosuke Kusaka, who was the true power behind the throne, the person who wielded most influence with Nagumo and it was he to whom most credit was due for Nagumo's unprecedented run of victories.

Nagumo looked to Kusaka for advice on many subjects, whether naval or not. On the occasion of his return to Tokyo from his devastating strike against Pearl Harbor, he was summoned, together with the two commanders of the attacking waves of aircraft, Mitsuo Fuchida and Shigekazu Shimazaki, to the Imperial presence. The Imperial household had submitted a number of questions the Emperor would ask. Kusaka had written down the answers so that Nagumo could learn them by heart and not slip into the common phrases of his native Aizu. But no one allowed for the Emperor's impromptu questions. The fifteen minute audience stretched into forty-five. Nagumo retreated further and further into colloquialisms, referring to the US admirals as 'this guy' and 'that guy' (*koitsu* and *aisu*), fascinating the Emperor but embarrassing Fuchida and Shimazaki. Fuchida later recalled the incident. Instead of answering questions through an Imperial aide, Fuchida, a relatively junior officer, replied directly to the Emperor: it was a miserable moment for him which he thought a worse ordeal than the raid itself.

The Emperor figured considerably in Japanese minds and especially so in the minds of servicemen. Veneration of the Emperor and his authority because of his divine essence was one of the basic concepts of the Japanese religion of Shintoism which also promulgated the belief that the Japanese people have a divine origin going back to the first Emperor who began his reign in 660 BC.* Emperor

*The Japanese calendar dates from then: the Christian year of 1940, therefore, related to the year 2,600 in Japan.

Hirohito was the 124th direct descendant of the Goddess Amaterasu, mother of the first Emperor.

Militarism and religion were always inseparable notions to the Japanese: the cultivation of great moral values and virtues through ancestor worship linked with the special reverence of the Japanese for the nobility of their warriors – and the wish to emulate them. The Bushido Code – the collection of principles that governed Samurai conduct – taught honour, loyalty, courage, the endurance of pain unflinchingly, reverence for the Emperor and a contempt for death. This code had been pursued for centuries by the Samurai but it was now adopted widely throughout the country, establishing a high moral attitude towards life by millions of Japanese. It also led to a curiously obedient acceptance of authority which meant that the officer class could count on the almost total submission of the masses of the population. The belief in the divine origin of the Japanese people led quite naturally to the belief in their being a chosen people with the pre-destined spiritual mission to dominate the world. The notions were embodied in the principle of Hakko Ichiu. Over the centuries this principle inspired the formation of a multitude of secret societies, groups, parties and committees, all ultra-nationalistic in concept, all – in their own way – engendering the idea of national superiority and the domination – economically, politically and militarily – of nothing less than the whole of Asia.

These were the inborn, basic beliefs which motivated Japanese servicemen to perform their duties with a blind obedience, with a calm acceptance of the possibility of death, beliefs that Westerners can never comprehend. Japanese servicemen expected no reward for valour or devotion to duty: bravery and heroism were required as a matter of course.

These were the qualities displayed by the sailors and airmen of Nagumo's much vaunted First Air Fleet. Coupled with the technical brilliance of the Fleet's aircraft, ships and armaments, they produced a redoubtable combination. The Allies were to discover this the hard way.

CHAPTER 2

Storming of Rabaul

VICE ADMIRAL CHUICHI NAGUMO hastened his fleet of carriers north-westerly through heavy seas and severe weather to the homeland leaving the destruction of Pearl Harbor far astern. Not even the gloom and severity of the weather could dispel the sense of jubilation that pervaded the warships' messdecks as the ships ploughed homeward: even the tedious proceedings of re-fuelling at sea from three oilers along the retirement route were completed uncomplainingly. The passage was accomplished uneventfully and went completely undetected and unmolested by even a single Allied ship, submarine or aircraft.

Nagumo and the ships' companies of the Carrier Striking Force, returning like Samurai warriors of old, were accorded a tremendous ovation for what was regarded as a bold and courageous blow which had been struck for their Emperor. Nagumo, as we have already seen, was summoned to His Imperial Majesty's presence in company with his air commanders. The whole nation rejoiced and euphoria swept across the islands of Japan. December 1941 was a time for exultation.

The severe weather which had battered the grey ships of Nagumo's *Kido Butai* or Carrier Striking Force caused the abandonment of a strike which had been planned for the aircraft of the 2nd Carrier Squadron, *Soryu* (15,900 tons) and *Hiryu* (17,300 tons), against Midway on 11 December. But five days later these two small carriers were detached to support the sorely pressed Japanese forces attacking Wake Island: they were accompanied by the heavy cruisers *Tone* (11,215 tons) and *Chikuma* (11,215 tons) of the 8th Cruiser Squadron and the 2,033-ton destroyers *Urakaze* and *Tanikaze*. The resounding din of their bombs and guns was added to the thunder of the Pacific surf along the beaches fringing the island. The bombardment went on almost continuously throughout 21 to 23 December.

On this last day, Rear Admiral Kajioka, commander of the Wake Island Invasion Force in the light cruiser *Yubari* (2,890 tons) in immaculate formal white dress uniform hung with medals and sword, took possession of the island in the name of Emperor Hirohito.

On Christmas Eve 1941, the 1st Carrier Squadron comprising *Akagi* (36,500 tons) and *Kaga* (38,200 tons), together with their screening units arrived at Kure to be followed the next day by the 5th Carrier Squadron, *Shokaku* and *Zuikaku*, both 25,675 tons, who had called briefly at Saeki. Three days later still *Soryu* and *Hiryu* also arrived safely at Kure to further scenes of jubilation, having been delayed by their Wake Island mission.

When the new year of 1942 dawned over the Japanese naval base at Kure near Hiroshima the whole of Nagumo's First Air Fleet command was still enjoying a respite from the rigours of seatime while the ships themselves were being prepared and replenished for their next mission. It was not long in coming.

Indeed, the whole plan for Japan's war in what the Japanese preferred to call the Greater East Asia Co-Prosperity Sphere, was dependent upon achieving a swift victory. Admiral Yamamoto had stated his opinion unequivocally in 1940: the schoolboy translation of the text makes amusing reading: 'If I am told to fight regardless of consequences, I shall run wild considerably for the first six months or a year, but I have utterly no confidence for the second and third years. The Tripartite Pact has been concluded and we cannot help it. Now that the situation has come to this pass I hope you will endeavour for avoidance of an American–Japanese war.'*

The main Japanese military thrust southward headed for the central section of ABDA Command,† but important assaults were also launched on both the eastern and the western flanks. It is the eastern assault, thrusting deeply like a lance, whose fortunes we shall follow, but before focussing upon its first targets, Rabaul and Kavieng in the Bismarck Archipelago, we must briefly turn to Guam and Truk.

Guam, an island under the sovereignty of the United States, is the

**Memoirs of Prince Konoye*: translation of extracts printed in *Asahi Shimbun*, 20–30 December 1945, issued by Okuyama Service, Tokyo, 1946.

†ABDA – standing for the initials of American, British, Dutch and Australian – Command based on Java was a hastily organised command doomed to failure even before it was formed. It survived only a few weeks.

largest of the Marianas. Virtually defenceless, it fell to the Japanese on the day of invasion, 10 December, and instead of becoming the bastion against Japanese aggression that it was hoped, it became instead a small naval and air base for the Japanese, playing an important role in the later Battle of the Philippine Sea.

Truk lies in the central group of the many hundreds of islands which make up the Caroline Islands. The Carolines were assigned to Japan under the mandate of the League of Nations and by the outbreak of war Truk could claim a small naval base. It was from this base that Admiral Inouye, Commander of the Fourth Fleet, commanded the invasion forces for both Guam and Wake.

It was at their own base at Truk and from the recently captured base at Guam that the Japanese assault forces for Rabaul and Kavieng assembled: those forces destined for Rabaul assembled at Guam and those for the invasion of Kavieng at Truk. Naval command for the whole of the Bismarck operation embracing both these landings and including the preliminary softening-up attacks was vested in Vice Admiral S. Inouye.

His Fourth Fleet comprised a force of forty-one transports, six minelayers, fifteen gunboats, two tenders, sixteen submarines and sundry small craft protected by the elderly 3,230-ton cruisers *Tenryu* and *Tatsuta* together with *Kashima* (5,890 tons) and *Yubari*'s 6th Destroyer Flotilla of eight destroyers of the *Kamikaze* (1,270 tons) and *Mutsuki* (1,313 tons) classes.

Support for these forces was given by Rear Admiral A. Goto's 6th Cruiser Squadron comprising the flagship *Aoba* (8,300 tons), *Kinugasa* (8,300 tons), *Kako* (8,100 tons) and *Furutaka* (8,100 tons). Rear Admiral Onishi in the depot ship *Jingei* commanded the 7th Submarine Flotilla in support of the operation: he deployed his boats like a defensive chain of redoubts between New Ireland and New Britain in the St George's Channel.

But the most impressive force assembled to give cover to the assaults on the Bismarck beachheads lay over the horizon, unseen yet menacing: Nagumo with his powerful Carrier Striking Force lurked, poised to strike at the Allied bases and ready to engage and crush any Allied opposition he might encounter.

By 9 January Nagumo's Force had re-ammunitioned and completed all routine maintenance at Kure. His new orders assigned his Force to cover the impending invasion of New Ireland and New Britain.

Truk, the designated destination for Nagumo's Force, lay almost 2000 miles south-east of Kure. The final objectives of Rabaul and Kavieng lay another 600 miles farther south of Truk. The operation was a huge undertaking. It pushed the Japanese point of advance to what must have been the prudent limit. Lines of communication would become vulnerable to enemy submarines and carrier striking forces. Nagumo was conscious of this vulnerability to raiding carriers and knew that it was due largely to his having failed to sink the US carriers at Pearl Harbor. It was a spectre which was to haunt him many times in the next few months.

Nagumo was a compulsive worrier. He was constantly being reminded by his Chief of Staff, Rear Admiral Kusaka, that on occasions such as this victory is wrested by running risks. '*Daiboju*', he would say, time and time again: 'Don't worry!'

It was the Australians and not Nagumo who had just cause for worry at the unfolding events. The Bismarck Archipelago and the lofty mountain ranges of New Guinea formed a natural defensive barrier for Australia. A penetration of this barrier would lay the continent open to invasion from the north. Australia was just as exposed to danger as all Japan's other conquests had been during the past few weeks of aggression, and, like them, Australia also displayed the same lack of preparedness.

Nagumo sortied from the Inland Sea and headed for Truk. He hoisted his flag as usual in *Akagi*, accompanied by *Kaga, Zuikaku, Shokaku*, and the 1st Division of the 3rd Battle Squadron *Hiei* (32,350 tons) and *Kirishima* (31,980 tons), the 8-inch gun *Chikuma* of the 8th Cruiser Squadron with the light cruiser *Abukuma* (5170 tons) leading the destroyers of the 1st Flotilla. This considerable force steamed south-east for five days and anchored at Truk in readiness for the Rabaul and Kavieng operation.

Independently, the 2nd Carrier Squadron *Soryu* and *Hiryu* with their supporting cruisers and destroyers left Kure to attack the island of Palau at the western end of the Carolines.

It was not clear to the British and the Americans exactly what the Japanese intentions were in this theatre. Although the Americans were privy to the Japanese signals because of their code-breaking successes the swiftness and violence of the Japanese onslaught was such that, almost before their intentions had been interpreted, the Japanese actions had overtaken events.

The British believed that the Fiji Islands were in jeopardy with their one airfield and a squadron of twenty-two out-dated aircraft: the few thousand British and native troops would be no match for the combat-experienced amphibious forces of the Japanese. Britain, disconsolate at this further threat to her colonial interests in the Pacific, appealed to the USA for help to protect these islands.

But the Australians considered that Suva rather than Fiji or Rabaul would be the target for the assault forces then massing at the Truk anchorage.

The Americans also guessed wrongly. They regarded Samoa as the likeliest objective, because the capture of this island would put the Japanese astride the US–New Zealand–Australia line of communication: this US view was lent credibility when a Japanese submarine shelled the US naval station on the Samoan island of Pago Pago on 11 January; it was believed that this was the prelude to a sea-borne assault.*

The Director of Naval Intelligence in Melbourne, Commander R. B. M. Long, in an appreciation in December 1941, predicted the possibility of a Japanese penetration to the New Hebrides, New Caledonia, Fiji and Samoa because of 'the strategic value of these areas to Japan vis-à-vis American–British trans-Pacific communications'.†

As early as 9 January a reconnaissance aircraft over Truk had brought the Allies warning of the assembling warships and transports. This, coupled with indications that four of Nagumo's carriers were in the area, and of more Japanese concentrations in the Marshall Islands, impelled the Australian Naval Board to ask Commander-in-Chief Pacific, Admiral Chester Nimitz, for naval action to be taken against these concentrations. But CINCPAC was in no position to help. Admiral Nimitz signalled the Naval Board regretting 'the inability of the US Pacific Fleet to operate against these Japanese naval concentrations in the Carolines and Marshalls in the immediate future owing to other commitments'.

The US Pacific Fleet was still recovering from the shock of the Pearl Harbor Attack barely five weeks before, and it was fully committed to the observance of its two primary tasks, the first of

*It was on this day, too, that another Japanese submarine successfully torpedoed the US carrier *Saratoga* 500 miles south-west of Pearl Harbor. She did not sink but she was put out of service for six months.

†*The Royal Australian Navy, 1939–1945* by G. Hermon Gill, Vol II, page 5. Australian War Memorial, Canberra.

which was to protect the Midway–Johnson–Hawaii triangle, and the second – of almost equal importance – 'securing communications along the lines Panama–Samoa–Fiji–New Zealand: and West Coast–Pearl Harbor–Fiji–New Caledonia–Australia'.

The vulnerability of these lines of communication was not lost on the Allied powers. Indeed, as we have just seen, their protection and the defence of Australia and New Zealand, coupled with the need to arrest the steam-rolling advance of the Japanese southward thrust were not only established prime Allied objectives, but US naval forces were soon operating in the early days of 1942 in the South West Pacific. The swift US reaction to Pearl Harbor and the adoption of a hard-hitting defensive role in the Pacific was a signal feature of the war at sea in that theatre.

Already the US task forces were being employed and even though their contribution to the overall war effort was minor, they demonstrated an aggression and latent threat which the Japanese were unable to ignore.

The US carriers had also been engaged in covering the US reinforcement of Samoa. When the Japanese submarine shelled this tropical island on 11 January the US forces were assembling in San Diego. They comprised four transports, an ammunition ship, a fleet oiler and a cargo vessel. They were escorted for the ocean voyage by Rear Admiral Frank Fletcher's new fast carrier force based on the carrier *Yorktown* (19,900 tons). On entering the war zone they were covered by Vice Admiral W. F. Halsey's *Enterprise* (19,900 tons) carrier group.

By 23 January all these US reinforcements were ashore on Samoa. By that date too all the Allied speculation over the destination of the massed Japanese shipping at Truk ended. Rabaul was revealed as Japan's primary target. Kavieng was the secondary objective. At about midnight on 22 January the Japanese assault upon Rabaul had begun.

New Guinea, New Britain, New Ireland and the British Solomon Islands form a vast 2000-mile-long barrier, with towering peaks and ridges rising to 15,000 feet, protecting Australia against marauders from the north like a natural Maginot Line. From Australia's northernmost point at Cape York across the dangerous shallows of the Torres Strait, New Guinea lies a mere sixty miles away, but elsewhere the distance lengthens to 1000 miles.

New Guinea, one of the largest islands in the world, is over 1000 miles long and just over 400 miles wide at its widest point. Administratively, the western half of the island was part of the huge Dutch colonial empire. The eastern half was administered by the Australians: the south-east portion comprising Papua and adjacent islands were defined as Australian territory: the northern portion, together with the islands of New Britain and New Ireland and the two northernmost islands of the Solomons – Buka and Bougainville – were held by Australia under a League of Nations mandate. The rest of the Solomons* were under a British Protectorate dating back to before the turn of the century. The population of all these islands – Mandated New Guinea, Papua and the Solomons – was less than 1,500,000 of which about only 6000 were Europeans.

The abundance of coral reefs close inshore make the seas around these islands hazardous for navigators: farther to seaward, coral reefs rise sharply and treacherously from the great depths providing a constant source of anxiety to seamen in waters never completely surveyed nor fully charted.

But it was the weather which dominated the scene both ashore and afloat. All these islands lay within the tropics – from the equator itself to 10 degrees South. With a heat made humid by the drenching monsoon rains, even the cooler lowland daytime temperatures remain steady in the nineties (32–37 degrees C). At sea this climate produced discomforts familiar to sailors of all nations who served under wartime conditions with hatches closed at night and air conditioning merely circulating warm air. Ashore the climate produced lush green vegetation and jungle with steaming, unhealthy swamps, and – to cap it all – active volcanoes. To Europeans, New Guinea was not a tropical island paradise.

The islands provide a number of good natural harbours, though most of them were undeveloped in 1942. There were three prominent ones: the harbour for Rabaul in New Britain called Simpson Harbour: Fairax Harbour in Port Moresby and Milne Bay.

It is Rabaul with which we are primarily concerned. It comprised a town on the north-east shore of Simpson Harbour consisting of bungalows for the thousand Europeans, with avenues of trees affording shade from the tropical sun: wharves lined the waterfront and there were shops and a few office buildings. The town was

*The main islands are Guadalcanal, Savo, San Cristobel, New Georgia, Choiseul, Shortland, Russell, Florida, Tulagi, Treasury, Vella Lavella and Rendova.

completed by a Chinatown of densely populated corrugated iron shacks for Rabaul's 3000 natives. This modestly sized town was the capital of the New Guinea Territory.

A volcanic eruption in mid-1941, following the 1937 eruption which showered Rabaul with pumice dust and volcanic debris a foot thick, impelled the authorities to transfer the capital to Lae, but the intervention of war prevented the completion of this transfer.

Rabaul's defences make curious reading: a battalion of Australians was supplemented by a detachment of just over 100 European volunteers: two 6-inch coastal guns were sited on Praed Point at the northern entrance to Blanche Bay: and north of Simpson Harbour lay a two-gun AA battery. A squadron of twenty-two Wirraway aircraft occupied two landing strips. The Navy was represented by a small base staff of ten men with Lieutenant MacKenzie in command.

It was against this target, curiously, that Japan had amassed a force as powerful as that which had attacked one of the world's biggest naval concentrations as Pearl Harbor on 7 December.

The main invasion force for Rabaul had assembled at Guam: it comprised the 19th Minelaying Squadron under Rear Admiral Shima's flag, with a landing party of 300 men. There were two auxiliary gunboats, *Nikkai Maru* and *Kongo Maru*, two destroyers and a number of transports. On 14 January the invasion convoy sailed due south from Guam and three days later it made a rendezvous with Rear Admiral Kajioka's force recently sailed from Truk which consisted of his flagship, the cruiser *Yubari* and an assorted collection of destroyers – *Oite, Yunagi, Asanagi* and *Yayoi* –; an auxiliary gunboat and two transports carried the landing force of Japanese marines. Two days later this combined force was further strengthened by the 6th Cruiser Squadron – *Kako, Furutaka, Aoba* and *Kinugasa*. Throughout the 20th and 21st this invasion fleet steered south-east heading for Rabaul.

Meanwhile, Vice Admiral Nagumo's four fleet carriers *Akagi, Kaga, Zuikaku* and *Shokaku* had sailed from Truk and on the 20th, in a position north-east of New Ireland, Commander Genda ordered a series of attack groups totalling ninety aircraft from the flight decks of the carriers. Commander Fuchida then led the powerful strike against Rabaul. The scene aboard the carriers bore all the signs of excitement and activity associated with a major fleet operation: the cream of Japan's naval air arm were waved and cheered off by their ships' companies, pilots with the experience of Pearl Harbor and many of them with the added experience of the air battles over China. Opposed to them were twenty-two outmoded aircraft and a virtually undefended harbour. Fuchida's force arrived over this harbour which lay unsuspecting and tranquil in the sunlight. He ordered his planes to attack.

The Norwegian cargo vessel *Herstein*, the only vessel of any size in the harbour was struck almost immediately and sank. Five of the defending RAAF planes were promptly shot down. Fuchida later reported only seeing two Allied planes, but certainly many more took to the air. After the initial dive bombing and gun-strafing runs the group of level bombers had no worthwhile targets to attack so their full complement of bombs was released upon the coastal guns at Praed Point.

While this softening-up attack was in progress at Rabaul, *Zuikaku* and *Shokaku* with *Chikuma* and three destroyers were detached from Nagumo's force. They proceeded into the Bismarck Sea and launched neutralisation strikes against Kavieng in New Ireland, and airfields in New Guinea at Lae, Salamaua, Bulolo and Madang, causing extensive damage.

On 22 January Nagumo's aircraft made another – superfluous – strike against Rabaul which induced the leader to comment: 'the employment of the Nagumo Force in this operation struck me as wasteful and extravagant. If ever a sledgehammer had been used to crack an egg, this was the time.'* Stranger still, it was these same officers, headed by Nagumo, who had timorously declined to launch a second strike against Pearl Harbor. Yet here at Rabaul only a little over six weeks later a second, needless attack was ordered. It was an error that Fletcher was to make later at Tulagi.

Simultaneously with the Rabaul invasion, another invasion force supported by the 18th Cruiser Squadron – *Tenryu* and *Tatsuta* – sailed from Truk for the assault upon Kavieng. Both the Rabaul and the Kavieng forces reached their destinations – 130 miles apart – at about midnight on 22 January.

With no Allied warships to contest the Rabaul and Kavieng invasions, with a mere handful of Wirraway fighters to oppose

***Midway* by M. Fuchida, page 56.

Fuchida's air squadrons,* and overwhelmingly outnumbered by the Japanese troops and marines, Kavieng and Rabaul succumbed. By dawn it was all over. Later on the 23rd both towns were completely in Japanese hands.

With these added successes tucked under his tunic Nagumo turned about and headed back to Truk with his cock-a-hoop force. Rabaul, in American terminology, had been a pushover. Nagumo had contributed to the establishment of a base for 'operations against New Guinea and Australia due to destruction of *important enemy's defence installations* by our powerful task force . . .'† And this statement, notable for its italicised inaccuracy, also gives a clue to a later operation – Operation MO against Port Moresby which led directly, fourteen weeks later, to the Battle of the Coral Sea.

Four days after the fall of Rabaul, on 27 January, the Australian Chief of Naval Staff, Vice Admiral Sir Guy Royle, disconsolate at the Japanese successes and apprehensive at the portents of disaster for Australia, signalled Admiral Chester Nimitz, CINCPAC, warning that the fall of Rabaul increased the threat to Port Moresby and New Caledonia. He added that a strong Allied naval concentration in the area was desirable as a matter of prudence to thwart any future Japanese action towards Australia and to preserve the line of communication between America and Australia. Royle's signal continued: 'On assumption that US flag officer will now assume command in Anzac Area and that one 8-inch and two 6-inch British cruisers will be available to join him, request that plans may now be concerted so that a sufficiently strong force may be concentrated in the area to deal with a force similar to that employed in the capture of Rabaul.'

The US view of the situation coincided closely with Royle's appraisal and resulted in a redeployment of ships at the direction of Admiral Ernest J. King, the Commander-in-Chief US Fleet – COMINCH.‡ He directed Nimitz to release Vice Admiral Wilson Brown's *Lexington* Task Force to reinforce the Anzac Area, under the command of Vice Admiral H. F. Leary.

*The commanding officer of the Wirraways, Wing Commander J. M. Lerew, when faced with the prospect of engaging Fuchida's Zero's signalled the Australian Air Board *Nos morituri te salutamus* – 'We who are about to die salute you.'

†ATIS Document: 'Full Translation of a Report of the Japanese Invasion of Rabaul.'

‡Originally CINCUS but the pronunciation of this unfortunate choice of title effected a quick change to COMINCH!

We are not concerned here with details of the activities of the US carrier forces but it is important as a matter of record to state that they were continually being employed to harass Japanese bases by striking at them whenever the opportunity presented itself. The three carriers around which these task forces were formed were *Yorktown*, *Lexington* and *Enterprise*. The *Saratoga*, as we have seen, was torpedoed on 11 January and had limped away for repairs and modernisation.

Rear Admiral Frank J. Fletcher commanded the *Yorktown* carrier force: Vice Admiral William J. Halsey, destined to rank with Cunningham as one of the world's greatest sea fighters of all time, commanded the group based on the equally famous *Enterprise* – the Big E: and Vice Admiral Wilson Brown commanded the force centred on *Lexington* – Lady Lex.

Enterprise, accompanied by three destroyers, struck at Wotje and Maloelap (the two enemy seaplane bases in the eastern Marshalls) and Kwajalein. Rear Admiral Raymond A. Spruance in the cruiser *Northampton* with *Salt Lake City* and a destroyer also bombarded Wotje while Captain Thomas Stock in *Chester* with two destroyers bombarded Taroa Island in the Maloelap Atoll.

Fletcher in *Yorktown* with *Louisville, St Louis* and some destroyers struck at the three southern islands of Makin, Mili and Jaluit.

Heralded though these offensive missions were for their damaging effect upon the enemy, it would be absurd to regard them as any more than useful combat experience for both the aircrews and for the crews aboard the carriers in carrying out their evolutions in active, wartime conditions. Their effect upon the morale of the US Navy was excellent. Their effect upon the enemy, of course, was minimal.

While these US carrier strikes were being conducted the Imperial Japanese Headquarters was preparing a directive which was issued to Admiral Yamamoto on 29 January, six days after the occupation of Rabaul. It read: 'The Army and Navy, working together, will occupy the Lae and Salamaua sectors as quickly as possible. At the proper time, the Navy, independently, will occupy Tulagi and secure an air base. . . . If possible, the Army and Navy will work jointly and occupy Port Moresby after the occupation of Lae and Salamaua.'*

*'Eastern New Guinea Invasion Operations'. Japanese Monograph No. 96 compiled

But it was to be another three months before the attempt to implement the directive to occupy Port Moresby and during that time great events were to occur in this theatre which need to be related. By then, too, there were signs that the impulsion was beginning to go out of the Japanese war machine.

Nagumo's Carrier Striking Force arrived at the Truk anchorage on 25 January where it was joined two days later by *Zuikaku* and *Shokaku*. A fleet was assembling in readiness for the next assignment. After an overnight stay at Truk, *Zuikaku* and *Shokaku* were detached to Palau and Yokosuka. They were followed two days later by *Akagi* and *Kaga* who arrived at Palau on 8 February. The sight that greeted them was exhilarating.

Deployed throughout the anchorage in impressive and purposive array, with a light breeze fluttering their red and white naval ensigns, lay the cruisers and destroyers comprising the main body of Vice Admiral Nobutake Kondo's Second Fleet. It comprised:

4th Cruiser Squadron: *Takao, Atago, Chokai, Maya,* all of them 13,400-ton cruisers.
5th Cruiser Squadron: *Myoko, Nachi, Haguro*, all of them 13,380 tons.
7th Cruiser Squadron: *Kumano, Mogami, Mikuma, Suzuya,* all of them 12,400 tons.
2nd Destroyer Flotilla: the light cruiser *Jintsu* and sixteen destroyers.
4th Destroyer Flotilla: the light cruiser *Naka* and twelve destroyers.

It was Kondo's force which had supported the Malay and Philippine invasions. Also in the anchorage were the *Soryu* and *Hiryu* fresh from yet another air strike, this time against the Dutch naval base at Amboina.

The next few days at Palau saw intense activity with many vessels entering and leaving harbour; there was much coming and going of staff officers and air unit commanders to the flagships as they planned their next bombing mission. Commander Genda discussed details with the air unit commanders: Commander Fuchida of *Akagi*, Lieutenant-Commander Kusumi of *Kaga*, Lieutenant Tomonaga of *Hiryu*, Lieutenant-Commander Egusa of *Soryu*, Lieutenant-Commander Shimazaki of *Zuikaku* and Lieutenant-Commander Takahashi of *Shokaku*.

by Commander Sakuji Mikami, Staff Officer in charge of operations during the period covered.

The new objective was the Celebes where Nagumo's Carrier Striking Force was to support the military operations against the south-west of the island. Date of departure was 1 February. But on that very morning Nagumo received reports of Admiral Halsey's three-pronged attack in the Marshall Islands, 1200 miles away to the east, and in particular, the carrier-borne air raid (from Halsey's *Enterprise*) at Wotje and Maloelap.

The departure for the Celebes was called off immediately and Nagumo was directed to head eastward with all despatch to try to intercept Halsey's force. But Halsey lay two days' steaming away. It seemed inconceivable that he would stay idle in one place, inviting retaliation, in the full knowledge that superior enemy forces – Nagumo's six carriers – were somewhere in the seas of the south-west Pacific. Nagumo reasoned that Halsey would use his task force skilfully and clear the area at speed once the strike was over.

Nagumo set out from Truk and headed east. Throughout the whole of the day of 1 February reports kept coming through to him giving details of the raids on the Marshalls, but by nightfall it was evident that the raids had terminated and that Halsey's force had withdrawn to safer waters. Nevertheless, Nagumo continued his easterly course throughout the 2nd until US radio news broadcasts were picked up announcing the execution of 'successful raids on the Marshall and Gilbert Islands'. Only then was it clearly evident that Halsey must have departed and that the groping hand of Nagumo was grasping at nothing. Nagumo's force turned about to a reciprocal course and headed back to Truk.

Genda, Fuchida – and many other Japanese officers – were unhappy about the turn around of the *Kido Butai* and the re-tracing of its wake back to Truk. While they had appreciated the absurdity and fruitlessness of a two day chase across 1200 miles of ocean, they had hoped for something better. They hoped for a change of strategy. The two day sortie east had given them hope. The about turn had dispelled any hope they nursed that Combined Fleet Headquarters might order Nagumo's force of fast carriers to seek out and engage the US carrier fleet in the Pacific. This, surely, was Japan's most logical target: to dispose of the remnants, albeit the most important elements, of the US Navy that Nagumo had failed to destroy at Pearl Harbor on 7 December. It was becoming increasingly clear to many senior officers that it was the carriers which must be destroyed if Japan was to win the Great East Asia conflict. But Genda and Fuchida, mere Commanders, were pre-empting history. The time for Nagumo's carriers to seek battle with the US carriers was to come – at Midway in June.

It is little wonder that the Allies were incapable of penetrating the inscrutable oriental minds of the Japanese planners. For there were three schools of Japanese thought on the next step.

Captain Sadatoshi Tomioka, Chief of the Admiralty Planning Staff, favoured the isolation of Australia by a southward advance to Samoa and Fiji to cut communications with the USA. Captain Kameto Kuroshima, Chief of the Operations Division of Yamamoto's Combined Fleet, recommended an offensive against Ceylon and into the faraway *western* Indian Ocean. While Admiral Yamamoto, the Commander-in-Chief, and his Chief of Staff, Rear Admiral Matoma Ugaki, with greater strategic perception, supported a third plan: to despatch his carrier fleet against Midway and Hawaii for a final, once and for all, confrontation with the US Pacific Fleet.

In the event, part at least of all three plans was implemented in turn and, paradoxically, it was the strategically most advantageous one for Japan – Yamamoto's plan for Midway and Hawaii – which provided Yamamoto, Nagumo and Japan itself with their great defeat at the Battle of Midway.

Though the eastward thrust from Truk to the Marshalls could well have become the sortie that many officers had hoped for, it in fact proved merely to be the chasing of a shadow: at worst a failure, at best a half measure.

Combined Fleet Headquarters at Hashirajima viewed the Halsey raids with some apprehension and over-reacted. In addition to sending Nagumo's powerful force to the Marshalls, now, on the retirement, the Combined Fleet detached *Zuikaku* and *Shokaku* to carry out defensive patrols east of the homeland in case Halsey might be emboldened to strike at targets nearer to Japan – conceivably even the homeland itself.

Nagumo's force, now reduced to *Akagi* and *Kaga*, returned to Truk to find the Celebes assault had been undertaken without his support and new orders were circulating for a strike against Australia.

Combined Fleet Headquarters continued to focus their attention upon the central thrust of the southern area where they displayed anxiety about the probable use by the Allies of north-west Australia as a base for impeding the Japanese seizure of the Dutch East Indies. This was a curious view because by the end of February the Japanese navy had inflicted grave losses upon the Allied warships taking part in the Battle of the Java Sea. Nevertheless, the decision had been taken to make a strike against Australia.

Darwin was to be the target. It was to become another Pearl Harbor. The objective was to neutralise the port as an Allied base and the signal to this effect reached Nagumo as he headed back to Truk from the abortive sortie towards the Marshalls. He promptly signalled Rear Admiral Yamaguchi with his two carriers *Soryu* and *Hiryu* to join him at Palau.

Yamaguchi with his two small carriers plus the 8th Cruiser Squadron and two destroyers had been busily engaged since the outbreak of war in the Pacific: after supporting the Wake Island invasion, the force proceeded south to support Admiral Takahashi's amphibious operations in the Banda Sea area and to protect the eastern flank in the attack on Kendari. On 24 January it carried out pre-invasion raids on Amboina with a force of seventeen bombers and eighteen fighters. On 4 February the carrier aircraft, now operating from newly captured airfields at Kendari in the Celebes surprised an Allied naval force of four cruisers and seven destroyers south of Kangean Island.

The force was commanded by Rear Admiral Karel W. F. M. Doorman with his flag in the Dutch cruiser *De Ruyter* (6470 tons). He was accompanied by the Dutch cruiser *Tromp* (3787 tons), the US heavy cruiser *Houston* (9050 tons), US light cruiser *Marblehead* (7050 tons), the four US destroyers *Stewart, Edwards, Bulmer* and *Barker* and the three Dutch destroyers *Van Ghent, Piet Hein* and *Banckert*.

Doorman was sheltering in the Bunda Roads immediately outside Sourabaya when reports indicated the presence of enemy forces at the southern end of the Makassar Strait. The enemy force comprised an invasion convoy of some twenty transports covered by three cruisers and several destroyers.

At midnight on 3 February, in the best traditions of his Dutch maritime ancestors, Doorman led his force towards the enemy in line ahead: *De Ruyter, Houston, Marblehead, Tromp* with the destroyers on either flank.

At 0935 Doorman radioed his ships that a force of about thirty-seven enemy aircraft were headed for the Sourabaya area having taken off from the captured airfield at Kendari. At 0949 the aircraft were sighted. They were Yamaguchi's planes from *Soryu* and *Hiryu*.

The morning was bright, though squally clouds scudded across the clear blue sky: visibility was so good that the faraway peaks of Bali and Lombok could be seen dimly more than forty miles away.

Doorman made the signal for his force to disperse and the ships promptly complied, scattering in all directions with the object of splitting the attacking aircraft into small, more vulnerable groups. These were still the pioneering days of AA tactics when dispersal and plenty of sea room were considered the prime needs for warships under attack. The later tactics of mounting an increasing number of AA guns aboard ships and concentrating the ships in company to increase the volume of fire were partly learnt in these inhospitable waters. These days, too, were the early days of radar as a weapon of war: only the bigger ships were fitted with sets which judged by any standards, were primitive. The defence of ships in these days rested solely and solidly upon the traditional gunnery methods taught in gunnery schools throughout the world.

Doorman's ships were still dispersing when at 0954 the first attack developed. It was directed mainly against the two large American ships. The first two attacks were repulsed without damage, but at 1019 events took an ominous turn when a stick of bombs fell close alongside *Marblehead* and gave her a good shaking.

At 1027 another group of bombers approached *Marblehead* from the port quarter: one of the straddling bombs shattered the motor launch, pierced the deck and exploded below, demolishing the sick bay, ward room and adjacent cabins, and starting several fires. A near miss for'ard damaged the bows and soon she was noticeably down by the head. A third bomb scored a direct hit well aft rolling back the armoured steel main deck like a sardine tin. The rudder jammed at hard-a-port and as she was making revolutions for 25 knots she started going round in circles, with a 10 degree list, down by the head and blazing aft. Dead and dying littered the compartments and the final tally showed fifteen killed and thirty-four seriously wounded.

A fourth attack which developed was directed at the flagship who suffered nothing worse than having her AA fire control knocked out.

In the meantime *Houston* had also received attention. During the earlier attacks near misses rendered her AA director useless and of sprung plates in the hull which caused her to start taking water aboard. But it was during the fourth and final attack that *Houston* nearly met her end.

Despite violent avoiding action she took a bomb aboard – the last of the salvo. It crashed through the two platforms of the mainmast and exploded just for'ard of number three gun turret aft. Commander Winslow, a young naval pilot at the time, later described the scene: 'Hunks of shrapnel tore through the turret's thin armour as though it were paper, igniting powder bags in the hoists. In one blazing instant all the hands in the turret and in the handling rooms below were dead . . . It was a hellish battle which ended with forty-eight of our shipmates killed and another fifty seriously burned or wounded.'*

Doorman and his savaged force retired from the area and dispersed, the two damaged US cruisers limping to Tjilatjap 'that stinking, fever-ridden little port on the south coast of Java'.† When Admiral Thomas C. Hart inspected the two cruisers he decided that *Houston* should remain in Java, for even with one turret knocked out she still matched the firepower of HMS *Exeter*. But *Marblehead*'s damage was so extensive that Hart ordered her temporarily patched up so she could reach Colombo. She eventually arrived at the Brooklyn Navy Yard three months later.

The *Hiryu* and *Soryu* pilots returned to Kendari understandably pleased with their morning's work which, they claimed, included the sinking of the two US cruisers and the damaging of two more.

After the Japanese pilots and aircraft had been re-assigned to their ships both of the carriers and all their screening units departed from Kendari to rendezvous with Nagumo in Palau in the western Carolines. Once there, the meetings aboard *Akagi* of the Air Unit Officers were full of excitement and tremendous confidence. Lieutenant-Commander Egusa of *Soryu* and Lieutenant Tomonaga of *Hiryu* were in specially good spirits after their successes against the US cruisers. Lieutenant-Commander Kusumi of *Kaga* and Commander Fuchida of the flagship made up the quartet of Air Unit Commanders responsible for executing the proposed strike against Darwin. When both the air and the naval plans for the attack had been completed the Nagumo Carrier Striking Force relished the prospect of the mission ahead of them.

*Commander Walter G. Winslow: see his *Galloping Ghost*, US Naval Institute Proceedings, February 1949.

†*Ibid.*

On 15 February the combined force left Palau and headed south-west, traversed the equator and then through blistering heat steamed through the Molucca Sea to Staring Bay, the outer harbour of Kendari where it paused momentarily before threading its way through the maze of islands and emerging unmolested into the Timor Sea.

Darwin, lazing in the languor of its arid climate and oblivious to the danger, awaited its day of destruction.

CHAPTER 3

Destruction of Darwin

DARWIN LENT NO enchantment to the tropical remoteness of the Northern Territory of Australia in 1942. It sprawled blistered and untidy, giving an air of impermanence like a dusty shanty-township. Yet this was Australia's northernmost mainland port, situated on the north-west corner of a huge 400-mile wide peninsula which separates the Gulf of Carpentaria from the Timor Sea.

The port of Darwin is vast with a seven-mile-wide entrance stretching between East Point and West Point. The land encloses a harbour which reaches inland with countless bays and small coves, with long arms of low-lying land fringed with mangroves and backed by low wooded shores. The Timor Sea, sometimes whipped to cyclone fury, provides Darwin with a capacious deep water port which in the early months of 1942 provided the township on the eastern side of the port with its main form of communication. Timor, 400 miles to the north-east was nearer than Alice Springs. Canberra and Sydney, overland by the most direct route, lay a continent away, very nearly as far distant as Singapore. A railway line thrust south-east into the barren wastes of the Northern Territory for 270 miles to Birdum, but thereafter a series of poor roads penetrated another 600 miles to the southern railhead at Alice Springs. This factor of isolation coupled with the general barrenness of the region, subjected as it was to the severity of a tropical climate, lent an atmosphere of 'frontier days' to Darwin and its outlying districts.

Thus the inhabitants of Darwin looked naturally to the sea as a normal and regular means of communication even to places like Fremantle, Brisbane and Sydney. A regular commercial monthly service of coastal passenger-cargo vessels operated east-about to Melbourne and another service to Singapore. The West Australian Government Steamship Service operated a regular service of 4000-ton motor ships from Fremantle to Darwin.

Because of its remoteness and obscurity in the north, it is little wonder that at the outbreak of war in the Pacific the port of Darwin lacked many of the facilities demanded by a modern port. There was one L-shaped wharf capable of berthing only two average-sized vessels. The cargo handling gear on the dockside comprised a 10-ton crane and sundry hand worked ones. All cargo was slung slowly by these cranes into railway trucks, for road transport was unable to use the wharf. Half-a-dozen or so lighters completed the port's facilities.

Thirty years before, a recommendation to develop the port as a naval base had been made but with little result.* Admiral Jellicoe in his *Report*, 1919, recommended that Bynoe Harbour just to the westward of Darwin should be developed as a temporary refuelling base and store because he visualised that any threat to Australia would come from the north and concluded that 'naval forces of the Commonwealth should naturally be based in Northern Australian waters'. But nothing came of this Bynoe recommendation other than a brief and cursory survey in 1922. Efforts were made in the late 1920s and during the 1930s to provide for the defence of Darwin. Considerable oil storage tanks were installed and approval was given for the installation of some coastal defence and AA guns and a District Naval Officer with a small staff was appointed to the port.

In 1938 the Darwin Mobile Defence Force of 300 men was raised and in the following year a scratch air force squadron was based at the small civil airfield while work proceeded on the construction of an air force station near by.

Early in 1939 a local Defence Committee consisting of the senior officers of the three services in the district was formed and began to prepare plans for local defence in the event of war. By the time war with Germany began in September of that year an Examination Service, Naval Control Service, local air reconnaissance patrols and other precautionary measures were put into immediate effect. The Defence Committee also initiated a number of longer term plans including the extension of the commercial wharf, the provision of coastal defences and AA guns, the construction of boom defences and a boom jetty.

During the early months of the war Darwin was gradually

***Recommendations* by Admiral Henderson submitted to the Commonwealth Government, 1911.

strengthened and put on to a more realistic war footing. The Senior Naval post of District Naval Officer was up-graded to Naval Officer in Charge, Northern Territory and in January 1940 a Captain Thomas took up this appointment. In May of the following year the submarine repair and depot ship HMAS *Platypus* (3455 tons) arrived from Sydney. As HMAS *Penguin* she had been the base depot ship at Sydney since 1929. And in November 1941 a floating dock arrived after having been towed all the way from Brisbane by two tugs. By the time of Japan's entry into the war Darwin had taken on the guise of a garrison town: a brigade of troops, 2000 air force personnel and a naval strength of 1105 officers and men were stationed in the Darwin area.

Some of the duties allotted to servicemen were the role of docker and railwayman and stevedore, for servicemen were regularly being called upon to maintain essential services during the rash of strikes which in both peace and war hampered all the defence projects and disrupted work in the port. The communist-dominated North Australia Workers Union controlled most of the labour force of Darwin and wielded power with damaging effect. Even the entry of Japan into the war, bringing danger much closer to home, did nothing to speed up the customary slow tempo of working in Darwin, let alone put an end to the strikes. It is an odd quirk of terminology that it took Nagumo's Striking Force to change all this. But then Nagumo changed everything about Darwin in February 1942.

The Federal Government of Australia was aware at the outbreak of war with Japan of the vulnerability of Darwin to some form of attack and as a matter of prudence the compulsory evacuation of women and children from the town was begun in December 1941. For two months a succession of shipping movements from Darwin took place taking evacuees to the relative safety of Sydney, Brisbane and Fremantle. By 19 February the civilian population of Darwin had been reduced to only 2500 comprising essential staff such as airport workers, civil servants, municipal employees, port workers and a small business community.

The fears of an attack – perhaps of invasion – grew as the weeks passed and the list of Japanese conquests lengthened. But unknown to the Allies – and the Australians in particular – an invasion of the mainland of Australia, often debated with heat and acrimony in Japanese naval and military circles as well as by Government leaders

Vice Admiral Chuichi Nagumo, commander of the Carrier Striking Force.

Commander Mitsuo Fuchida, idolised bomber pilot, photographed here in 1970 as a lay preacher after his conversion to Christianity.

Flagship of Vice Admiral Nagumo's Carrier Striking Force, the 36,500 ton fleet carrier *Akagi* at sea in 1941.

IJN *Kaga*, the 38,200 ton carrier, accompanied her flagship *Akagi* on all her wartime missions and together they were both sunk at the Battle of Midway in June 1942.

The small carrier *Hiryu*, 17,300 tons, took part in the Darwin strike and the sortie into the Indian Ocean, helping to sink the two British cruisers and a carrier, and striking at Colombo and Trincomalee. April 1942.

of the day, had been firmly rejected. Strangely, this rejection stemmed largely from a personal feud between General Tomoyuki Yamashita, victor of the Malayan campaign, and a member of his staff, Colonel Masonobu Tsuji. They first fell out over out-flanking tactics along the Malayan peninsula: Tsuji lost face before his fellow officers and the differences increased until the breach was unbridgeable. The colonel pursued a course of vilification against the general which was pursued in Tokyo and at court by Tsuji's patron and protégé, Prince Mikasa, no less a person than Emperor Hirohito's brother. So strong was the prince's influence that even when Singapore fell just two months later – perhaps the greatest Japanese military feat of arms – Hirohito treated his ablest general with near scorn, denied Yamashita a triumphal entry into Tokyo and had him posted back to his old command in Manchuria. But, more importantly, the Emperor turned a deaf ear to a plan of Yamashita's as audacious as the Malayan blitzkrieg itself: the invasion of Australia.

Yamashita wanted to land an expeditionary force on Australia's undefended, almost measureless northern coast if only to terrorise the country with a division or two of Japanese troops. Yamashita was anxious to lead such an invasion personally. Despite the vastness of the sub-continent – an area five-sixths the size of America – he considered it would be feasible to land a division at Darwin to speed like a javelin down the north–south road and rail links to Adelaide and Melbourne 2000 miles away on the southern shores of the country. A second division, Yamashita proposed, should land on the east coast and leap frog from port to port until the final prize of Sydney could be reached. Opposition, he reasoned, would only come from the Australian civilian population and tough though they may be they would be no match for seasoned Japanese veterans from Singapore. An officer in Darwin half-expecting a landing at any minute, commented at the time that all his men needed to do was to kill twenty Japs each to win the day. Australian troops in their own country numbered a mere 7000 regulars, for the bulk of the Australian Army was already committed in England, the Western Desert, the defence of India and Burma: in Singapore alone more than double this figure – 15,000 Australians – had surrendered and now languished in notorious prison camps on the naked island.

Prime Minister Tojo and most of the elders on the General Staff opposed the Yamashita plan on several counts but mainly on the inability to provide air superiority and on the logistics problems, placing expeditionary columns in jeopardy.

Hirohito agreed that the plan to invade Australia should be postponed – until after the conquest of Burma: and in terms of global strategy he ruled that the proposed advance towards India and the Middle East and the division of the world with Hitler should take precedence over an Australian campaign. Hitler was more sanguine about this concept.*

Despite the American cryptanalyst's breaking of the Japanese code, the Allies were unaware of the Japanese intentions regarding Australia and the Australians braced themselves for the worst. January and February saw many comings and goings of US warships in Darwin. In early January the submarine depot ships or tenders in harbour were *Holland* (8100 tons) and *Otus* (3600 tons): there were also the destroyer tender *Black Hawk* (5600 tons) and the seaplane tenders *Langley* (11,050 tons), *Heron* (an ex-minesweeper of 840 tons) and *William B. Preston* (an ex-destroyer of 1190 tons). Also in harbour were the oilers *George G. Henry* and *Trinity*.

However, the US naval authorities soon became disillusioned about the use of Darwin as a base and they soon decided to shift to Tjilatjap to speed the turn-around of submarines and also 'because Darwin, not entirely suitable from the beginning, was becoming intolerable'.† The depth of water was accounted a disadvantage: in the event of any tenders being sunk the great depth would make chances of salvage well nigh impossible. Accordingly, early in February, *Holland, Otus* and *Black Hawk*, accompanied by the oiler *Trinity* were despatched to Tjilatjap. They were escorted by the destroyers *Alden* and *Edsall*. *Heron* followed them a week later on the 10th. The next day *Langley* and *George G. Henry* sailed for Fremantle where the seaplane tender was to embark aircraft for the defence of India.

On 15 February, shortly before 0200, the US cruiser *Houston*, destroyer *Peary* and the RAN sloops *Warrego* (1600 tons) and *Swan*

***Hitler's Table Talk 1941–1944: His Private Conversations*, Weidenfeld and Nicolson, 1953. Hitler said: 'I can well imagine that Japan would put no obstacle in the way of peace on condition that the Far East were handed over to her. She's not capable of digesting India and I doubt whether she has any interest in occupying Australia and New Zealand . . . both of us need fifty to a hundred years for the purpose of digestion: we for Russia, they for the Far East.'

†*The United States Navy at War 1941–1945: Official Reports to the Secretary of the Navy*. USGPO.

(1060 tons) departed from Darwin with a convoy of four transports filled with troops to reinforce threatened Timor. US General George Brett had expressed US concern since mid-January about the failure to reinforce the island, but the Australians, understandably with their eyes fixed on the New Guinea scene where events were developing alarmingly, were not prepared to send a force from their depleted reserves to support what many believed to be a lost cause anyway. Brett persisted and was rewarded by an Australian concession to send a force comprising in the main a Pioneer Australian battalion, a troop of anti-tank guns and a detachment of US field artillery. This force embarked in the transports *Meigs* (12,568 tons), *Mauna Loa* (5436 tons), *Talagi* (2300 tons) and *Port Mar* (5551 tons). These transports and their escorts set course westward, a course well southward of the direct route to Kupang. A little after 1100 the convoy was sighted by a four-engined Japanese reconnaissance flying boat and shadowed. Three hours later, in a position about ninety miles west of Darwin, an ineffectual raid developed and no damage was sustained.

The next day the shadowing was resumed and soon after 1100 – about 330 miles from Darwin – the convoy and escorts were subjected to an hour long attack by thirty-six twin-engined bombers and more four-engined bombers from Kendari.

Houston distinguished herself by throwing up a barrage 'like a sheet of flame'; the flash of her guns, related an observer, 'was so constant that she appeared to be ablaze the whole time'. This strenuous defence, plus that contributed by the sloops and destroyer gave the convoy an immunity from the high level bombers which would never have been so against dive bombers. In the event, the only achievement of the bombers was slight damage to the *Mauna Loa*. However, the combination of these attacks, the deteriorating situation in Timor and the suspected presence of heavy Japanese naval forces in the Banda Sea prompted General Wavell's staff to cancel the convoy operation. Captain Rooks led his cruiser round at 1515 and headed the convoy back to Darwin, reaching this busy port in the forenoon of the 18th.

Admiral Doorman, in dire straits in the Java Sea, had urgent need of the US warships so *Houston* and *Peary* were directed to join him: they departed later that day. *Houston* reached Tjilatjap safely and joined Doorman's hard-pressed and ill-fated Striking Force. Soon after leaving Darwin, the destroyer *Peary* parted company with

Houston to hunt a suspected submarine in the course of which she consumed so much fuel that Lieutenant-Commander Bermingham was compelled to return to Darwin to replenish her tanks from the fuel bunkers. She arrived there early in the morning of the 19th. By a strange quirk of fate this abortive submarine hunt was to lead directly to the loss of the destroyer and the majority of her crew.

Thus, on 19 February the only remaining US naval vessels in the port of Darwin in addition to the refuelling *Peary* was the seaplane tender *William B. Preston.* The other vessels in port comprised the three US transports *Meigs, Mauna Loa* and *Port Mar* of the returned Timor convoy, and the Australian coastal trader *Talagi* which made up the fourth member of the convoy.

Another US ship, *Admiral Halstead*, a freighter of 3289 tons, was a recent arrival in port. There were also two tankers: *British Motorist* of 6891 tons and the Norwegian vessel *Benjamin Franklin* (7034 tons). Both were loaded with oil fuel to replenish the Darwin tanks. There were three more Australian ships: the *Neptuna* (5952 tons), the *Zealandia* (6683 tons) and the *Barossa* (4239 tons). The latter was loaded with timber for wharf extensions in the harbour. The *Neptuna* carried materials for the extension of the boom plus an explosive cargo of 200 tons of depth charges. The *Zealandia* had arrived in Darwin on 6 February with stores from Sydney, but by the 19th she was still only partially unloaded.

Also in harbour, shining bright and clinically clean, so clearly recognisable as a hospital ship was the *Manunda*, awaiting instructions because her original destination, Singapore, now lay in Japanese hands.

A number of small Australian naval vessels contributed to the congestion in the harbour, notably the depot ship *Platypus* which, as we have already seen, had recently arrived from Sydney, and the sloops *Warrego* and *Swan* from the Timor convoy. In addition there were corvettes of the 24th Minesweeping Flotilla, one of whom, the *Katoomba*, was under repair in the floating dock, having survived a collision with the US tanker *Pecos*: and the *Deloraine*, shackled like a prisoner to a buoy near her sister corvette in the dock, boilers dismantled and immobilised, she was destined to be a spectator of great events. Finally, there were a number of smaller boom working vessels, gate vessels, channel patrol boats and sundry small harbour craft.

The harbour's deficiencies and in particular the inability of the wharf to berth more than two vessels at a time began to cause problems of congestion with resultant delays in unloading. Conditions of working were made intolerable for a period of eight days by a cyclone which hit Darwin on 2 February and virtually brought the harbour to a standstill. In an effort to speed up the unloading of ships those in the stream tediously discharged their cargoes into lighters and small harbour craft: these harbour craft then had to be unloaded, thus twice handling thousands of tons of stores and equipment on to makeshift landing sites on the beach and on to the incompleted boom jetty.

Two ships were withdrawn from their minesweeping duties – the *Tolga* and *Terka* – in order to act as water carriers to the ships at anchor because the only water pipe for ships lay on the only wharf, accessible only to ships alongside.

On the morning of 19 February the normal activities of a busy harbour were proceeding at a leisurely pace. The gate vessel *Kara Kara* and boom working vessel *Kookaburra* were in position at the eastern and western end of the boom, the main section of which was nearing completion. In the vicinity of the boom there were the other three boom working vessels, *Karangi, Koala* and *Kangaroo*, the 300-ton examination vessel *Southern Cross* and the little 34-ton patrol craft *Coongoola*. Close by were the two auxiliary minesweepers *Gunbar* and the *Tolga*.

Seawards, beyond the boom, a light westerly breeze barely ruffled a smooth sea and a clear tropical blue sky patterned by a few slow-moving fine weather clouds gave promise of yet another sunny day: and soon enough a bright sun rose from out of the waters of the Arafuta Sea, bathing it in hues of yellow, gold and pink. Visibility was extreme.

As already recorded, the wharf was fully occupied with the *Barossa* alongside occupying the inner berth with an oil lighter secured outboard of her. On the outer leg of the wharf was the *Neptuna* with the sloop *Swan* having secured outboard of her just that morning.

The floating dock with *Katoomba* safely inside her was sited some thousand yards south of the wharf. *Platypus* was anchored not far away and the antiquated 14-ton lugger *Mavie*, a relic of Victorian days, was alongside. On the townside of the harbour, north-west of the floating dock there were at anchor the *Zealandia*, dutifully exercising her ship's company at boat drill, the Australian hospital ship *Manunda* and the tanker *British Motorist.* Farther to the westward lay the four ships from the abandoned Kupang convoy which had all disembarked their troops – *Port Mar, Meigs, Mauna Loa* and *Talagi.* Scattered around the harbour in various berths were the USS *Peary*, the *William B. Preston*, the corvettes, about twenty small craft and tenders, plus *Warrego* with working parties over the side chipping away her rust and re-painting.

Far out of Darwin, towards Bathurst Island, two small Filipino vessels, the *Florence D* (2638 tons) and *Don Isidro* (3200 tons), were steaming northwards in an attempt to run the Philippine blockade.

When the sun rose from the Arafuta Sea and bathed Darwin and all these vessels in its warmth, it also shone upon the *Houston* hastening to Tjilatjap: farther away it brought into sharp relief the assault forces of Rear Admiral Tanaka's Timor invasion convoy. More menacingly, it cast shadows among the dive bombers and fighter aircraft assembled on the flight decks of Nagumo's Carrier Striking Force.

We had left the ubiquitous admiral sortieing with his Force from Palau and we must briefly re-trace our steps and follow his fortunes to see what brought him to within striking distance of Darwin.

His Force left Palau with the instruction to neutralise Darwin as a base for Allied operations against the proposed Japanese occupation of Java. The Force stopped momentarily at Staring Bay, the outer harbour of Kendari in the Celebes, then proceeded southwards across the Banda Sea. The Forces now under Nagumo's command for the Darwin operation and heading for the launching point in the Timor Sea comprised an impressive fleet of warships:

PORT DARWIN STRIKING FORCE Vice Admiral Chuichi Nagumo in *Akagi*.
Chief of Staff Rear Admiral Ryunosuke Kusaka.

Carrier Group Vice Admiral Chuichi Nagumo 1st Carrier Squadron

Akagi Captain Taijiro Aoki

Air Unit Commander	Commander Mitsuo Fuchida
Zero Fighters	Lieut.-Commander S. Itaya
Dive Bombers	Lieutenant Takehito Chihaya
Level Bombers	Lieut.-Commander S. Murata

Kaga Captain Jisaku Okada
Air Unit Commander Lieut.-Commander Tadashi Kusumi
Zero Fighters Lieutenant Masao Sato
Dive Bombers Lieutenant Schoichi Ogawa
Level Bombers Lieutenant Ichiro Kitajima

2nd Carrier Squadron Rear Admiral Tamon Yamaguchi
Hiryu Captain Tameo Kaku
Air Unit Commander Lieutenant Joichi Tomonaga
Zero Fighters Lieutenant Shigeru Mori
Dive Bombers Lieutenant Michio Kobayashi
Level Bombers Lieutenant Rokuo Kikuchi

Soryu Captain Ryusaku Yanagimoto
Air Unit Commander Lieut.-Commander Takashige Egusa
Zero Fighters Lieutenant Masaharu Suganami
Dive Bombers Lieutenant Masahiro Ikeda
Level Bombers Lieutenant Heijiro Abe

Support Group Rear Admiral Hiroaki Abe in *Tone*
8th Cruiser Squadron 8 Rear Admiral Abe
Tone Captain Tametsugu Okada
Chikuma Captain Keizo Komura

Battle Squadron Captain Masao Nishida in *Hiei*
Hiei Captain Masao Nishida
Kirishima Captain Sanji Iwabuchi

Screen Rear Admiral Sentaro Omori
1st Destroyer Flotilla Rear Admiral Omori
Abukuma Captain Seiroku Murayama
Destroyers: *Tanikaze Urakaze Isokaze Hamakaze Shiranuhi Kasumi Kagero Arare Akigumo*

The composition of this Darwin Striking Force has been a source of much dispute and controversy. Roskill[1] quotes without identification four carriers, two battleships and three cruisers: Morison,[2] quoting Commander Isawa[3] under interrogation in October 1945, says a force comprising the same number of ships, but adds that Admiral Kondo commanded the Battle Squadron. Fuchida and Okumiya,[4] clearly state the same number of ships but Fuchida later

1. Captain S. W. Roskill, *The War at Sea*, Vol II
2. S. E. Morison, *The Rising Sun in the Pacific*, Vol III
3. United States Strategic Bombing Survey (USSBS) No. 94 (Navy 19) 12 October 1945
4. *Midway* by Fuchida and Okumiya

contradicted himself in discussions with Lockwood[1] when he substituted the heavy cruisers *Maya* and *Takao* for the two battleships and went so far as to allow Lockwood to sketch a sailing plan showing four heavy cruisers and no battleships. Rohwer,[2] the War History Division of the National Defence College, Tokyo and Tabular Record of Movements (TROM)[3] all agree on the composition of the force as set out above.

The original plan for the destruction of Darwin had not got off to a smooth start. There had been some personal rivalry between the flag officers Nagumo and Yamaguchi. It was the latter who had asked the Commander-in-Chief, Admiral Yamamoto, if his Carrier Squadron (*Hiryu* and *Soryu*) could mount the raid. At the time there was some indecision as to whether Darwin or Ceylon should be raided first. Commander Genda was asked for his opinion. He regarded Darwin as the major threat to the Japanese Netherlands East Indies campaign: intelligence reports indicated a build up of naval and air forces* in the Darwin area and Genda concluded that it should be eliminated as an offensive base as a matter of urgency. Yamamoto accepted the advice and gave the order for the strike, but Yamaguchi was dismayed at the stipulation that it should be a joint operation by the 1st and 2nd Carrier Squadrons – with the overall command Nagumo's.

On 9 February Nagumo received the signal detailing Order No. 92: it comprised a situation appraisal and the order to attack Darwin:†

> Owing to our air attacks at the beginning of February, the enemy, with its main base in Java, lost most of its naval and air strength. It is highly probable that they are planning escape to Australia, India and South Africa. It is also probable that the naval strength of Britain, the United States, the Netherlands and Australia will appear in the eastern Indian Ocean to pick them up. It appears that a part of the enemy strength is already taking refuge in the vicinity of Port Darwin. Intelligence shows that part of the US air reinforcements, together with British and Australian forces are based there.

1. Douglas Lockwood, *Australia's Pearl Harbour: Darwin* 1942
2. J. Rohwer and G. Hummelchen, *Chronology of the War at Sea 1939–1945*, Vol I 1939–1942
3. Tabular Record of Movements (TROM) – See Appendix A – Sources and Bibliography

*The reference to the build up of air forces was, of course, wrong.

†Quoted in Lockwood's *Australia's Pearl Harbour* and credited to Japanese naval historian Hitoshi Tsunoda.

At an opportune time, the carrier task forces will conduct mobile warfare, first in the Arafuta Sea and next in the Indian Ocean endeavouring to annihilate the enemy strength in the Java area from behind.

For the surprise attack on Port Darwin on 19 February, the task force will advance to the Arafuta Sea. After the surprise attack it will return to Staring Bay for supply.

The document goes on to detail submarine operations to be executed in the Indian Ocean, Malacca Strait, the south coast of Sumatra and the Torres Strait.

The Darwin raid was to be the greatest naval air strike since Pearl Harbor. Nagumo was according Darwin the rare honour of launching 188 strike aircraft, just one less than the number that attacked Pearl Harbor.*

Commander Mitsuo Fuchida, idolised by the fleet for his leadership of the Pearl Harbor strike, prepared to lead the groups of aircraft about to be launched for the first strike against a new continent. Tension was running high aboard the carriers. Aircraft had been brought to a state of preparedness since before dawn: mechanics fussed over their aircraft and tuned engines to a high pitch. Pilots, like Japanese warriors of earliest times embarking upon battle, had partaken of the traditional meal of rice, soybean soup, pickled plums, chestnuts and *sake*. Now, they stood about engaged in nervous banter while the aircraft lifts hoisted their bombers and fighters to the flight deck where the aircraft were manhandled into position.

Officers on the *Akagi*'s bridge watched the activity with keen interest: Nagumo, stocky, fierce and formidable: Captain Taijiro Aoki, the commanding officer: Chief of Staff Kusaka, plump and anything but agile: Commander Shogo Masuda, the Air Officer: Commander Miura, the fleet navigator stood, as always, in his carpet slippers: he reported to the Captain that the flagship was in position 9 degrees S and 129 degrees E, the position for launching the attack.

The carriers altered to a reciprocal course – north-westerly – to take advantage of the light breeze for flying off.

*The number of aircraft calls for comment. Roskill quotes 'some 150 attack aircraft' and fighters: Gill states a mere 81 carrier borne aircraft. Bergamini's *Imperial Japanese Conspiracy* convincingly states 189, but ATIS document 'Invasion of the Dutch East Indies' quotes '36 fighters, 71 carrier bombers and 81 carrier attack planes' which totals 188, precisely the figure Fuchida quotes. True figures are: 36 Zero fighters, 71 Type 2599 and 81 Type 2597 bombers.

Commander Minoru Genda, Air Unit Commander, planner of the whole air strike, watched the air fleet assemble under the leadership of his Academy classmate, Fuchida.*

The flagship's loudspeakers blared 'All hands to launching stations', and then 'Start engines'. Activity on the flight deck flared even as the exhausts themselves vented flame and smoke. The softness of the dawn was ruptured.

Aoki ordered 'Commence launching' and Commander Masuda swung his green signal lamp in a wide arc over his head. The leading Zero crawled forward, engine roaring, gathered speed rapidly down the flight deck, dipped momentarily then climbed aloft. It was 0845 on 19 February 1942. Lieutenant-Commander Haya Shigura, veteran combat pilot and idolised fighter ace, led his group of escorting Zeros. Waving and shouts of '*Banzai*' from flight deck crews cheered each aircraft on its way.

Aboard the massive *Kaga* and the smaller carriers *Hiryu* and *Soryu* the identical routines were being observed while the air fleet assembled glistening in the rays of the rising sun, then, led by Fuchida, the air fleet set course 148 degrees for Darwin.

Darwin was unaware of the impending attack. It had not been a difficult decision, therefore, to release ten US Kittyhawk fighters from Darwin for the defence of Timor. At 0915 these fighters took off for Kupang under the command of Major F. S. Pell, but about fifteen minutes later an adverse weather report induced Major Pell to cancel his flight and to reverse course for Darwin. It was at about this time that the first evidence of an air raid was received by Darwin. It came in the form of a teleradio message from the aborigine mission station on Bathurst Island, reporting the sighting of Nagumo's formations of aircraft heading south.

Hardly had five of the returning Kittyhawk fighters landed at Darwin than the first Japanese fighters struck. The Zero's pounced upon the five remaining Kittyhawks like falcons, destroyed four of them in as many minutes and then strafed those which had landed and were making frantic efforts to take off again. All were destroyed. The lone Kittyhawk which survived the first attack managed to land, claiming to have shot down one fighter and two

*Douglas Lockwood in *Australia's Pearl Harbour* quotes the amusing story of his meeting Fuchida in Hollywood: he asked the Japanese flyer to define the roles of Genda and Fuchida. 'Genda wrote the scripts,' he replied, 'I directed. My pilots did the shooting.'

dive bombers. But even this aircraft was destroyed later in the day.

The first sighting of the enemy aircraft from Darwin itself came when Lieutenant G. Robertson commanding an AA post on the heights overlooking the harbour at Darwin Oval, identified the approaching aircraft as enemy by their large red roundels, and taking a leaf from Rear Admiral Bellinger's book at Pearl Harbor signalled 'This is no drill. This is fair-dinkum.'

It was the leading group of fighters which first struck at the harbour and strafed the ships with machine gun fire. The auxiliary minesweeper *Gunbar* was passing through the boom gate when she was attacked at 0957 and suffered damage and casualties. The fighter attacks ended at 1010. During this spell all the boom working vessels and the gate vessel *Kara Kara* suffered damage or injuries.

At 0958 the air raid alarms ashore began their wailing, and within a minute the bombs began to fall. They were released from the leading group of high level bombers from a height of about 14,000 feet. The planes approached the harbour from landward, over the back of the town, having made a wide sweep to port in their approach. The bombs rained down and exploded with flashes and columns of water and smoke. In the first few minutes hits were scored on the wharf severing oil fuel and water pipe lines. The oil fuel ignited and spewed over the wharf, blanketing the area like a smoke screen.

'The wharf labourers had knocked off for the ten o'clock smoke-oh and were bunched at the elbow of the jetty. A bomb hit near by, hurled a locomotive into the sea and took away an entire span, effectively trapping the surviving workers.'*

Ashore, early hits were scored on government offices, shops and homes, on the hospital, the post office and police station.

Within minutes of the initial attack the high level bombers gave way to Lieutenant-Commander Egusa's dive bombers which attacked either singly or in small groups of two or three.

By this time, too, all ships with any defence armament had opened fire and shell bursts, gunfire and the noise of machine gunning added to the general din. Fuchida's planes found the opposition's AA fire ineffectual, the element of surprise had caught

*G. Hermon Gill, *Australia in the War of 1939–1945*, Australian War Memorial, Canberra.

the defences unprepared and the response was fragmentary and un-coordinated. The severity of the attack was overwhelming. Fuchida later criticised Nagumo for using an anvil to crack a nut.*

In the first minutes of the initial attack the *Neptuna* and *Barossa* alongside the wharf were struck by bombs. Both vessels were secured alongside the wharf with wires, and both had vessels secured outboard of them. HMAS *Swan* had tied up to the *Neptuna* only minutes before the attack developed to take on explosives. She still had steam up and prudently cast off rapidly.

The *Barossa* had an oil lighter alongside and it stayed there throughout the raid.

Neptuna, destined to produce the most gigantic explosion of the day had also only gone alongside that morning. The intention was to unload her cargo of explosives which principally comprised 200 tons of depth charges. It was Egusa's dive bombers which brought disaster. The first bomb to strike *Neptuna* penetrated the bridge and exploded between decks. The second struck aft, plunged through the decks into the boiler room and exploded. The death roll was high. The ship blazed like a bonfire. She was doomed. Those still alive abandoned ship but the wharf – and escape route to safety – had now been severed and the only hope for survival was to swim for the shore. Oil and debris littered the water, patches of burning oil killed and maimed many seamen, the majority of whom were Chinese. The end was inevitable. When it came, the explosion rocked the town. Smoke rose in a mushroom fashion to a height of 300 feet and red hot fragments of the vessel, as lethal as shrapnel, showered the harbour.

The corvette *Deloraine*, immobilised by dismantled boilers, secured to a buoy near by, heeled over in the explosion as if rocked by a violent Atlantic storm. She survived the blast with nothing more than splinter damage from the flying debris of *Neptuna*.

The warships *Swan, Warrego, Peary* and *Willian B. Preston* all with steam up managed to get under way, but their AA gunfire, though vigorous, was not a deterrent. The pilots pressed home their attacks courageously. The *Swan* was heavily damaged by a bomb which exploded close alongside as she strove to get away from the *Neptuna*. But one of the earliest and most tragic episodes of the whole day centred on the four-funnelled destroyer USS *Peary*.

Although the Pacific war was only weeks old, this gallant old

**Midway* by M. Fuchida and M. Okumiya, page 58.

destroyer had already experienced an eventful war. On 10 December at Cavite she was struck by a bomb in the crow's nest above the bridge; nearly all those on the bridge were killed, the captain, Lieutenant-Commander Harry Keith being peppered with shrapnel and splinters. He was replaced by Lieutenant-Commander Bermingham, under whose command she survived another air raid on 26 December. Two days later she was mistakenly bombed by an Australian aircraft. On the flight south from Manila she sought sanctuary by a small tropical island, some of her crew sleeping ashore to escape the heat aboard ship: many caught malaria and died.

Now, in Darwin's harbour under attack, she suffered a direct bomb hit almost before she had managed to open fire against her attackers. Her steering gear was demolished. Another bomb, taken amidships, demolished the galleydeck-house, caused extensive damage and many casualties. A huge blaze was started which quickly enveloped the whole ship. A third bomb pierced the main deck, entered Number 2 fireroom and went out through the hull plating without exploding. It mattered not at all. The fourth bomb created the second worst explosion on this convulsive day in Darwin. The bomb struck a for'ard magazine. A fifth bomb – superfluous, for the destroyer was already doomed – exploded in the engine room. These bomb hits caused fearful damage and casualties.

Lieutenant-Commander Bermingham strove to make the open sea – as most seamen would – rather than fight in the confines of a crowded harbour, but *Peary* began to settle by the stern and seemed 'like a hunted deer trying to escape while shot in the hindquarters'.* Her guns were still firing even while her decks became awash. She never made the open sea. Mr T. Minto, Chief Officer of the hospital ship *Manunda*, later recalled that only ten minutes after the first bombs struck Darwin, the *Peary* 'was on our port side a solid mass of flame with burning oil all around her and what was left of the crew jumping into the burning oil. We manned our lifeboat . . . and went to their rescue and eventually picked up over thirty badly burned and wounded men'.† *Southern Cross* also managed to rescue some of *Peary*'s men. But even as she lowered her boats Zero

***Report* by Chief Officer T. Minto of *Manunda*, quoted by G. Hermon Gill in *Australia in the War of 1939–1945*, Vol II page 593.

†*Ibid.*

fighters machine gunned the 300-ton examination vessel.

The death toll was high. Lieutenant-Commander Bermingham and all his officers except Lieutenant R. L. Johnson were killed or drowned in the action together with seventy-six of the ship's company. For several days thereafter the dead bodies of *Peary*'s sailors were washed up on the inhospitable Darwin beaches. It was a long way to come home.

Peary was not alone in her ordeal. Although the seaplane tender *William B. Preston* also managed to get under way, she too took a bomb aboard well aft, damaging her steering gear. Mr Minto reported 'An American destroyer [the seaplane tender was, in fact, a converted destroyer] went dashing across our bows, missing us by inches and steering with her engines.'

The seaplane tender's commanding officer, Lieutenant-Commander Etheridge Grant, was ashore at the time of the raid. He was not aware that his first lieutenant had got the ship under way. But under way she was, and she managed to reach twenty knots in a harbour congested with shipping under dive bombing attack, itself an achievement. Then, with the wheel hard over in an effort to make the bombers miss, the tender took three direct hits. One, on the main deck aft, killed eleven men. Damage was extensive but strenuous efforts to control the fires and the damage were successful. *Preston* got through the boom at twenty-five knots and made good her lucky escape to Broome the next day. The first lieutenant sent a Catalina to pick up the commanding officer who himself had survived a day of remarkable adventures crewing a launch rescuing survivors from disabled and sinking ships in harbour.

Mr Minto's eye-witness account from *Manunda* at the time of the *Peary* sinking reported the fate of other ships in harbour. The tanker *British Motorist*, off the hospital ship's bow, was sinking by the head, her valuable oil cargo still aboard. The *Tolga* took off survivors and the tanker was left to sink. The transport *Mauna Loa* had her back broken and was down by the stern. Another transport, the *Meigs*, was on fire aft and beginning to settle. She had taken a tremendous pounding. Upwards of twenty bombs struck her, and possibly a torpedo as well. Her captain, Master F. S. Link was wounded in the throat, chest, back and thigh. He gave the order to abandon his ship and she settled in a depth of eighteen fathoms.

The master of the *British Motorist*, Captain E. C. Bates, and the wireless operator J. Webster, were killed when the first bomb struck the bridge. A second bomb hit the tanker for'ard. She began to list to port and the fires which were started amidships raged uncontrolled. Ship was abandoned. Blazing fuel oil swept across the harbour engulfing men and rescue boats.

Dive bombers continued to wreak havoc. The antiquated little lugger *Mavie*, secured alongside the depot ship *Platypus*, was struck and sank. The depot ship herself suffered three more near misses and machine gunning, but fought off every attack with her AA guns. She became immobilised by damage to the engine room, the result of the bomb blasts.

The harbour had become the scene of incredible activity with all the small vessels taking whatever action they could to succour the damaged and sinking ships. *Southern Cross* with *Peary*'s survivors aboard also collected wounded from the US transport *Port Mar*, now beached in an effort to save herself, then helped the *Admiral Halstead*, laden with a cargo of aviation spirit, and damaged by near misses.

The two minesweepers *Tolga* and *Terka* with some patrol boats stood by the *Zealandia*. She had been struck and set ablaze aft. As she swung to the tide and brought the light breeze aft the fire swept through the ship until she blazed unchecked throughout her whole length. Her crew abandoned ship and she became a total loss. The corvette *Katoomba* in dry dock fought off a dive bomber so spiritedly that the Japanese pilot missed his target.

The ancient 292-ton naval tug *Wato* gallantly managed to secure a line to the oil lighter alongside the burning *Barossa* by the wharf and managed to get her clear.

While all this activity was going on the hospital ship came under attack and suffered extensive damage from the effect of two bombs. The first was a near miss. It exploded with a thunderous roar, rocked the ship, killed four people and peppered the ship with 'seventy-six holes and over a hundred deep scores in our plating overside and played hell with our gear and upperworks'.* The next bomb was almost fatal. It struck squarely amidships, shattered the after end of the bridge, caused severe internal damage and resulted in a number of casualties, including twelve killed.

The hospital ship was readily recognisable as such, painted gleaming white with prominent red crosses. Fuchida later agreed

Report by Chief Officer T. Minto.

that he had seen the crosses. He added that his flyers had been instructed not to attack hospital ships. Seven fires erupted throughout the vessel only one of which proved serious. Water mains were severed making fire fighting difficult. 'The after end of the bridge,' Mr Minto reported, 'was blown away, along with our wireless equipment, the direction finder and echo sounder. The chart room was adrift . . . the compasses were all to hell . . . the steering gear controls . . . were badly cut by shrapnel.' Despite all this damage the *Manunda* continued to function as a hospital ship. Indeed, it was fortuitous that she was in Darwin on this dreadful day for the wounded and dying were ferried across to her. By nightfall she had seventy-six patients.

The decision to sail the *Manunda* was soon taken and she embarked 190 more patients from the hospitals ashore. She sailed late at night on 20 February with 266 patients aboard. Nineteen died on the passage to Fremantle and were buried at sea.

After the *Neptuna* had exploded the *Barossa* was helped clear of the wharf by a tug then managed to beach herself where her cargo of timber was allowed to burn itself out. She herself was salvaged and finally towed away to Brisbane.

It was about 1100, just twenty minutes after the all clear sounded in Darwin, when Wyndham radio station received a distress signal from *Don Isidro*: 'Am being attacked by aircraft' off Bathurst Island. The other Filipino ship, *Florence D*, was also attacked by the same squadron of dive bombers. *Don Isidro* was struck by five bombs and set ablaze, but she managed to beach herself on the south-western extremity of the island of Fourcroy. Seventy-three people were rescued from her the next day by the *Warrnambool* who herself survived an attack by a four engined bomber before collecting more survivors from the *Florence D*. Other survivors from the *Florence D* managed to scramble ashore on Bathurst Island. There, the aboriginals believed the seamen to be Japanese and the Filipinos thought the aboriginals savages. But good sense prevailed and the survivors were cared for and eventually reached Darwin safely.

In a little less than one hour, Commander Fuchida's last aircraft had left the scene at Darwin. In the harbour ships were blazing, sinking or beaching themselves. The toll of ships and men was heavy. See Appendix B for the full details of losses. The USS *Peary* was sunk as were the merchant ships *British Motorist, Neptuna, Zealandia, Mauna Loa, Meigs*, and the small naval craft *Mavie* and

Kelat. The *Barossa, Port Mar* and *Talagi* were all beached, but later salvaged. Ships were damaged in varying degrees; these included *Admiral Halstead, Manunda, William B. Preston, Swan, Warrego, Platypus, Gunbar, Kara Kara, Kangaroo, Kookaburra* and *Coongoola*. The loss of life totalled 250, of which *Peary*'s contribution was eighty and *Neptuna*'s forty-five.

Ashore the scene was one of utter devastation. Darwin was a shambles. The civil hospital was severely damaged. The police barracks had been reduced to rubble. The post office and telephone exchange had been destroyed and the postmaster's residence severely damaged. Houses, shops and offices were destroyed. Government House was damaged and the Administrator's office in the grounds was demolished. The army camp out of town was badly damaged. Fires blazed. Smoke obscured much of the damage. Rubble, bricks, plaster and dust littered the streets. Dead, dying and wounded were tended as best as could be. The final toll was heavy.

Darwin's fierce ordeal for the day was not yet over. At five minutes before noon the air raid sirens wailed once more and within minutes a second raid began. The official war history commented:*

> To most of the people of Darwin the rapidity with which the second raid followed the first meant only one thing – it was a pre-invasion bombardment. Therefore it is not too surprising that many left as fast as they could. The siren was the starting signal for civilians to enter the Adelaide River Stakes. The exodus, though disgraceful in many ways, was in the best interests of the Armed Services.

The reference to Adelaide River was to the township seventy-two miles south of Darwin. The road south ended there.

For this second raid Lieutenant-Commander Toshie Irisa and Lieutenant-Commander Takeo Ozaki each led a flight of twenty-seven twin-engined shore-based bombers from Ambon and Kendari.

They sought out the airfield four miles outside Darwin. The dense black smoke of blazing ships and oil from the harbour – and the stench of burning fuel oil – was drifting across Francis Bay to the RAAF airfield. In minutes, more smoke and flames were to erupt.

Ozaki and Irisa led their flights in a pattern bombing operation of

*G. Hermon Gill, *Australia in the War of 1939–1945*, Australian War Memorial, Canberra, page 595.

great intensity and accuracy. The target was smothered. The hospital, recreation huts and airmen's dormitories, administration block and houses were all hit. Hangars and equipment stores were blasted to steelwork skeletons. The runways were cratered like a Flanders battlefield. The nearby oil storage tanks were hit, exploded and added impenetrable black smoke to the scene of devastation.

Ozaki and Irisa led their flights back to base. They were well satisfied. By now, Fuchida and his aircraft had traversed the Arafuta Sea and had safely alighted aboard their carriers. Nagumo's Force, flushed with the glow of another triumph, set course for Staring Bay. Their victory had been achieved at derisive cost. Figures of Japanese aircraft losses are always difficult to reconcile, but the probable figure is five aircraft lost. Fuchida in later years quoted seven but Tsunoda, despite his assurance that the figure was two aircraft, is unlikely to have been right.

A mystery also surrounds the pilot of a Zero fighter from *Hiryu*. He was first class pilot Hajime Toyoshima. He was seen to crash land on Melville Island. On the flight back to *Akagi*, Fuchida broke radio silence to tell Nagumo of the success of the operation and of Toyoshima's forced landing. Nagumo ordered a float plane away from a cruiser and its crew landed on the beach – the first and only landing on Australian soil by the Japanese. The crash landed pilot was not found although he was believed to have survived and to have been taken prisoner by the aborigines. Mystery now attends the story. Toyoshima's name never appeared in Australian prisoner of war records, nor in the list of repatriated prisoners, nor of those who died in captivity. As far as Australia is concerned Toyoshima never existed.*

Darwin, savaged beyond description, survived Nagumo's attentions. Australia, too, survived. But she was to be threatened again in ten weeks time when the Battle of the Coral Sea developed. In these intervening weeks more sombre events lay over the horizon and it is to these events we must now turn our attention.

*See Douglas Lockwood's *Australia's Pearl Harbour*, Appendix III, page 218, for a fuller account of this mystery.

CHAPTER 4

Collapse of the Indies

25 FEBRUARY 1942 was a day of destiny in the Indies. For the purposes of attempting to unravel the complexities of the politico-military–naval situation both north and south of the Indonesian barrier with the carrier squadron, screening units, amphibious forces, together with the mass of Allied merchant shipping and warships constantly shifting in moves of considerable complexity, it is this date which is convenient to take as a datum point in time. It was a day of shattered fortunes, of staggering triumphs, depending upon whether one was the vanquished or the victor.

Nagumo's Carrier Striking Force recovered its air fleet from the sweep of blue sky above the Arafuta Sea and returned from the Darwin strike in buoyant mood to Staring Bay. Nagumo's star, like those of his commanders, remained at its zenith. The pilots, officers and ship's companies, bound by their great sense of duty and exhilarated by their martial triumphs, were developing an attitude of invincibility bordering on complacency which contributed to what was later to be termed Victory Disease.

On 25 February Nagumo's force left Staring Bay with the two-fold task of cutting off Allied escape from Java and of preventing reinforcements reaching the island from India, Ceylon and Australia. The force, in fact, was a double one. It comprised Nagumo's majestic Carrier Striking Force consisting of the carriers *Akagi, Kaga, Hiryu* and *Soryu*; the battleships *Hiei* and *Kirishima*; the 8th Cruiser Squadron, *Tone* and *Chikuma*; and the light cruiser *Abukuma* leading the destroyers *Tanikaze, Isokaze, Hamakaze, Urakaze, Shiranuhi, Kasumi, Arare, Kagero* and *Akigumo*; and six supply ships. This force was followed out of Staring Bay by Vice Admiral Kondo with his Support Group, with his flag in the heavy cruiser *Atago*: he had with him *Takao* and *Maya*, the battleships *Kongo* and *Haruna* and the six destroyers *Arashi, Nowake, Hagikaze, Maikaze, Akatsuki* and *Hibiki*.

For the next few weeks they were to operate in unison in the seas to the south of Java and Sumatra astride the escape route for vessels fleeing from Java.

Before we consider the depredations of these two Japanese forces south of Java we must turn our attention – if only cursorily – to the savage struggles of the British, American, Dutch and Australian naval forces north of Java.

Java was the main prize which the outstretched arms of Japan hoped to embrace and it was this island which, from the outbreak of the Pacific war, held the key to so many Allied hopes. Admiral Hart, fleeing from the collapsing Philippine campaign, arrived there in December as did, technically, the US Asiatic Fleet which, in fact, was not a fleet at all. Admiral Sir Geoffrey Layton, Commander-in-Chief East Indies, left threatened Singapore in January to set up his headquarters in Java taking with him Rear Admiral Palliser as Senior Naval Officer, Batavia, with the main duty of convoy direction duties.

This was a period of bustling organisational activity both in London and Washington. Changes in national and inter-Allied high commands were being made with bewildering rapidity to meet situations which were quickly and constantly changing – and, indeed, deteriorating in the face of the relentless Japanese advances. Stability of a sort was achieved when Winston Churchill visited Washington to consult with President Roosevelt. It was agreed to set up an Allied Supreme Command in the South-West Pacific. The selection of Field Marshal Sir Archibald Wavell, then C-in-C India, as Supreme Commander with the title ABDACOM came at the suggestion of the Americans. It was evident at the time that with the military-naval situation deteriorating so steadily that the appoint-was a stop-gap one destined for failure even before the organisational command could be implemented. No doubt there is some truth in the accusation that the Americans were happy that a British or even a Dutch C-in-C would have to accept the odium of defeat which assuredly lay ahead.

Wavell arrived at Singapore from India on 7 January and with General Pownall as his Chief of Staff proceeded to Java where he set up his HQ at Lembang near Bandoeng on 10 January.

Admiral Thomas Hart was given command of the Allied Naval Forces with the title of ABDAFLOAT while Admiral Karel Doorman, who enjoyed the support of the British, was appointed Commander Combined Striking Force of the Allied navies.

Hart did not enjoy a harmonious relationship with his Allied colleagues: he did not endear himself to Admiral Layton by insisting upon having Rear Admiral Palliser as his Chief of Staff, compelling Layton to seek a replacement SNO Batavia. He chose wisely in selecting Captain J. A. Collins RAN with the rank of Commodore. But Hart was unhappy with his appointment: with a HQ up country, remote from the seat of operations, with a deplorable communications network often extemporised by radio and wire, and, like many Americans, he probably felt that the battle was not his, that fighting to save an outdated colonial empire was none of his business. Very soon he was sent home on the pretext of ill health* which diplomatically allowed the appointment of Admiral Helfrich as the Allied Naval Commander who declined the title ABDAFLOAT and resumed the title of Commandant der Zeemacht (CZM). So many changes were taking place that even the admirals themselves hardly knew what their status really was.†

By 25 February the carefully organised Supreme Allied Command in the South-West Pacific, with only six weeks of fragile existence, with its nicely balanced international sub-structures, was crumbling like timber plagued with dry rot. A few days previously the Combined Chiefs of Staff in Washington had instructed Wavell to defend Java with the utmost resolution by all available combatant troops. 'Every day gained is of importance. There should be no withdrawal of troops or air forces of any nationality and no surrender.' Their instructions were unequivocal. But only one day later Wavell was told to leave his HQ – and Java – at his discretion.

Prior to all this high level activity, Helfrich had confessed to Wavell on 20 February that he was unable to defend Java with the forces at his disposal and asked for diversionary demonstrations to the east and west of Java by the British Eastern Fleet and by the Anzac Force in the Pacific, but these diversions were not practical.

On 25 February Wavell dissolved his command as hopeless and with most of his HQ staff flew from Java to India where he resumed command as C-in-C India. The other Allied members of the ABDA Command dispersed. ABDA had collapsed.

*Only days before, when visiting *Houston* and *Marblehead*, he had displayed the agility of a midshipman when inspecting these cruisers.

†S. E. Morison's *History*, Vol II page 279.

The resolute and courageous Dutch refused to surrender their island home without a determined fight but Helfrich and Doorman knew that the Allied naval forces available to form a Combined Striking Force to defend the island were completely inadequate for the task. Annihilation faced them yet still they were prepared to sail and fight. We are not concerned here with the melancholy details of the Battles of the Java Sea and the Sunda Strait, but it was in these engagements that the Allied losses mounted alarmingly: *De Ruyter*, *Java*, *Exeter*, *Perth* and *Houston* plus several British, Dutch and American destroyers were all destroyed.

If there had been any chance of saving Java before, then the defeat and dispersal of all the Allied naval forces north of the island by 1 March dispelled all hope. The best that could be hoped for was to flee to the sanctuary of Ceylon or Australia. Resistance crumbled fast and on 9 March Java surrendered.

CHAPTER 5

South of Java

THE GALAXY OF Japanese admirals – Takahashi, Kurita, Takagi, Hara, Tanaka and Nishimura – had swept the seas north of Java free of Allied surface vessels with almost disdainful ease in the first major Japanese naval engagement since Tsushima in 1905. It remained for Vice Admiral Kondo and Vice Admiral Nagumo lying in wait to the south of Java with their powerful forces to mop up the fleeing remnants of the Allied forces. The Japanese net was spread wide. Their patrolling aircraft ensured that the mesh was fine. And their harvest was rich.

It was on 25 February, as already related, that Nagumo's Carrier Striking Force had sailed from Staring Bay, skirted Timor's north west coast, passed into the Indian Ocean and steamed west for a position south of Java. It was on this same day that Field Marshal Wavell had given up the fight for Java basing his decision largely on the lack of air protection for the island. But with stubborn Dutch optimism Helfrich believed that aircraft could be brought in to save the day. Before the island of Timor fell on 23 February, pilots hazarded their aircraft in landing on the tiny staging strip on that island before attempting the flight to Java, but after the 23rd the only way to get aircraft to Java was by sea.

The US aircraft tender *Langley*, captained by Commander R. P. McConnell, was the ideal vessel for such a task. She had enjoyed a chequered career. Built as a collier thirty years before, she was converted to a carrier in 1922 but was later consigned to the duties of an auxiliary. Now, in a belated effort to reinforce Java with aircraft, thirty-two P 40 fighters were shipped aboard her in Fremantle. They were already assembled, prepared for flying off. Twenty-seven more P 40's were crated into the holds of the freighter *Sea Witch*. Also aboard *Langley* were thirty-three new pilots. These two vessels departed Fremantle on 22 February as part of a convoy whose destination was Bombay. The US light cruiser

Phoenix was released from the Anzac Force as escort. Arrangements had been made for a British cruiser of the Eastern Fleet to take over escort of the convoy in the vicinity of the Cocos Islands at which juncture *Langley* and *Sea Witch*, accompanied by *Phoenix* should peel off from the convoy then head almost due east to Tjilatjap.

But with the situation deteriorating rapidly in Java Helfrich gave a desperate, and on the face of it a foolhardy order which was to have grave consequences. He ordered Commander McConnell in *Langley* and Lieutenant-Commander Hatfield, master of the *Sea Witch* to detach from the convoy much sooner than planned and to make a dash independently at best speed for Tjilatjap. In due time HMS *Enterprise* relieved *Phoenix* who turned about and arrived in Fremantle the same day that *Enterprise* delivered the convoy safely to Colombo.

At Tjilatjap there was no airfield. There was not even a rudimentary air strip from which the ready assembled fighters aboard *Langley* could fly off. But Tjilatjap was the only port still safe in Allied hands capable of accepting the ship without the certainty of immediate bombing and probable loss. With a mounting sense of desperation spaces had to be cleared ashore to enable a long straight road to be employed as a makeshift air strip; the approach roads had to be widened, trees lopped or felled and native huts removed to make way for the spread wings of the P 40's. They would have to be towed all the way, principally by Dutch and US personnel because panic was already affecting the natives who were deserting the scene in their thousands. It was hot, humid work.

Under the original plan, *Langley*'s ETA at Tjilatjap was 28 February, in the early morning. Helfrich's new instructions – detaching *Langley* on the 23rd to make best speed for the port – gave a revised ETA of the late afternoon of 27 February. Helfrich's order – both rash and forlorn – bore the stamp of desperation for even he could not have believed that these few fighter aircraft could have saved Java from defeat.

McConnell had been told that he could anticipate escort on the final leg of the run for Tjilatjap by the US destroyers *Whipple* and *Edsall*. Both were on the sick list. *Whipple* had been in collision with *De Ruyter* and was confined to light duties. *Edsall* had developed bad leaks after exploding a depth charge too close astern. Both were regarded as not fit enough to sail with Doorman's Combined Striking Force.

Instead of the two destroyers making an appearance two Dutch float planes contacted *Langley* on the afternoon of 26 February and reported that the 1390-ton Dutch minelayer *Willem van der Zaan* was only twenty miles to the westward and was to act as escort.

McConnell was in a dilemma: should he await the minelayer or press on unescorted in the expectation of meeting the two destroyers? His original orders had not been countermanded so he gave orders to press on, zig-zagging, hoping to meet the destroyers, and out-stripping the minelayer. After dark on the 26th McConnell received a signal from Java confirming that the *Willem van der Zaan* and the two float planes were to be his escorts.

Dismayed at this unhappy turn of events, McConnell reversed course to try to locate the minelayer, losing many precious hours in the process. Eventually he came across the two float planes circling protectively over – not the minelayer – but the two US destroyers!

It was now well past 0700 on the 27th and more valuable time was lost while the destroyers hunted down a submarine contact. *Langley* stood off impatient to get away to Tjilatjap. Hours later all three ships resumed course for their destination.

At 0900 *Langley* was sighted by Japanese aircraft from a wide sweep of blue sky marred only by high scattered clouds. A fresh breeze streamed the ensign astern stiffly. McConnell realised that it was ideal weather for carrier aircraft and, sensing the danger, he signalled Java for air cover. None, of course, was available. It was all lashed aboard his own tender.

At 1140 more planes were sighted and *Langley* went to action stations. McConnell signalled his plight.

When *Langley* left the convoy on 23 February Admiral Nagumo's force of carriers was close by, within striking distance, and in the ensuing days air patrols must have failed to detect *Langley* by the narrowest of margins. In the end it was not Nagumo's planes which intercepted Langley but aircraft from Kendari and Bandjermasin flying air patrols into both the Java Sea and the Indian Ocean. The sighting aircraft called for reinforcements. It was not long before they appeared.

Nine two-engined bombers approached the tender at a height of about 15,000 feet and began their dive bombing attack. *Langley* and the two destroyers opened fire, but the destroyers' main armament comprised a single 3-inch AA gun apiece. As the first and then the second flights of aircraft dived at the ship at an angle of about

80 degrees McConnell ordered the ship hard-a-starboard and managed to avoid the bombs which burst close alongside. But the third run proved deadly. Of seven bombs directed at her, five scored direct hits and the other two near misses. The resultant damage was devastating. Many of the deckload of aircraft were destroyed and the shattered remains burst into flames, the bridge steering was damaged, the gyro compass wrecked and the site of each bomb burst became an inferno. *Langley* took in water and developed a list of 10 degrees to port.

McConnell reduced speed to minimise the fanning of the flames but in the stiff breeze this had little effect. Much of the blazing wreckage was jettisoned and counter flooding of some starboard compartments rectified the list.

Commander McConnell faced another agonising decision. He realised that *Langley* could probably make Java but she would not be capable of negotiating the treacherous narrows marking the approach to Tjilatjap: he decided to set course for the nearest point of Java in the hopes of beaching his ship. Soon after setting the new course a further inrush of sea water flooded both main motors and the ship came to a dead stop. At 1332 McConnell ordered the crew into the lowered lifeboats and abandoned ship while the escorts were still in company to rescue survivors. Admiral Glassford's subsequent *Report* implies that the abandonment of *Langley* was premature and that the ship might have been saved. There had been other criticisms of premature abandonment of ships in the early months of the war at sea in the Pacific but in this case it is likely that *Langley*'s pumps were quite incapable of containing the flood water.

The two destroyers rescued all but sixteen of the ship's company and air personnel. *Langley* was scuttled and helped to the bottom by torpedo and gunfire. It was a sad loss. She sank just seventy-five miles from Tjilatjap.

If McConnell's luck had run out it was compensated for by Lieutenant-Commander Hatfield's, whose command, *Sea Witch*, had a luckier passage. She eluded the Japanese, reached her destination, discharged her cargo, collected forty refugee soldiers and escaped safely to Australia.

On the day that *Langley* sank, the US oiler *Pecos* departed Tjilatjap bound for Colombo. Her astute commanding officer, Lieutenant-Commander Abernethy, had ordered lashed up top on the upper decks a cargo of large bamboo poles; these, he believed with foresight, would serve as life savers should the ship go down. Embarked upon *Pecos* were casualties from *Houston* and *Marblehead* and the crew of the destroyer *Stewart*, abandoned as a total loss in the dry dock in Sourabaya.* The total aboard numbered 342 compared with her normal complement of about 125.

Soon after leaving Tjilatjap she was ordered to rendezvous with *Whipple* and *Edsall* then steam to a position about 200 miles south of the Christmas Islands in order to take aboard the *Langley* survivors from the two destroyers. Commander Crouch in *Whipple* led the vessels to the southward and the transfer was affected satisfactorily on 1 March. The three ships then parted company.

Tjilatjap was a hive of activity to which land convoys of cars and trucks filled with retreating naval base staff from Batavia with documents and equipment were descending – including a train with survivors from the sunken British destroyer *Jupiter*.

A convenient date to dwell on the scene south of Java is 1 March. The seas were a mass of shipping movements. Admiral Helfrich had ordered merchant ships from Tjilatjap following the Java Sea defeat and on the last two days of February no less than thirty-four vessels sailed from the harbour, the majority of them Dutch merchantmen, supplemented by a few US warships. In the next three days there were thirteen arrivals and twenty-one departures. Thus, during the five days ending 3 March fifty-five vessels cleared the harbour. On 1 March the ships in harbour included the US destroyers *Pillsbury* and *Parrott*, the gunboat *Tulsa*, the old British destroyer *Stronghold* and two of the many merchantmen were the Dutchmen *Zaandam* (10,909 tons) and the *General Verspyck* (1213 tons).

Approaching the harbour from the westward were the 650-ton escort sloops *Burnie* and *Bendigo* and astern of them what can be termed the HMAS *Yarra* convoy. It comprised the 1060-ton sloop herself and the RIN sloop *Jumna* as escorts for the ships *Anking*, *Francol* and *MMS 51*. The previous evening one of the convoy, the tanker *British Judge*, had been torpedoed south of the Sunda Strait but had remained afloat. She was now some way astern of the convoy

**Stewart* was not, in fact, a total loss. She was salvaged by the Japanese and this old four-stacker – now with one funnel removed – served her new masters for the remaining years of the war as Patrol Boat No. 102.

with the brand new 650-ton sloop *Wollongong* as escort, both of them crawling towards Tjilatjap. Also heading for the port were four ships of the 21st Minesweeping Flotilla, *Maryborough, Toowoomba, Ballarat* and *Goulburn*. Farther away at Padang HMAS *Hobart* embarked more than 500 refugees and set out for Colombo with *Tenedos*: *Danae* and *Dragon* with the little *Scout* were to follow later.

Two hundred miles south of Java was HMAS *Warrego*, the 1060-ton sloop, heading for Tjilatjap, and 200 miles south of her Commander Crouch was completing the transfer of *Langley*'s survivors to the *Pecos*. Four hundred miles south-west of Christmas Island, USS *Phoenix*, having handed over her convoy to the *Enterprise* the previous day, was steaming for a point 15 degrees S 113 degrees E, the position designated as a rendezvous point for vessels escaping from Tjilatjap.

Another 400 miles west of *Phoenix* the graceful *Mount Vernon*, a US transport with 4668 Australian troops aboard, was making best speed towards Australia, the first of a number of transports returning the Australian Imperial Forces from the Middle East to the threatened homeland. Spread around these seas were other vessels, sailing independently, bearing equipment, motor vehicles and supplies for the AIF.

Farther away, to the north-west, lay a prize that Nagumo would dearly have loved to intercept. It was the Convoy SU1 escorted by HM ships *Royal Sovereign* (29,150 tons), *Cornwall* (9750 tons), the destroyer *Express* (1375 tons), the corvette *Hollyhock* (925 tons) and the RAN ships *Manoora, Nizam* and *Vampire*. The convoy comprised twelve ships* carrying 10,900 troops out of Colombo for Australia.

All these – and many more ships of trade – were still carrying out their lawful voyagings throughout the Indian Ocean on the routes linking Australia with South Africa, Ceylon, India and the Middle East.

Nagumo's presence was known by virtue of the code-breakers, but it was unclear what were his precise intentions. Much was made clear on the afternoon of 1 March when the first sighting of the Force was made by aircraft of the Dutch Naval Air Service.

***Eastern Prince* (10,926 tons), *City of Paris* (10,902 tons), *City of London* (8956 tons), *Esperance Bay* (14,204 tons), *Kosciusko* (6852 tons), *Egra* (5108 tons), *Salween* (7063 tons), *Silverwillow* (6373 tons), *Penrith Castle* (6369 tons), *Mathura* (8890 tons), *Madras City* (5092 tons), *Empire Glade* (7006 tons).

Earlier that morning *Pecos, Whipple* and *Edsall* after heading south at thirteen knots, lay to and began transferring the *Langley* survivors by boat in heavy seas, a tedious proceeding which lasted three hours. Once completed, *Edsall*, with the thirty-three *Langley* pilots aboard, headed for Tjilatjap and *Whipple* set course for the Cocos Islands. *Pecos* now began her ordeal by battle.

At about noon a formation of nine bombers from *Soryu* located her in a position only about thirty miles SSW of *Akagi* and began an attack. *Pecos* – an oiler – was ill-equipped to repel an air attack and her puny AA defence proved ineffective against the ensuing onslaught. Despite all Abernethy's efforts to avoid the bombs, the ship was struck and severely damaged. Strenuous efforts were made by damage control parties to keep the old ship in action. A second flight of aircraft from another of Nagumo's carriers added to the damage about an hour after the first attack. But it was the third attack, from yet another of Nagumo's carriers, which put paid to the ship. Five direct hits and six near misses reduced her to a blazing wreck littered with dead, dying and wounded. *Pecos* died hard. As she went down, what remained of her bamboo poles floated clear: she also got off a distress signal and a position report. The sea was littered with the debris of a sunken ship, with the dreaded oil fuel that contaminated the sea at every sinking and with the survivors of *Pecos, Langley, Stewart, Houston* and *Marblehead* who now lay awash on life rafts, others clinging to lifelines, more aboard the single lifeboat to get clear, and others kept buoyant by the bamboo poles.

The rest of the afternoon passed with a lowering of spirits until darkness descended and added to the dismay of the survivors. Then a light appeared. The survivors were anxious in case the vessel might be Japanese. Nevertheless, a Very light was fired. The vessel which came upon the scene was *Whipple*. Knotted ropes and willing hands helped the survivors aboard. Two hundred and twenty men had survived the ordeal and were rescued, but they represented probably only one third of the number aboard *Pecos* at the time of her sinking. At 2130 rescue was brought to a dramatic end when an Asdic echo demanded action. Commander Crouch set in motion a depth charge attack and effectively killed any hope of further rescue. With every compartment and flat crammed with US seamen, the destroyer *Whipple* sped for Fremantle at a rattling speed. It was ironical that fuel caused dreadful privations to the rescued seamen and it was the depleted fuel tanks of *Whipple* which soon necessitated a considerable reduction in speed in order to reach her destination safely.

Whipple made it, but *Edsall* failed. On her way to Tjilatjap she stumbled into the mighty Nagumo Striking Force. At 1747 in a position 14 degrees 34′ S 106 degrees 51′ E the battleships *Hiei* and *Kirishima* and the cruisers *Tone* and *Chikuma* detached themselves from the main body of the force and chased *Edsall*. She was never heard of again. There is a dearth of information from the Japanese on many episodes and engagements south of Java between 1 and 4 March. What information is available is culled from the records of the interrogations of Japanese officers after the war.

Many years later, research unearthed a poor quality film by a Japanese officer of the last moments of the *Edsall*. Rough seas pounded the old destroyer as she endeavoured with the desperation born of fear to flee her pursuers as heavy shells burst close alongside, straddled then finally struck home, reducing her speed and setting her up for the kill. She sank at 1906. There were no survivors from the gallant *Edsall*. The thirty-three pilots had gone by a roundabout route to their deaths.

USS *Asheville*, gunboat relic of an imperial age, survivor of years of overseas service in Chinese waters and the seas of the Pacific, also fell victim to Nagumo's force. Only two radioed words 'Raider. Raider,' were heard from her: then the silence of doom. She had been seen last by HMS *Bendigo* at 1720 in a position 10 degrees 30′ S 110 degrees 10′ E – about 140 miles NNW of Nagumo on 2 March. After the war a *Houston* survivor related the story of Fred L. Brown,* whom he met as a fellow prisoner of war. There had been no alarm aboard *Asheville*. The first announcement of the enemy was shells falling close by and some exploding aboard. Brown went up top in the general confusion and rush to action stations to find the bridge and fo'c'stle heavily hit and dead and wounded littering the decks. Soon the gunboat sank under the hail of fire from three destroyers. Brown was the only survivor hauled from the sea by the Japanese. He was transferred to a captured Dutch hospital ship then to a prison camp at Makassar. Four years later, the lone *Asheville* survivor died.

. . . . .

*Quoted by Admiral Kemp Tolley in his remarkable book *Cruise of the* Lanikai, Naval Institute Press, Maryland, 1973.

The US destroyer *Pillsbury* suffered a similar fate. She disappeared without trace. In fact, it was units of Nagumo's force who sank *Pillsbury*, probably Admiral Kondo's own cruiser flagship *Atago* with *Maya* and *Takao*. It is probable too that the Japanese genuinely wrongly identified the old four-stacker destroyer as the light cruiser *Marblehead* – also a four funnelled ship. This is possible if the visibility was as poor as the weather conditions at the time suggest, and if it was a night engagement. No one survived the *Pillsbury* sinking. On 11 March Imperial Headquarters issued a communiqué announcing 'A Japanese cruiser formation, operating in the Indian Ocean west of Australia on 2 March sank the 7050-ton United States cruiser *Marblehead* which was fleeing towards Australia.' Thus ended *Pillsbury*'s career in the anonymity of the friendless wastes south of Java. But the record of Allied losses is not yet complete.

HMS *Stronghold*, destroyer of another, bygone age, departed Tjilatjap on the evening of that dreadful day of 1 March. She delayed her departure so that she could provide anti-submarine escort for the Dutch *Zaandam* who had spent the day embarking refugees. They sailed in company at 1800 for Fremantle. *Stronghold* provided escort until midnight when *Zaandam* forged ahead independently at a higher speed while the destroyer was compelled by reason of fuel economy to keep below fifteen knots. At about 0900 on the 2nd Japanese patrolling aircraft sighted the destroyer. The weather was fine, visibility good, but there was a heavy swell. *Stronghold* was shadowed by aircraft throughout the forenoon and afternoon. Just before 1800 in a position about 300 miles south of Java, the Japanese heavy cruiser *Maya* and the destroyers *Arashi* and *Nowake*, both modern vessels of over 2000 tons, intercepted her. The other two cruisers of Kondo's force – *Atago* and *Takao* – were present at the execution, but were content to stand off at some distance and watch the engagement as if at a firework display. The one-sided action did not last long. *Stronghold* fought to the end with her puny armament of one 4-inch and one 3-inch gun against her heavily armed adversaries. She took a severe battering by gunfire. Lieutenant-Commander Pretor-Penney, her captain, was fatally wounded on his bridge. The old destroyer soon lay stopped, immobilised and vulnerable. Ship was abandoned while *Maya* steamed slowly only 3000 yards off the starboard bow with the destroyers only 2000 yards abeam to port. A few minutes after abandoning ship the twenty-year old destroyer blew up and disappeared. The enemy ships, with heartless disregard for the survivors in the oil-coated heavy swell, turned away to rejoin their main force.

Soon after dawn on 3 March the *Stronghold* survivors were still clinging to Carley floats when a small Dutch KPM steamer, captured by the Japanese the previous day, came upon the scene and started rescue operations. Fifty men had been clawed aboard from two Carley floats when the cruiser *Maya* came along, stopped further rescue attempts and took the fifty survivors aboard. One of this party subsequently related that the treatment meted out to them was good: medical attention was given to the wounded and all were allowed up top several times daily for a smoke.

On the afternoon of the rescue of *Stronghold*'s survivors the modern sloop HMAS *Yarra* with her small convoy was ploughing her way SSE through the heavy swell at a mean speed of 8½ knots in a position about 180 miles NW by N of Nagumo's force. Although Nagumo's presence was unknown to *Yarra*, the Japanese had been shadowing the convoy since the previous day. On the 3rd *Yarra* sighted lifeboat sails and rescued Dutch and Javanese survivors from the Dutch merchantman *Parigi* (1172 tons) sunk by submarine *I-2* on 1 March. The rest of the 3rd and that night passed uneventfully except for a suspected submarine contact by *Yarra* who dropped two depth charges.

March 4th dawned with a glorious tropical sunrise but the beauty of the morning was dispelled by the clangour of the alarms for action stations. Over the horizon, to the NNE, three of Kondo's cruisers and destroyers hove into sight coming upon the convoy at speed. The encounter was in a position 12 degrees 15′ S 110 degrees 10′ E.* *Atago*, *Takao* and *Maya* and destroyers *Arashi* and *Nowake* in the words of a brief Japanese report of the incident 'sighted two enemy transport vessels under escort of two light naval units which were attacked by gunfire and sunk. None of the Japanese ships suffered any damage.' The Japanese report gave the bare bones of the story.

As soon as the British convoy was sighted two aircraft were catapulted from two of the Japanese cruisers to give general spotting help. Lieutenant-Commander Rankin turned his *Yarra* for the

*The position quoted is the Japanese. *Anking, MMS 51* and a later rescue ship *Tjimanoek* all recorded positions of considerable variation.

The Darwin Air Strike February 19th 1942:

(a) The detonation of *Neptuna*'s 200 tons of depth charges produced the biggest single explosion of the day. The corvette HMAS *Deloraine* in the foreground rocks to the blast.

(b) The gallant destroyer USS *Peary* suffered heavy casualties when dive bombed. She is seen here sinking by the stern while a merchantman blazes and lists heavily nearby.

(c) The pall of smoke rising from burning oil storage tanks merges with smoke from burning ships. A listing freighter is being abandoned.

Heavy cruiser HMS *Cornwall* sinking in the Indian Ocean on 5th April 1942 after a display of incredib accurate dive bombing by Nagumo's Val aircraft.

HMS *Hermes* was the only British carrier to be sunk by aircraft during World War II.

enemy to interpose the sloop between the cruisers and his charges, ordered smoke from the engine room in a vain attempt to cloak the convoy's movements. The ships were ordered to scatter. But the outcome of the encounter was predictable. With overwhelming superiority of firepower the Japanese were able to use the scattering vessels as target practice.

The first to succumb to the barrage of fire was *Anking*. She sank just after 0630. By then *Yarra* herself was heavily damaged, on fire and listing to port, but still engaging the enemy with her three 4-inch guns. *MMS 51* was on fire and being abandoned by her crew: scuttling charges had been set. As the survivors left her to her fate a cruiser came close by and riddled her with pom pom gunfire and she went down. At about 0730 the other merchant vessel, *Francol*, sank and the last to go was *Yarra*. Soon after 0800 Rankin ordered 'Abandon ship' and a few minutes later an 8-inch shell exploded on the bridge structure killing Rankin and creating awful damage. To the gunfire was added bombs from the spotting aircraft. Two Carley floats and thirty-four survivors – including the Dutch captain of *Parigi* – got away and watched in stunned silence the melancholy sight of heavy close range shelling to destruction of their ship.

Other witnesses of the sinking were survivors of *Stronghold* aboard the cruiser *Maya*. At the start of the action they had been secured below under guard but later they were allowed up top to witness the end of the *Yarra*. A New Zealand survivor later reported: '*Yarra* was the only ship left afloat and we could see flames and a good deal of smoke. The two destroyers were circling *Yarra* which appeared stationary and were pouring fire into her. She was still firing back as we could see odd gun flashes . . . The last we saw of *Yarra* was a high column of smoke . . . we were vividly impressed by her fight.'

The five Japanese ships steamed off to the NNE pausing only momentarily while one of the destroyers hoisted aboard twelve survivors from the *Francol*. Over the rest of the battle area the pitiful flotsam and jetsam of war at sea rose and fell to the swell. Fourteen of the crew of sixteen of *MMS 51* clung for life to floats. Forty-seven from *Anking* fared better in a lifeboat. One Chinaman clung to a raft in lonely solitude. Another two floats bore up the thirty-four *Yarra* survivors. All brooded unhappily on their plight but buoyed their spirits with the hopes of rescue.

Anking's lifeboat was sighted on 4 March by the Dutch *Tawali* (8178 tons) who took the fifty-four men aboard then steamed off, apparently unaware of other survivors in the area. The fourteen survivors of *MMS 51*, now augmented by the lonely Chinaman, survived the hot days and chilly nights until 7 March when they were rescued by the Dutch *Tjimanoek* at 1400. She, too, hastened on her way to safety.

The less fortunate *Yarra* survivors were compelled to endure another two days and nights before the low silhouette of the Dutch submarine *K 11* appeared. But those awaiting rescue now numbered thirteen: the captain of *Parigi* and twenty-one of the *Yarra* crew had perished. No other survivors of this convoy incident were ever found.

All survivors paid generous tribute to their Dutch rescuers for their customary kindness and generosity: 'No men in the world could have been kinder to us,' one *Yarra* man wrote of the Dutch submariners. The officers and crew of the *Tjimanoek* were similarly praised by the men of *MMS 51*: 'Our wounded were tended, we were given clothes and every attention possible and the kindness and hospitality of the Dutch captain, officers and crew were beyond praise.' These minesweeper survivors landed in Fremantle on the 13th. It was not until the 22nd that *K 11* arrived at Colombo and Admiral Layton was able to signal Australia that of *Yarra*'s crew of 151 only thirteen had survived their ordeal.

There were another dozen ships which must have missed destruction by a hairsbreadth for Nagumo's aircraft and Kondo's cruisers sectored their areas in planned searches, criss-crossing the seas in extreme visibility. The total number of ships accounted for by Nagumo and Kondo south of Java are listed in Appendix C. The fortunes of six of these have been followed – HMS *Stronghold*, USS *Pecos*, USS *Pillsbury*, USS *Edsall*, USS *Asheville* and HMAS *Yarra* – plus another eleven, including the ships of the *Yarra* convoy.

With the benefit of hindsight, it is a wonder that Nagumo and Kondo failed to achieve even more successes with such a dominating command of the seas. The situation compares with the end of the *Afrika Korps* when the remnants of the German army sought to flee Africa and Cunningham signalled to the Royal Navy 'Sink, burn, destroy. Let nothing pass.' Virtually nothing did.

By 10 March those ships which had managed to evade Nagumo's

net had all arrived safely in Fremantle: it was quite an impressive list: the US destroyer *Parrott*, the gunboats *Tulsa* and *Isabel*, HMAS *Warrego*, the sloop *Burnie* with the unaccustomed broad pennant of Commodore Collins, *Bendigo* with the survivors from *Jupiter* aboard; and the 650-ton minesweepers *Wollongong, Maryborough, Ballarat, Goulburn* and *Toowoomba*. The Dutch merchant ship *General Verspyck*, manned by a scratch crew of British naval evacuees, was another safe arrival. And it was on this day, too, that the *Mount Vernon* with her thousands of troops arrived at Adelaide. Other ships carrying evacuees from Java also made good their escape to Colombo.

For those vessels which remained at Tjilatjap there was no respite. On 5 March they met disaster at the hands of Nagumo's aircraft. Dive bombers and level bombers escorted by fighters from *Akagi, Kaga, Soryu* and *Hiryu* were launched to effect a neutralising strike against Tjilatjap. It was another sledge hammer operation like those against Rabaul and Darwin. A total of 180 strike aircraft were employed and the heavy bombardment reduced the town to ruins. Two hundred buildings were bombed to destruction or gutted by fire. Almost everything floating in the harbour was sunk or damaged. The following day many of the damaged ships were scuttled by their own crews to prevent the ships being captured by the Japanese. All these losses appear in Appendix D.

When Nagumo's aircraft struck at Tjilatjap on 5 March Japanese troops were firmly entrenched on the island, Japanese aircraft ruled the skies and Japanese ships dominated the seas. It could hardly be more than hours before the island fell. In the event, on 8 March Tjilatjap was occupied by triumphant Japanese soldiers and the following day General ter Poorten, now in command of the island following Helfrich's departure to Colombo, surrendered unconditionally.

Java, the prize of the Indies, lay submissively in Japanese hands. The whole of the Malay Barrier, Indonesian chain of islands and parts of the Bismarck Archipelago now formed a huge, natural defensive perimeter for their conquests. It was to be a long time before this barrier was to be penetrated in force by the Allies. Japan was reaching the prudent limit of her advance and would soon consolidate behind this natural, defensive wall.

. . . . .

Kondo and Nagumo, their powerful forces intact, returned to Staring Bay in the Celebes: the only scar of battle borne by the warships was the blistered paintwork on overheated gun barrels. These admirals had wrought destruction and now sought a period of what they regarded as well-earned rest.

CHAPTER 6

The British Eastern Fleet Assembles

ADMIRAL SIR JAMES Fownes Somerville, KCB, KBE, DSO retired from the Royal Navy in July 1939 terminating a distinguished career of forty-two years. But he was recalled to active wartime service and two-and-a-half years later he was appointed Commander-in-Chief of the newly constituted British Eastern Fleet. He had just completed a spell as commander of the famous Force H at Gibraltar with a heightened reputation little short of that attained by his Dartmouth classmate Admiral Sir Andrew Cunningham.

Lord Rodney, victor of the Saints, is part of the Somerville ancestry, as is Admiral Lord Hood; and another ancestor from whom Somerville took his middle name, commanded a sloop, the *Bulldog*. Somerville's own career progressed along normal Royal Navy channels until World War I. In 1915 he was promoted to the rank of Commander in the same year as he won a DSO at the Dardanelles. The rank of Captain came in 1921 and Rear Admiral twelve years later. In 1936 he was awarded the coveted appointment of Rear Admiral (Destroyers) Mediterranean, taking over from Cunningham. Two years later Somerville became C-in-C East Indies, but in the following year – 1939 – only weeks before the outbreak of World War II he was knighted and placed on the retired list on account of ill health.

Yet less than a year later, only weeks short of his 58th birthday and in recovered health, he was recalled to take command of Force H* at Gibraltar which was perhaps the most important appointment of his whole career.†

*The Force comprised a powerful array of ships including the carrier *Ark Royal*, the battleships *Malaya, Ramilles* and *Nelson*, the battlecruiser *Renown* and the cruisers *Berwick, Sheffield* and *Newcastle*.

†This period was highlighted by Force H's participation in a number of engagements including action against the French Fleet at Oran, convoys to Malta, the raid on

The choice of this man to command a new British Eastern Fleet was an appropriate one – a fighting admiral – the very title chosen by his biographer.* But even he was depressed at the prospect of his new command. He had just completed a strenuous eighteen months at Gibraltar when he received the signal of his new appointment on 15 December 1941 with the initial, incredible Japanese *Banzai's* still ringing around the world.

After a spell of home leave he saw the Prime Minister. 'You quite realise, my dear admiral,' Mr Winston Churchill confided to him, 'that you enjoy the confidence not only of the Admiralty but of the Government.' They then briefly discussed the strategy of the eastern theatre and how the Allies were to fight back. 'No adventures!' the Prime Minister adjured the C-in-C designate; an uncharacteristic piece of advice from the pugnacious Churchill who probably then, a few weeks after the event, still brooded disconsolately over the loss of the *Prince of Wales* and *Repulse*.

The defensive role being foisted upon him was hateful to Somerville who relished taking the fight to the enemy: to evade battle, to preserve his Fleet 'in being' was anathema to him. He was, after all, perhaps the most knowledgeable admiral in the Royal Navy on carrier operations and the tactical use of their aircraft. And carriers, by their very nature, were offensive weapons of war.

He was highly critical of one of the new carriers to join his command, the most up-to-date carrier in service, the *Formidable*, was 'green' and judged by the standards set for the *Ark Royal* in Force H was improperly worked up and unfit for offensive operations.

Somerville was aware of the many dangers about to face him but even he was not fully aware of the violent fury and deadliness of Nagumo's onslaught. The surrender of Singapore had a salutary effect upon him, as upon all other senior serving officers, but it had added impact coming as it did on the eve of his departure for the east on 17 February.

He sailed from the Clyde aboard *Formidable*, recently returned from a refit in a US Navy Yard and for the next few weeks on the outward passage via Capetown Somerville was to receive many

***Fighting Admiral* by Captain D. MacIntyre, Evans, 1961.

Cagliari, the Action off Cape Spartivento, the strike against Genoa and Atlantic operations in pursuit of the *Bismarck*.

signals cataloguing the list of Japanese triumphs: even before *Formidable* left home waters there came the news of the destructive Darwin strike.

The composition of the British Eastern Fleet had been the subject of considerable discussion at the Admiralty and of correspondence between the First Sea Lord and the Prime Minister many months before Japan was even an adversary in the war.

Fleet dispositions were a complex issue fraught with problems and ramifications of the utmost gravity. For example, a battleship damaged off Crete needs escorting to a United States Navy Yard for repair: her replacement must be drawn from the Home Fleet: cover for *her* detachment is sought from the US Navy which delays dispositions in the Pacific in order to make possible the temporary loan of a capital ship: a lurking, modern German battleship in a Norwegian fjord necessitates the deployment of no less than three 14-inch gun battleships to contain her: three, because two must be on station at any one time in order to engage in battle with a degree of superiority, the third to allow of refitting, repairing or resting one of the other two: remove one of these three at peril, for the Atlantic convoys are thereby jeopardised. The complicated war game proceeded in ever-changing scenes and demands, expediency and political pressures sometimes over-riding prudent professional assessments.

Winston Churchill wrote to the First Sea Lord, Admiral Sir Dudley Pound, on 25 August 1941, three-and-a-half months before Japan's 'day of infamy', on the subject of fleet dispositions in the Indian Ocean.*

It should be possible in the near future, to place a deterrent squadron in the Indian Ocean. Such a force should consist of the smallest number of the best ships . . . The most economical disposition would be to send *Duke of York* as soon as she is clear of constructional defects . . . She could be joined by *Repulse* or *Renown* and one aircraft carrier of high speed. This powerful force might show itself in the triangle Aden–Singapore–Simonstown. It would exert a paralysing effect upon Japanese naval action. The *Duke of York* could work up on her long, safe voyage to the east . . . I do not like the idea of sending at this stage the old 'R' class battleships to the east . . . the old ships are easy prey to the modern Japanese vessels, and can

*Winston S. Churchill, 'The Second World War', Vol III, *The Grand Alliance*, Appendix K.

neither fight nor run . . . I am however in principle in favour of placing a formidable, fast, high-class squadron in the aforesaid triangle by the end of October and telling both the Americans and the Australians that we will do so. It would always be an advantage, if possible, to change the armoured *Victorious* for the *Ark Royal* for service in the narrow waters of the Mediterranean, and I suppose you wish to strengthen Force H with one of the *Nelsons* as well as either *Repulse* or *Renown*. Naturally, C-in-C Home Fleet will require a first call upon an aircraft carrier, preferably *Ark Royal*. *Furious* will have to do some more work on ferrying aircraft to Takoradi. *Victorious* would be well placed in Force H. This would leave *Illustrious*, *Formidable* and *Indomitable*, as they came to hand, together with *Eagle* and *Argus*, for the needs of the Eastern triangle and the Mediterranean.

Churchill concluded with the touch of a schoolmaster: 'You ought to be very well off by the end of the year.'

This minute, which on the face of it appears plausible, was not to Pound's liking. Churchill could not, of course, take into account the loss of *Ark Royal* later in the year, but the minute did overlook a number of vital issues which Pound was quick to point out. His reply three days later was a comprehensive survey of the Royal Navy's global dispositions in capital ships and aircraft carriers, but we need only concern ourselves here with the Far East. The final dispositions being worked to, with the dates of ships' arrival on station were:

TRINCOMALEE	*Nelson*	end of November 1941
	Rodney	end of January 1942
	Renown	mid-January 1942
	Hermes	now: August 1941
	Ark Royal	April 1942
	Indomitable	in emergency
INDIAN OCEAN	*Revenge*	mid-September 1941
TROOP CONVOY	*Royal Sovereign*	mid-November? 1941
ESCORT	*Ramilles*	mid-December 1941
	Resolution	early January 1942

Pound justified these proposals to send *Nelson, Rodney* and *Renown** to Trincomalee or Singapore for the following reasons:

(a) *Nelson* and *Rodney* will eventually form part of the Eastern Fleet, when it is possible to form one, which is dependent upon the availability of cruisers and particularly destroyers.

*The trinity forever preserved in the lower deck lament 'Roll on the *Nelson*, the *Rodney, Renown* . . .'

(b) *Nelson* and *Rodney* will give the best backing to the 'R' class when the Eastern Fleet is formed . . .

(c) Until we can form a fleet in the Far East which is capable of meeting a Japanese force of the strength they are likely to send south it is necessary to deter Japanese action in the Indian Ocean.

By sending capital ships to escort our convoys . . . we hope to deter the Japanese from sending any of their battleships to this area.

By sending a battle-cruiser and aircraft carrier . . . we hope to deter the Japanese from sending their 8-inch gun cruisers to attack our trade . . .'

Pound did not consider the substitution of one of the *KGV* [*King George V*] class for the *Nelson, Rodney,* or *Renown* would give sufficient added advantages to outweigh the disadvantages of her absence from the Home Fleet would entail. And even a *KGV* did not have the speed to outrun an 8-inch cruiser. Pound proposed, further, that the three capital ships and the carrier should be despatched to Singapore as the greatest form of deterrent, retiring to Trincomalee in the event of war breaking out. Pound's appraisal continued:

(e) Owing to the necessity to refit *Ark Royal* it would not be possible to send a large carrier to join the force until April '42 unless we take *Indomitable* away from Force H.

INDIAN OCEAN TROOP CONVOY ESCORTS: It is proposed to send the four 'R' class to the Indian Ocean now for the following reasons:

(a) They are no longer required for the North Atlantic escort duties.

(b) They will eventually form part of the Eastern Fleet and until this time it is desirable to keep them in waters where they will be free from air and U-boat attack.

(c) By employing them for escorting troop convoys they will relieve the cruiser situation.

(d) Their presence in the Indian Ocean together with *Nelson*, *Rodney* and *Renown* will go some way to meet the wishes of Australia and New Zealand for the Far East to be reinforced.

Pound concluded that the spare or unallocated battle-cruiser *Repulse* would escort Convoy WS 11 and subsequently arrive at Trincomalee on 7 October.

Churchill's reactions to these proposals were predictably prompt and critical, deploring the creation of a fleet considerable in numbers but consisting of slow, obsolescent or unmodernised ships which could neither fight a fleet action with the Japanese nor act as a deterrent to modern, fast raiders acting singly or in pairs like the convoy raiders *Scharnhorst* and *Gneisenau*. These old vessels, Churchill commented, would leave themselves and their convoys easy prey. The 'R's' he warned would be floating coffins. The best use, he considered, even at this late stage was to armour them against air attack for use as a slow squadron for the Mediterranean to sustain Malta. Churchill concluded, that the inclusion of a *KGV* could well be a decisive deterrent to the hesitant Japanese.

A few weeks after this exchange of views the *Nelson* suffered damage which necessitated three or four months in dockyard hands. By October, too, other political matters began exerting an influence. Prince Konoye's government in Japan fell and was succeeded by General Hideki Tojo's who took upon himself the triple offices of Prime Minister, Minister of War and Minister for Home Affairs: he wielded almost as much power as Churchill in Britain.

On 16 October Anthony Eden, Foreign Minister, in a memorandum to Winston Churchill warning of the mounting dangers in the political situation in the Far East, urged upon the Prime Minister the necessity of despatching a deterrent force to the Far East and the desirability of including a modern battleship rather than any number of obsolescent capital ships in an effort to reassure the worried Australian and New Zealand governments.

At a resumed Defence Committee meeting on 20 October the weight of argument by the Prime Minister, the Foreign Secretary and the First Lord of the Admiralty, Mr A. V. Alexander, prevailed and Sir Dudley Pound agreed to a compromise solution. *Repulse* was already allocated to Trincomalee – she was there having completed escorting Convoy WS 11. *Prince of Wales* should replace the damaged *Nelson* and *Rodney*, sailing as far as Cape Town subject at any time to recall in case of need. The final decision as to her destination would be taken when she reached Cape Town. *Indomitable* would be despatched from the West Indies to join the *Prince of Wales* on passage.

Thus was the debate conducted and finalised. The deterrent force was despatched. Vice Admiral Sir Tom Phillips boarded the *Prince of Wales* in Greenock and hoisted his flag on 25 October. With the destroyers *Electra* and *Express* the flagship steamed through the drizzle for Cape Town. But only nine days out, Phillips received a signal notifying him of damage to the carrier *Indomitable* by running aground while completing her working up trials.

Phillips in the *Prince of Wales* arrived at Colombo on 28 November where *Repulse* was already moored in the capacious harbour. Awnings were spread, gangways rigged and the routine of a tropical harbour adopted with quick and accomplished ease despite the fact that sixty per cent of the ship's company were young men in their first sea-going commission.

Within fourteen days war had erupted in the east, the *Prince of Wales* and *Repulse* were sunk, more than 800 of their men dead or drowned, their admiral lost and the myth of the deterrent dispelled for ever in the inhospitable waters of the Gulf of Siam.* An unbelieving nation, headed by Churchill himself, mourned the loss. Only Pound could hold his head high with any justification, but above all he was a sailor and he too mourned younger comrades.

The loss of these two ships now demanded urgent replacement just at a time when the Royal Navy was least able to provide them.

Both *Ark Royal* and *Barham* had just been sunk in the Mediterranean and hard on the heels of the loss of Force Z Cunningham was to lose the *Valiant* and *Queen Elizabeth* to the intrepid Italian human torpedomen. Thus all three modernised battleships in the Mediterranean were out of commission. Churchill's August prediction to Pound of 'being very well off by the end of the year', simply proves the undesirability of making forecasts in wartime.

All that could be done to retrieve a situation almost past recall was to arrange to despatch the modernised veteran of Jutland, HMS *Warspite*, recently recovered from her Cretan battle wounds in Bremerton Navy Yard, Puget Sound, USA, to Ceylon to join the waiting *Resolution, Ramilles, Royal Sovereign* and *Revenge*. Churchill endeavoured to reassure the Prime Ministers of Australia and New Zealand and their Commonwealth governments, alarmed by the disastrous turn of events in the east, of the resolute determination of the British government to defend their interests to the utmost. At the time, the 'utmost' seemed to reside in two ships approaching Ceylon, *Warspite*, which had just left Spencer Gulf in South Australia on 9 March. And an ocean away – on 13 February – the carrier *Formidable* sailed from Cape Town with Vice Admiral Sir James Somerville aboard.

The British Eastern Fleet was moving to its station.

*See *The Hunting of Force Z* by Richard Hough for the detailed story.

CHAPTER 7

Somerville Assumes Command

VICE ADMIRAL SIR James Somerville completed the last ninety miles of his passage to the east in flamboyant style aboard an aircraft from *Formidable*. He arrived in the tropical heat of 24 March, the day after Japanese forces landed in the Andaman Islands. He was received at the airfield by Commodore Ralph Edwards who was to be his Chief of Staff and who had been Admiral Layton's Chief of Staff through the painful days of the loss of Force Z and the fall of Singapore. He was an ideal aide for Somerville.

The admiral was taken straightaway to see Layton who was presiding at a meeting of the Commander-in-Chief Ceylon.

Somerville quickly formed a favourable impression of the masterful activity of the C-in-C who gave every appearance of being in command of the situation sombre though it was. With Layton in charge ashore and his staff responsible for the organisation and administration of the bases at Colombo and Trincomalee Somerville felt free to concentrate on the sea-going aspect of his command. It needed his undivided attention.

On 26 March at 0800 Somerville hoisted his flag in *Warspite*, the veteran twenty-seven-year-old battleship newly arrived in Colombo, and formally assumed command of the British Eastern Fleet. Rear Admiral Denis Boyd was appointed Rear Admiral Aircraft Carriers with his flag in *Indomitable*. The fleet organisation was as shown on opposite page.

All Somerville needed now was time to train his fleet. It was the one thing denied him. Two days after assuming command Somerville received a report that a Japanese force intended to attack Ceylon by air on or about 1 April. He had barely a few hours before the anticipated attack on the island.

. . . . .

BRITISH EASTERN FLEET

Taking part in Naval Operations off Ceylon
29 March–10 April 1942
Commander-in-Chief Vice Admiral Sir James Somerville

FORCE A

Battleship:	*Warspite*	Captain F. E. P. Hutton
Carriers:	*Indomitable*	Captain T. Troubridge
	(12 Fulmars)	
	(9 Hurricanes)	
	(24 Albacores)	
	Formidable	Captain A. W. La T. Bisset
	(12 Martlets)	
	(21 Albacores)	
Heavy Cruisers:	*Dorsetshire*	Captain A. W. S. Agar
	Cornwall	Captain P. C. W. Manwaring
Light Cruisers:	*Enterprise*	Captain J. C. Annesley
	Emerald	Captain F. C. Flynn
Destroyers:	*Napier*	*Panther*
	Nestor	*Hotspur*
	Paladin	*Foxhound*

FORCE B

Acting Vice Admiral A. V. Willis

Battleships:	3rd Battle Squadron	
	Resolution	Captain A. R. Halfhide
	Ramilles	Captain D. N. C. Tufnel
	Royal Sovereign	Captain R. H. Portal
	Revenge	Captain L. V. Morgan
Carrier:	*Hermes*	Captain R. F. J. Onslow
	(12 Swordfish)	
Light Cruisers:	*Caledon*	Captain R. J. Shaw
	Dragon	Acting Captain H. J. Haynes
AA Cruiser:	*Heemskerck* (R.Neth.N.)	
Destroyers:	*Griffin*	*Norman*
	Arrow	*Vampire*
	Decoy	*Fortune*
	Scout	*Isaac Sweers* (R.Neth.N.)

Note: The carrier *Hermes* was slow and unsuited to fleet operations. Many of the other ships in these Forces were past their prime and were unfitted for a major fleet action. HMS *Dorsetshire* was undergoing refit at Colombo and was operationally unfit.

Before Somerville arrived in Colombo there had been much intense political activity ashore which has a bearing on this story.

On 25 February when ABDA Command disintegrated Field Marshal Wavell fled from Java to resume his appointment as C-in-C India. Another more radical change was made on 5 March: Vice Admiral Sir Geoffrey Layton was appointed C-in-C Ceylon. Churchill was well aware of the fragmentation of commands in the east which had contributed to the fall of Singapore and he determined that Ceylon should not suffer the same fate. It was largely at his instigation that Layton was given almost dictatorial powers including power over the Governor of Ceylon and over all naval, military air and civil authorities. He had the full backing of the UK government and of the Chiefs of Staff. 'Do not ask permission to do things,' he was instructed by the First Sea Lord. 'Do them first and report afterwards what you have done.' It was a unique appointment. It demanded a unique man. Layton proved the man for the job.

Layton had been profoundly shocked at the general state of unpreparedness of almost every aspect of defence on the island. In the busy port of Colombo go-slow strikes disrupted the organisation with the result that at times there were as many as fifty vessels lying in the exposed outer anchorages awaiting an opportunity to discharge their cargoes. The civil defence organisation was woefully inadequate: no gas masks existed: fire fighting arrangements were rudimentary: there was no radar warning system. Life in Ceylon proceeded at the leisurely pace normally associated with the peacetime routines in a beautiful tropical island.

Layton soon changed all this. Within a few short weeks he got all the defence services humming with activity. The working of the port was overhauled and ships and cargoes were soon being turned around with a speed and on a scale never seen before in Colombo. An improvised air raid warning system was installed and the civil defence and fire fighting services were re-organised. By 30 March the race course at Colombo sported an air strip which was to be put to effective wartime use within days of its completion. To this improvised air strip came some of the two squadrons of Hurricane fighters from the carrier *Indomitable* originally destined for Java but diverted by Layton to Ceylon.

These aircraft were just some of the reinforcements being despatched in all haste to Wavell in India and to Layton in Ceylon.

Wavell, curiously, had responsibility for the air defence of Ceylon. By the end of March the Chiefs of Staff in London promised Wavell fifty-seven crated Hurricanes for Karachi followed by another forty Hurricanes, forty Blenheim and ten Wellington bombers. By the middle of April the operational strength of aircraft for the defence of India and Ceylon would reach 182 and by the end of April 268. A strong fighter force was to be located in Ceylon at the expense of the defence of north-east India; the army in Ceylon was to be built up to such a strength as to act as a deterrent to a Japanese assault upon the island.

But numbers of aircraft was not the sole need. Air defence demanded an efficient technical and administrative organisation which India was sadly lacking – and needed time to establish. It was a laborious and time-consuming task.

On 13 March Wavell gave as his opinion to the Chiefs of Staff that although Ceylon 'would be threatened and raided it would not be attacked in force'. He recommended that the defences of Ceylon should be sufficient only to repel surprise strikes like those at Darwin and Pearl Harbor and to combat small commando-type landing parties.

But the real remedy to the defence problems of India and Ceylon lay in the sea. The War Cabinet were emphatic in their opinion that the defence of the naval bases in Ceylon was paramount.* The Chiefs of Staff advised Wavell that by the end of March the British Eastern Fleet under the command of Admiral Sir James Somerville would consist of five battleships, three aircraft carriers, eleven cruisers and fourteen destroyers concentrated in the Ceylon area. Just how deceptive this statement is will be seen later.

Wavell was much relieved by this promise of – what looked on paper, at least – a substantial fleet to protect Ceylon and India. He was advised by the Chiefs of Staff that the function of the fleet would be to maintain control of sea communications in the Indian Ocean. Somerville's fleet, it was made quite clear, was to act as 'a fleet in being', avoiding unnecessary attrition and the risk of crippling losses. The Chiefs of Staff accepted the fact that India might be at risk from attack by the Japanese invading Burma and that Ceylon might be savaged like Darwin.

On paper Somerville's new fleet looked impressive: five battleships, three aircraft carriers, a substantial force of cruisers and

*See Field Marshal Wavell's *Despatch*, para 3.

flotillas of destroyers. Many fears were allayed and morale received a fillip both at the arrival of such naval majesty and the Commander-in-Chief himself with his envious reputation of fearlessness and list of outstanding achievements in the Mediterranean. Somerville was delighted and touched by the reception he received aboard some of the ships he visited: he was among many old Force H friends and spontaneous cheering throughout ships of the Fleet occurred whenever he appeared aboard to address ships' companies. All this was good for morale, but in itself was dangerous for it simply helped perpetuate the illusion of strength displayed by the Fleet. 'I have an uneasy suspicion I'm regarded as a White Hope,' was Somerville's comment. This worried him slightly but what caused him the most anxiety was the miracles expected of him by Wavell who knew little of naval matters, and by the Admiralty who should have known better. Somerville could only assert that he could do nothing until his Fleet was trained and he was not prepared to use his forces offensively until he was satisfied they were in a fit state.

On 28 March he despatched a comradely signal of greetings to Admiral Nimitz, C-in-C Pacific Fleet: 'My Fleet,' he signalled, 'consists for the greater part of ships that have been employed almost exclusively on independent duties or are newly commissioned. I am engaged in giving them intensive fleet training and hope before long to report them as fit for offensive operations.' On this same day Somerville received notice of Nagumo's intended attack on Ceylon. Time had already run out – even before it began.

On 30 March Somerville went aboard his flagship in Trincomalee. It was pouring with rain. A gale whipped the rain across *Warspite*'s decks and added to the discomfort as seamen embarked great quantities of rifles aboard. This was an evacuation operation: taking guns aboard to save them from falling into enemy hands. It was a dispiriting duty.

A few hours later, embarkation of the rifles complete, Captain F. E. P. Hutton took the flagship to sea and headed for a fleet rendezvous for the evening of 31 March in a position eighty miles south of Dondra Head, the most southerly point of Ceylon. The fleet lay scattered over the Indian Ocean. Some, like *Warspite*, were steaming south from Trincomalee: others were leaving Colombo: the major part of the fleet, including the squadron of four 'R' class battleships, had departed Addu Atoll in the Maldive Islands, lying 600 miles south-west of Ceylon, a secret base established as a 'funk hole' in the event of Colombo and Trincomalee being attacked. Addu Atoll was flat, barren, a coral atoll as desolate as a desert island with only a scattering of palms to afford shade from the blistering sun.

Vice Admiral Algernon Willis, until recently Chief of Staff to Admiral Cunningham, was Somerville's second in command in the Eastern Fleet. It was he who had insisted that the battle squadron should spend all available time in training routines.

From Addu Atoll, too, emerged the carrier *Indomitable*, Rear Admiral Boyd's flagship, still engaged in badly-needed training for her aircraft squadrons and pilots.

All these ships were converging on the point south of Dondra Head.

Somerville's intention in the event of battle was to avoid a day action between opposing battle squadrons: to keep within aircraft range, keeping his distance by day and closing in at nightfall in order to launch aircraft for torpedo attacks by the light of the full moon. This intention was partly based on the belief, quite commonly held, that the Japanese, like the Italians, disliked night action.* It was also based largely on conjecture because Somerville was unaware of the size and composition of Nagumo's Force but his belief was that the enemy force comprised a powerful and balanced task force and he assumed, quite correctly, that it had been tempered in the heat and flame of battle and honed as finely as a Samurai sword. If subjected to daylight battle, Somerville believed his fleet to be, by comparison, little short of what Winston Churchill described as 'floating coffins'. His judgement was absolutely correct. The wonder is that the main fleet managed to evade detection. Had it been located by Nagumo's pilots a disaster of tremendous proportions would have overwhelmed the British Eastern Fleet. The relatively few British ships spotted by reconnaissance aircraft were attacked and sunk almost as a matter of course.

*With the benefit of hindsight we now know that Somerville was proposing a fatal course of action. Later events proved the naivety in believing that reconnaissance aircraft could keep Somerville informed of the Japanese daylight movements: Zero fighters patrolled above Nagumo's Force sweeping the skies clear of enemy aircraft. Indeed, it is fair to say that these Zeros would have been more successful in locating Somerville than vice versa. The belief that the Japanese disliked night action was wrong, of course, as was demonstrated in the night battles among the islands of the South Pacific.

CHAPTER 8

Ceylon: Target for Nagumo

THE FLEET THAT assembled at 1600 on 31 March in a position 4 degrees 40′ N 81 degrees E, 80 miles SSE of Dondra Head, bore all the trappings of admiralty and might. Not since the days of peace had a British Fleet of such substance assembled as a force. Massive twin 15-inch guns were trained fore and aft aboard the four 'R' class battleships as Vice Admiral Willis led them in impressive line ahead to the rendezvous. The battleships were accompanied by two fleet carriers, also displaying power, but none of the grace and majesty of the battleships, nor the style of the slim cruisers and the even leaner destroyers. Carriers enjoy no symmetry, their flat tops and one-sided island structures make them the ugly ducklings of a fleet: and, offensive vessels though they were, they themselves were vulnerable to attack from the sky.

But Somerville's command was like a scene from a Gilbert and Sullivan comic opera. The 'R' class battleships at full power could only make about eighteen knots. At this rate fuel consumption was so great that four days would find their tanks empty. Equally problematical was the question of water supplies: they were unable at anything above a medium speed to distil enough water to replace boiler losses. Water rationing imposed great hardships upon the crew who were restricted in their dhobeying and their personal washing in tropical temperatures which soared over the 100 degrees F (38 degrees C) mark between decks. Upper works became almost too hot to touch. Heat, sweat, smells, prickly heat – and the spectre of engaging Nagumo: even with the fillip of having Somerville around with his brand of charisma had already worn thin. 'Poor old girls,' Somerville commented about his battleships, 'they were much more at home in the North Sea: the tropics got them down.'

The carriers, too, suffered from the heat with their huge acreages of steel flight decks making the compartments between decks as hot as ovens. At night, for black-out reasons, scuttles and hatches were closed and the airless heat became intolerable.

The aircraft aboard these carriers were as outclassed by Nagumo's aircraft as the 'R' class battleships by Kondo's capital ships. The old Swordfish biplanes had at last been replaced by Albacore torpedo bombers but even this aircraft's performance made it easy prey for the Japanese Zero. Nor did the Martlets and Fulmars inspire confidence. Almost in every department Nagumo's aircraft and air crews enjoyed a superiority over their British counterparts.

Somerville's Fleet was a collection of variegated warships, not yet organised into squadrons and flotillas, for seniority lists of commanding officers had not yet been promulgated. As this random collection of ships assembled south of Dondra Head Somerville signalled his second in command: 'So this is the Eastern Fleet. Never mind, many a good tune is played on an old fiddle.'*

To be fair to Willis, he had put his few days at Addu Atoll to good use in training his battleships, to such an extent that Somerville was pleasantly surprised on seeing his 'old "R" class battleships squaring up for the fight. They manoeuvred as if they'd been together for weeks, not days.'†

But there was no disguising the fact that Somerville in 1942, like the Russian Admiral Rojdestvensky at Tsushima in 1905, also opposing the Japanese, led a force that was a travesty of a fleet.

For the purposes of meeting Somerville's battle intentions his Eastern Fleet was organised into two forces, the fast one designated Force A and the slower one Force B. The exact composition of these forces has already been presented in Chapter 7.

Throughout the night of 31 March Somerville led Force A south and east of Ceylon while Willis with his slow Force B positioned himself to the westward of Somerville as a support force. At daylight on 1 April the Forces turned about in the hope of keeping beyond the sight of any enemy patrolling aircraft which might be reconnoitring ahead of the Japanese fleet. In the absence of any firm enemy reports Somerville's course of action was pure conjecture based on the flimsiest of information. This was the original report received on 28 March warning that a Japanese force of two or more carriers, several cruisers and a large number of destroyers,

*_Fighting Admiral_ by Captain D. Macintyre, Evans Bros, 1961.
†Ibid.

possibly supported by battleships of the *Kongo* class, might attack Ceylon about 1 April.

Six Catalina flying boats – all of Ceylon's long range reconnaissance aircraft – maintained patrol sectors to the south-east of Ceylon for four days without any sight of the enemy. They flew a distance of 420 miles from Colombo between bearings of 110 degrees and 154 degrees but, of course, only three Catalinas were on patrol at any one time.

Throughout this period Somerville was completely devoid of information about any enemy movements. But the days at sea were not being wasted: Somerville put them to good use by exercising his ships continuously, training ships and officers in fleet movements until at the end of four days they were beginning to shape up nicely and he had every hope that before long they would be in some sort of fighting trim. But the short endurance of Force B now imposed additional problems. On 2 April Willis signalled that his battleships must return to harbour quickly as they were running out of water.

Fate now took a hand in Somerville's deliberations. If the slow battleships were compelled to return to harbour, then it was probably the right decision to take the opportunity to re-fuel the rest of the Fleet rather than be caught with the enemy over the horizon and near-empty fuel tanks. Furthermore, by dusk on 2 April Somerville believed that Nagumo had called off the raid, perhaps temporarily, but probably permanently. He based his belief on the complete absence of any sighting reports. Somerville decided, consequently, to abandon his own operation and return to base.

But to which base? Colombo was the obvious choice, but Somerville selected Addu Atoll as the less likely to be attacked by Nagumo's Force if indeed such an enemy force really was in the vicinity and likely to launch an attack at all. He ordered the Fleet to Addu.

He also made these dispositions: Captain A. W. S. Agar* was ordered to detach *Dorsetshire* back to Colombo to resume her refit: Captain Manwaring in *Cornwall* was directed to accompany Agar to Colombo and then to take over escort duties for Convoy SU 4, an Australian troop convoy comprising the US transport *Holbrook* and the Australian *Duntroon*, arriving Colombo on the 8th.

*Captain Agar won the VC in Kronstadt in 1919 by sinking the Russian cruiser *Oleg* with a torpedo from his coastal torpedo boat.

The antiquated little *Hermes*, accompanied by the old Australian destroyer *Vampire*, were detached to Trincomalee to resume their part in the projected venture to invade Madagascar.

Both Force A and Force B were now fragmented and dispersed with all ships low on water and fuel. Somerville referred to the Japanese force in a letter home: 'I fear they have taken fright,' he wrote, 'which is a pity because if I could have given them a good crack now it would have been very timely.'* With historical detachment we can now see the absurdity of the C-in-C's over-confidence: his statement demonstrates how sadly ill-informed he must have been about Nagumo's Force and its capabilities. And, of course, he was quite wrong about Nagumo's intentions: far from having aborted his Ceylon operation, Nagumo was on the point of launching his attack.

We left Nagumo in company with Vice Admiral Kondo returning to Staring Bay. On completion of their strikes against shipping to the south of Java the forces had then launched a destructive surface bombardment against Christmas Island on 7 March. They arrived back at their temporary base in the Celebes and anchored in the Bay on 11 March.

A few days later the battleship *Kongo* was detached from Staring Bay to return to Sasebo for an overdue refit which was carried out during March and April. The depleted Striking Force was reinforced by the return of *Zuikaku* and *Shokaku* who had departed from the Inland Sea on 17 March and reached Staring Bay on the 24th. These two carriers were part of the powerful fleet marshalling in preparation for a major foray into the Indian Ocean.

On 9 March Kondo and Nagumo had received orders to prepare plans for an attack upon the British naval bases in Ceylon and to seek out and engage the British Eastern Fleet. The prime objective of the operation was to neutralise the British naval and air forces in the waters around Ceylon with the intention of safe-guarding the Burma venture. A secondary objective was to disrupt sea communications in the Bay of Bengal. Finally, there was a subsidiary political objective: India was in the throes of dire internal political unrest. A powerful body of opinion headed by Mahatma Gandhi sought Indian neutrality in the war. Hindu leaders in Congress sought

Fighting Admiral: quoted by Captain Macintyre on page 187.

recognition of India's sovereign status and the formation of an All India National Government. Moslem leaders opposed this proposal. Other stresses and turmoils prevailed. In an endeavour to resolve the situation Sir Stafford Cripps headed a Mission to India with the promise to grant full independence if demanded by a Constituent Assembly after the war. Japan sought to add to the Mission's and Britain's difficulties in attempting to settle these thorny problems. The Cripps Mission failed. The Japanese certainly did not contribute towards a settlement of the India problem: they may possibly have hindered negotiations.

By the end of March Nagumo's plans were running according to schedule, but his time table was just a few days later than that which Somerville had been led to expect. The Ceylon raid – or 'C' Operation as the Japanese called it – was proceeding as planned and the force allocated to the task was mighty indeed.

'C' OPERATION

Naval Operations in the Indian Ocean
March–April 1942

Commander-in-Chief Vice Admiral Nobutake Kondo

Carrier Striking Force: Vice Admiral Chuichi Nagumo

Carriers:	*Akagi*	Captain T. Aoki	
	Soryu	Captain R. Yanagimoto	
	Hiryu	Captain T. Kaku	
	Zuikaku	Captain Yamaoto	
	Shokaku		

Battle Squadron: Vice Admiral Gunichi Mikawa

Battleships:	*Kongo*	Captain T. Koyanagi	
	Hiei	Captain M. Nishida	
	Kirishima	Captain S. Iwabuchi	
	Haruna	Captain T. Takama	
Cruisers:	*Tone*	Captain T. Okada	
	Chikuma	Captain K. Komura	
Light Cruiser:	*Abukuma*	Flagship of Rear Admiral Omori Captain S. Murayama	
1st Destroyer:	*Isokaze*	*Tanikaze*	*Urakaze*
Flotilla:	*Hamakaze*	*Shiranuhi*	*Kasumi*
	Kagero	*Arare*	*Akigumo*

At dusk on 2 April when Somerville dispersed his two forces to their various destinations, the Japanese Striking Force which he judged had abandoned its projected attack on Ceylon, was in fact, rounding the southern tip of Sumatra steering for the very area Somerville had been patrolling. Unknown to Somerville another Japanese force was also venturing into the Bay of Bengal. Vice Admiral Ozawa had instructions to disrupt Allied shipping in the Bay and to launch air raids upon Indian ports. Again, just as Somerville's forces were dispersing south of Ceylon and Kondo's battleships with Nagumo's carriers were rounding Sumatra, Ozawa was in the vicinity of the Nicobar Islands having departed Mergui in Burma at 1300 on 1 April.

The decision to strike at shipping in the Bay of Bengal was a shrewd one. Britain was in a state of considerable confusion because of congestion in ports throughout the Indian Ocean. At the end of 1941 it was not unusual to have 20–25 ships anchored outside Durban awaiting berths and a dozen or so in Table Bay. The situation in India and Ceylon was worse, with Bombay and Calcutta particularly hard hit. But the worst congestion was at Colombo where in the first few months of 1942 100–110 vessels berthed in the harbour's official berthing capacity of forty-five. Ships berthed like destroyers in their trots. There were, too, all the attendant problems of such congestion. The sea lanes, too, were busy and the unprotected, un-convoyed vessels were easy prey to a marauder. Such a marauder appeared in the form of the Malaya Force.

MALAYA FORCE

Commander: Vice Admiral J. Ozawa

Light Carrier	*Ryujo*	Captain T. Kato
Heavy Cruisers	*Chokai*	Flagship Rear Admiral Kurita Captain M. Hayakawa
	Kumano	Captain K. Tanaka
	Suzuya	Captain M. Kimura
	Mogami	Captain A. Soji
	Mikuma	Captain S. Sakiyama
Light Cruiser	*Yura*	Captain S. Sato
Destroyers	*Fubuki, Shirayuki, Hatsuyuki* and *Murakumo* set out with the Malaya Force but were replaced on 4 April by *Amagiri, Asagiri, Shirakumo* and *Yugiri*.	

Covering Force — The light cruiser *Sendai*, Captain N. Morishita, took up a covering position with the following destroyers: *Fubuki, Isonami, Hatsuyuki, Murakumo, Shirayuki, Uranami* and *Ayanami*.

Note: Much confusion has arisen over the composition of this force and few sources agree possibly due to the confusing movements of the destroyers and their light cruiser leaders.

On the same day that Somerville dispersed his Fleet, with Kondo and Nagumo heading for Ceylon and Ozawa about to strike at shipping in the Bay of Bengal, the British Chiefs of Staff in London discussed reports they had received dealing with the Japanese threat to India and the Indian Ocean. Winston Churchill had already set the scene in a minute to the Chiefs of Staff on 27 March: 'Nothing,' he emphasised, 'must be taken from Ceylon which endangers the naval base or deters the Fleet from using it.'

The report that was being considered warned that the present British weaknesses coupled with the US inability to give immediate help would enable Japan to cause 'irreparable damage' in the area. 'An invasion of Bengal, an assault on Ceylon or an attack on our Eastern Fleet, would each, if successful, prove a devastating blow to us . . . we are in danger of losing our Indian Empire – with incalculable consequences to the future conduct of the war.'* Another report gave the conclusion that the Japanese threat to India was even greater than the German threat to Malta. 'All available warships should be sent to the Indian Ocean: local defence of Ceylon should be built up as fast as possible.'

Even as these minutes were being typed powerful Japanese naval units were descending upon the area.

The Nagumo plan for the attack upon Ceylon was to strike at the port and installations of Colombo on a Sunday, hoping – as at Pearl Harbor – to catch the port and ships at a Sunday routine, especially as Sunday 5 April was Easter Sunday. In particular, Nagumo hoped to catch the Eastern Fleet at anchor and, again, hoped to repeat the destruction he wrought on 7 December 1941. He planned to employ the bombers and fighters of the 2nd and 5th Carrier Squadrons as strike aircraft and to keep the aircraft of his own flagship,

*War Cabinet Minutes CAB/79/19 and Chiefs of Staff Memoranda CAB 80.

Akagi, in reserve. Thus it was planned to be a raid on a slightly smaller scale of intensity than at Pearl Harbor and Darwin. The aircraft were to be launched from a position about 200 miles south of Ceylon. This position, incidentally, and the course steered by Nagumo were outside Somerville's patrolling area and although the designated Catalinas reconnaissance sectors do not coincide with Nagumo's track chart, one Catalina did in fact sight the carriers at 1600 on the 4th. This was the first confirmation that Somerville had of Nagumo's presence.

The sighting report was by Squadron Leader Leonard J. Birchall, RCAF. He reported a large enemy force heading north-west in a position 360 miles SE of Dondra Head. But before the composition of this force could be signalled the message ended abruptly as a force of six patrolling fighters from *Hiryu* fell upon the lone scout plane and shot it down. The survivors were hauled from the sea on to the decks of the destroyer *Isokaze*. The hour of reckoning for Ceylon was at hand. Colombo was about to undergo her baptism of fire. On receipt of Birchall's signal, Admiral Layton set in motion the reorganised defence systems and awaited the onslaught.

Layton had already cleared the port of Colombo of all ships which could possibly sail and dispersed them to anchorages in southern India. The number of vessels remaining in the harbour totalled twenty-one merchant ships, eight fleet auxiliaries and five naval vessels including the 11,198-ton armed merchant cruiser *Hector* and the antiquated little destroyer *Tenedos*.

Somerville was now in a quandary. Rarely can a Fleet commander have been caught so helplessly on the hop. He had just arrived for the first time at Addu – and the shock persisted. Its blistering, sun-glaring tropical heat and barrenness numbed the senses: 'Scapa Flow – with bloody palms,' was the sailor's jocular description of the deep water lagoon at Addu. *Warspite* had just anchored and launches were still busily criss-crossing the anchorage bringing flag officers and commanding officers to conferences aboard the flagship when the Catalina's report was received by Somerville.

The first signal bore an error which must have added to the general confusion: only when 'south-east of Dondra Head' was substituted for 'south-east of Addu Atoll' did the signal make much sense.

Somerville reviewed his situation: he was 600 miles from the enemy, far from a position from which he could defend Ceylon. He presumed that the Japanese intention would be to launch a dawn attack against Colombo and possibly Trincomalee, too, before a retirement eastward. Somerville's capital ships and carriers were short of water and fuel: tankers and water boats were hurrying to replenish the warships. Force A, the fast squadron, could be got under way almost immediately – except for the cruisers *Enterprise* and *Emerald* who would not be ready for sea until midnight. *Cornwall* and *Dorsetshire* were far away heading for Colombo. Force B – the old battleships and slow cruisers – would not complete topping up empty tanks until the following day. The whole of Force B's departure would have to be delayed.

Somerville instructed that Force A should proceed to sea as soon as *Enterprise* and *Emerald* had completed taking aboard fuel and water. The two heavy cruisers under Agar's command were recalled at once and ordered to rendezvous with the admiral south-west of Ceylon. Admiral Willis was instructed to sail his Force B as soon as possible. *Hermes*, a liability rather than an asset, was ordered to get clear of Trincomalee and keep to the north-east.

Admiral Somerville and his staff considered their tactics. The paramount need – in conformity with Admiralty orders – was to keep the Eastern Fleet 'in being' and not to subject it to unnecessary or crippling losses. The defence of Ceylon against a strike was a secondary consideration. This view was strengthened by the knowledge that the island was now aware of the impending attack and preparations would already have been made to use the Hurricane fighters to defend the island and for the small force of Blenheim bombers to attack the Striking Force – with the possibility of damaging some of the Japanese ships.

Throughout the clear night of 4 April Force A steamed at nineteen knots on a converging course with the enemy force. But, providentially for Somerville, contact was never made.

Aboard Nagumo's carriers excitement was rising fast as the Striking Force approached Ceylon. The passage across the Indian Ocean had been pleasant and uneventful, distinguished only by the re-fuelling of the ships south of Java. Pilots, officers and air crews enjoyed the sight of five ungainly but majestic carriers cleaving a course north-westerly through the smooth seas towards the equator: four ponderous but powerful battleships and their screening cruisers and destroyers made an awesome sight. By the evening of 4 April as Force A shaped a converging course, preparations aboard the carriers were almost complete for another major strike against yet another Allied naval base: Pearl Harbor, Rabaul, Darwin, Tjilatjap – and now Colombo.

Pilots and air crews aboard the carriers had already written letters for their parents and many – as was customary for Japanese warriors entering battle – had preserved little packages of snippets of hair and even of nail clippings in their lockers for their families in case of death in combat.

At dawn on 5 April the activity and excitement was even more intense. Many pilots had put on clean *mawashi* or loincloths and many more fixed their 'thousand-stitch' belts: these wide body- or belly-bands were worn as good luck charms: they were made by loving mothers, wives or sisters who then stood on street corners and invited passers-by to add a stitch until one thousand had been collected: each stitch was meant to represent a prayer for good luck – and a good fight for the warrior.

The mood aboard the carriers was buoyant. In the pre-dawn beauty of the equatorial waters of the Indian Ocean south of Ceylon the Dragons and the Cranes made ready for the strike. *Soryu* and *Hiryu* were the Dragons; their names meant 'Green Dragon' and 'Flying Dragon'. *Shokaku* and *Zuikaku* meant 'Soaring Crane' and 'Happy Crane'. Even aboard the flagship *Akagi* the mood was light-hearted even though her aircraft would not be taking part in the actual raid, with one exception, Fuchida, the strike leader.

The pilots and air crews of the 'Crane' carriers were specially proud of their association with their Emperor, for the Crane was the symbol for the Emperor on the throne in much the same manner as in Britain the crown is synonymous with the monarch. But for the Japanese this link with their Emperor, albeit tenuous, was an emotive and important association. Hirohito in 1942 – or on the Japanese calendar Showa 17 – was a vital and living part of a serviceman's existence: Showa was the name Hirohito had given to his reign and Showa 17 was the seventeenth year of his reign. Showa, ironically, means Enlightened Peace.

Commander Mitsuo Fuchida, ace destructor of Pearl Harbor and of Darwin, once again led the strike force. Thirty-six fighters streaked from the flight decks amid cheers and *Banzais*. As they marshalled above the fleet like migratory birds the bomber squadrons totalling ninety-one high level and dive bombers took off and set course for Colombo. One hundred and twenty-seven aircraft were on their way.

As these squadrons approached their target they encountered changeable weather. When – at 0740 on Easter Sunday – they arrived over Colombo thunderous storm clouds still hung over the port and gusty winds accompanied the heavy squalls of rain. 'Still wet from a recent squall of rain,' Fuchida recalled later, 'the city lay glistening in the sun.'*

Ashore in Colombo various reports of sightings of battleships and cruisers had been coming through from Catalinas but Nagumo's carriers, keeping south of Kondo's force, were not sighted. Admiral Layton had expected a raid to develop during the moonlight period of the early hours of 5 April and ordered defence services to stand-to at 0300.

As already mentioned, Colombo's radar system was incomplete, but it was manned in expectation of the attack which developed just a few hours later than Layton had predicted. The radar, in fact, successfully picked up the approaching Japanese aircraft, but owing to an error no alert was given until the Japanese aircraft were visible by the score to the naked eye. Fuchida reported: 'As we closed the target flying through dense but occasionally broken cloud, I suddenly spotted a formation of twelve enemy Swordfish-type torpedo planes. They were flying at a much lower altitude, without any fighter escort and obviously had not noticed us.' All British records refer, in fact, to six aircraft of 788 Squadron. They happened upon the scene at the beginning of the raid on their way to Ratmalana from Trincomalee armed with torpedoes. They were not as Fuchida believed at the time on their way to attack Nagumo's carriers. Fuchida quickly signalled Lieutenant-Commander Itaya, the fighter group commander flying to port, to close him. He pointed to the Swordfish formation and motioned Itaya to attack. Itaya veered off to lead his fighters against the unsuspecting Swordfish and in a swift and violent attack shot down every one of them.

Believing that British fighters must be aloft to intercept his bombers, Fuchida led the whole of his bomber force round to the north of Colombo to launch his attack, passing on the way Ratmalana airfield at a height of 7000 feet.

*_Midway_ by Fuchida and Okumiya, page 60.

The dive bombers started their attacks upon the harbour, its installations and shipping both inside and outside the breakwater. These bombers dived as low as fifty feet, machine gunning as they completed their bombing runs. They were quickly followed by the high level bombers which took as an additional target the airfield at Ratmalana.

Colombo's defences, alerted to the attack and now benefiting from Admiral Layton's dictatorial badgering over the past few weeks, reacted swiftly to the raiders' approach. AA batteries were in action quickly. Fighter pilots were in their cockpits awaiting the alarm to scramble. Forty-two fighters took off: twenty-two Hurricanes of 30 Squadron, six Fleet Air Arm Fulmars of 803 and 806 Squadrons all of which took off from Ratmalana, and another fourteen Hurricanes which took off from the hastily constructed airstrip on the racecourse.

All the Ratmalana aircraft were quickly engaged by Itaya's fighters which soon displayed their superiority in the ensuing dog fights. The racecourse Hurricanes fared better probably because their airstrip was unknown to the raiders. They managed to get among the bombers over the harbour but were themselves fiercely engaged by Zeros. The British losses in aircraft were heavy. Four of the six Fulmars were shot down. Fifteen Hurricanes were lost but five of the pilots saved. Two Catalinas had been destroyed earlier. In addition, the six Swordfish biplanes were all destroyed.

British claims of the raiders' losses were excessive and the actual losses sustained amounted to one fighter from *Soryu*, one bomber from *Shokaku* and five bombers from *Zuikaku*. *Hiryu* lost none but logged nine planes as damaged. Ceylon's Hurricanes had provided Nagumo's aircraft with the severest opposition encountered so far in the five months of war.

But the blows struck at Colombo were severe. Railway workshops were damaged. The quays in the harbour and the workshops were severely damaged: piers, Government buildings, a repair shop, several hangars and buildings at the airfield were damaged. Fortunately the loss of life was small: shops and offices were shut, streets empty and the working population of Colombo out of town because it was Easter Sunday.

Havoc in the harbour was extensive. Two warships were sunk, another damaged and a merchant ship set ablaze. HMS *Hector*, the armed merchant cruiser, was undergoing refit in the harbour. She was struck by several bombs, set ablaze and burned till gutted. She became a total loss.

The old destroyer *Tenedos* was hit and quickly sank in the harbour. The submarine depot ship *Lucia* was struck by a bomb which penetrated her thin deck plating and exploded just below the waterline. The 5943-ton merchant ship *Benledi* was set afire and damaged but the fire was quickly extinguished.

By 0835 – less than one hour since the raiders arrived over Colombo – the strike was over and the last of the raiding aircraft had cleared the area. As they shaped course for their carriers the departing Japanese pilots could see the palls of smoke rising from burning ships and harbour installations.

The damage to the airfield at Ratmalana was not severe. Within half-an-hour of the end of the raid a squadron of ten Blenheim bombers managed to take off from the airfield to seek out and attack Nagumo's Striking Force. But they failed to locate the carriers and returned to base with their bomb loads.

At the end of the attack on Colombo, Fuchida was about to signal Nagumo that a second attack would not be necessary when he overheard a short message from a reconnaissance plane to the south-east of Ceylon. 'Two enemy heavy cruisers sighted heading south.' Fuchida believed these ships to be part of a fleet or squadron sent out to locate Nagumo's Force: he hastened his return to the carriers, leaving Itaya's fighters behind still engaging Hurricanes.

Only when he got back aboard *Akagi* did Fuchida learn that the two cruisers were sailing independently and were fleeing not attacking.

Lieutenant-Commander Egusa of *Soryu*, leading a force of eighty bombers, had already been despatched to attack the cruisers.

The enemy sighting report intercepted by Fuchida came from a float plane from the heavy cruiser *Tone* which gave the position of the cruisers as 3 degrees 01′N 77 degrees 58′E. The sighting report set in motion a chain of events, starting with the despatch of Egusa's bombers, resulting in tragedy for the British and triumph for the Japanese. It was a common enough story in the early weeks of the war in the east.

CHAPTER 9

Sinking of the Cruisers

WHILE THE ATTACK on Colombo was still in progress Admiral Somerville's Force A was heading ENE from Addu Atoll with the intention of being in a position 250 miles south of Ceylon at dawn on the 6th. He ordered *Dorsetshire* and *Cornwall* to join him in latitude 0 degrees 58′N and longitude 77 degrees 36′E at 1600 on the 5th.

Dorsetshire and *Cornwall* were already at sea when they received the C-in-C's signal to rendezvous and at 0700 they altered course to comply. Agar was heading his two cruisers at a comfortable speed to the southward to meet the 1600 deadline but at about 0800 he received a signal timed 0648 warning of heavy enemy forces about 150 miles to the eastward. Agar increased speed to *Cornwall*'s maximum of 27½ knots to join Force A as soon as possible.

More than 100 miles astern of the C-in-C was Willis' Force B which had left Addu Atoll at 0700 on the 5th. After being caught so dangerously on the wrong foot the previous day, the situation began to look a bit more encouraging for Somerville. What he sought so anxiously now was accurate information of the enemy's movements. Early in the forenoon it seemed that his luck might be changing when he received the signal that impelled Agar to increase speed.

This signal reported Japanese battleships in a position 300 miles to the north-east of Force A. Somerville decided that this was probably the Japanese battle squadron covering the carrier force which probably lay to the eastward recovering aircraft from the strike on Colombo. Of the carriers' whereabouts Somerville was ignorant, but he believed they would withdraw to the eastward as soon as the aircraft were recovered.

On the plot the reported Japanese battleships were somewhat to the eastward of the track of Agar's two cruisers and about 150 miles farther to the north. Agar seemed safely past any danger. There was no need to change any plans. But Somerville's luck – and more so that of Agar – ran out almost before he could enjoy it by the intrusion of *Tone*'s reconnaissance aircraft.

The weather conditions in the area were unlike those over Colombo. At sea the sky was clear with practically no cloud. Visibility was extreme, and the sea barely ruffled.

Cornwall had no radar. *Dorsetshire*'s set was not one of the sophisticated models which heavy cruisers enjoyed later in the war: the early models were rudimentary and unreliable. At about 1130 *Dorsetshire*'s radar registered the *Tone* aircraft and it even became visible to the lookouts. There was little that Agar could do about it: he did not break radio silence to report the sighting.

Nagumo acted differently. There was much he could do and he acted decisively. He turned his carrier force to the south and prepared to launch the reserve formation for the second-wave attack on Colombo led by Lieutenant-Commander Egusa to strike against the cruisers.* With the despatch of Egusa's aircraft, the fate of Agar's cruisers had been decided.

When, at 1300, the cruisers were sighted by two more aircraft, Agar decided that as he was now only seventy miles from the admiral the sighting jeopardised Force A. He broke W/T silence and made a shadowing report. Captain Agar recorded 'Sea calm. Visibility maximum, little or no clouds, slight haze over the sun.' Agar was then in a position 2 degrees 12′N, 77 degrees 47′E, about 220 miles from Colombo.

This signal was received by *Warspite* in a mutilated form and it was not until 1400 that it was identified as from *Dorsetshire*. By that time both *Dorsetshire* and *Cornwall* had been sunk.

Force A itself had come close to detection. At 1344 *Warspite*'s radar detected a formation of aircraft. The echoes soon faded from the radar screens. These echoes were Egusa's bombers: they were sinking the cruisers.

. . . . .

*Composition of this force is quoted by Fuchida in *Midway* and Okumiya in *Zero!* as eighty Vals. Eighty bombers alone is unlikely, but neither sources mention fighter escorts. Masanori Ito in his *The End of the Imperial Japanese Navy* quotes fifty-three torpedo planes, thirty-eight bombers and thirty-six fighters, totalling 127 planes. Out of a total aircraft force of 403 aircraft aboard Nagumo's carriers, 180 committed to the first strike on Colombo and 127 for the back-up strike seem probable. But, contrarily, there is no evidence whatsoever of torpedo aircraft being employed in the cruiser attack. Ito was certainly correct in referring to Takashige Egusa's attack as 'a startling demonstration of aerial marksmanship and effectiveness'.

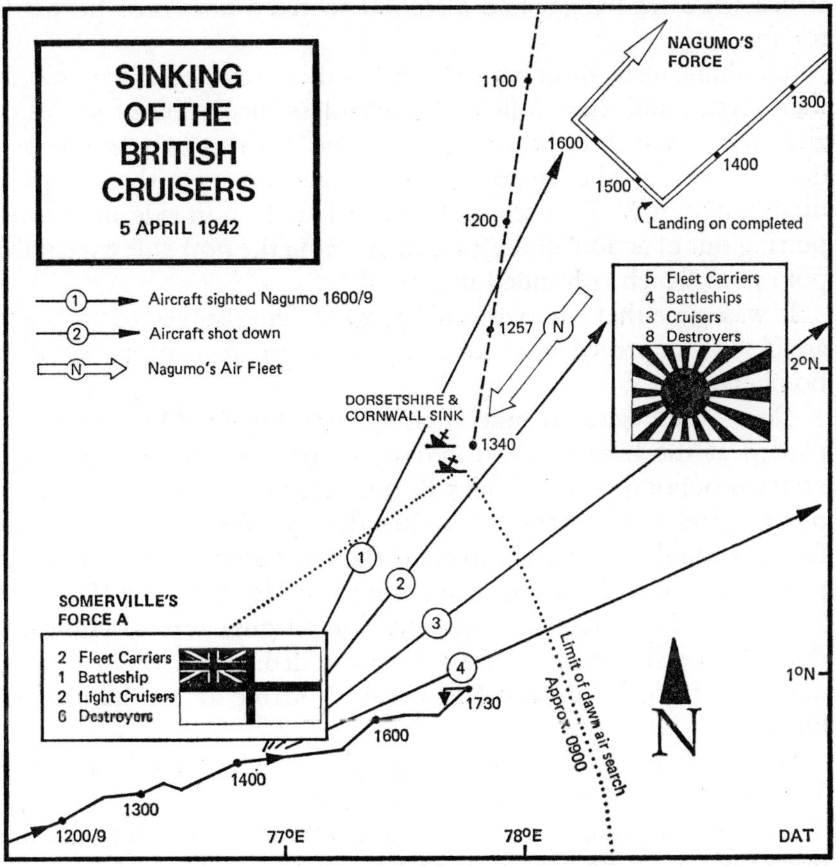
SINKING OF THE BRITISH CRUISERS
5 APRIL 1942
Aircraft sighted Nagumo 1600/9
Aircraft shot down
Nagumo's Air Fleet
NAGUMO'S FORCE
1100
1300
1600
1400
1500
1200
Landing on completed
5 Fleet Carriers
4 Battleships
3 Cruisers
8 Destroyers
1257
2°N
DORSETSHIRE & CORNWALL SINK
1340
SOMERVILLE'S FORCE A
2 Fleet Carriers
1 Battleship
2 Light Cruisers
6 Destroyers
1730
1600
1400
1300
1200/9
77°E
78°E
DAT
1°N
Limit of dawn air search
Approx. 0900
N

It was 1340 when Agar's cruisers began their last ordeal. Three aircraft were sighted at a high altitude, assumed to be hostile and fire was opened immediately. They were part of Egusa's formation. Egusa signalled Nagumo: 'Enemy vessels sighted.' Within a few seconds the three aircraft dived through the shell bursts at HMS *Cornwall* and released their bombs at a low altitude. One bomb struck the after hangar and a second scored a near miss port side for'ard.

Simultaneously three more dive bombers selected *Dorsetshire* as their target, and there followed a relentless succession of waves of aircraft. All first three bombs struck home 'one through the quarter-deck, disabling the steering, the second through the catapult, disabling both W/T offices, and the third on the port side amidships, putting out of action all the AA armament on the port side except the pom pom which continued in action'.*

It was clear that the two cruisers were being subjected to heavy attacks of unprecedented accuracy by large formations of dive bombers.

Dorsetshire began to take massive punishment. One bomb exploded at the base of the foremost funnel putting out of action S1 HA mounting and A Boiler Room: another on the quarterdeck put X turret out of action: another through the base of the after funnel brought it down, exploded the HA magazine and put both pom poms out of action. The accuracy of Egusa's bombing was frightening in its clinical accuracy. Later Egusa was to comment that it was easier to count the misses and deduct the total from the number of bombs dropped in order to arrive at the number of hits.

'Just before the first bomb burst,' a survivor recalled later,† 'Captain Agar gave instructions to hoist the silk battle ensign. Great efforts were made to do this and although the ensign did not reach the top of the mast it was flying when the ship sank.'

In his *Report* Agar stated:

At this stage five minutes had elapsed, by which time the ship had taken a heavy list to port, there were large fires on the upper deck and stoker's mess deck, all the anti-aircraft armament except the 0.5-inch machine guns were out of action, there was no W/T communication and the ship had

*Captain Agar's *Report* to the Commander-in-Chief Eastern Fleet, 8 April 1942.

†Quoted by Chief Canteen Manager NAAFI A. G. Elsegood in *Illustrated*, 12 September 1942.

lost both speed and steering . . . I gave orders to cast off the rafts and stand by the boats.

Firing the only remaining machine guns was Royal Marine Bugler G. W. Timms. Despite the later order to abandon ship, he continued firing his guns through the smoke and flames. He did not survive the battle.

Another four hits were taken in rapid succession making a total of at least ten, plus a number of near misses. A severe list to port worsened and Agar had no option but to order abandon ship.

In his *Supplementary Report** Agar amplified the situation aboard his cruiser after four minutes of attack:

It was also about this time that the HA magazine blew up and the ship's list increased. All communication between bridge and other parts of the ship had gone, and looking down from the bridge aft all that could be seen was flames and smoke extending to the stern. By about Z + 6 [minutes] I realised it would be a matter of minutes only before the ship sank, so gave orders to be passed verbally to everybody to throw overboard rafts and cut the boats' falls . . . I also ordered 'All hands on deck'. I then gave order to 'Abandon ship' at about Z + 6½ by which time the ship was slowly turning on her beam ends . . . Enemy aircraft were still flying low over the ship using their machine guns and it was possible to get a clear picture of them and their occupants . . . It was incredible how quickly the ship sank. She took just one plunge by the stern and as we were thrown into the water the bows towered up almost vertically alongside us.

Captain Agar reported how only two leaking whalers were got away and floated nearly down to their gunwales, together with the skiff and many Denton and Carley floats. At one time there were fifty-two in one whaler and forty-seven in the other.

By about 1700 all the survivors numbering about 500 men were collected together into one compact party. They were warned by Agar to be prepared for a twenty-four or forty-eight hour wait.

A mile or two away could be seen boats, including a power boat, containing survivors from *Cornwall*, for she too had undergone a similar devastating attack. Bombers peeled off into their dives in an almost continuous stream. There was little that Captain Manwaring could do, for his ship was overwhelmed by the fierceness and intensity of the attack and within minutes she too was blazing

*Captain Agar's *Supplementary Report* to Commander-in-Chief Eastern Fleet, 13 April 1942.

almost from stem to stern and was evidently about to sink. Abandon ship was ordered and the survivors took to the water.

Morale was given a boost at about 1730 when an Albacore aircraft sighted the survivors and signalled 'Hold on'.

Four of the *Dorsetshire* men died before nightfall, five died in the skiff during the night and another three the next day. Their dead bodies had just to be pushed over the side to make way for others. Exhausted swimmers were taken aboard for spells of rest.

During the morning the breakfast ration was issued. It comprised half a biscuit each and a sip of milk and water from the standard barricoe of water in each whaler. Distribution was not easy but as far as possible everyone got a fair share.

The day was spent in conserving energy, but even merely treading water for several hours on end was exhausting. At about 1730 on the 10th another Albacore was sighted and put good heart into the survivors and shortly afterwards the masts of a cruiser and two destroyers appeared over the horizon to the south-west: the *Enterprise* and the two destroyers *Paladin* and *Panther*. Within only one hour 1129 weary survivors were clutched to safety, *Cornwall*'s men aboard *Enterprise* and *Dorsetshire*'s aboard the two destroyers. Agar scrambled aboard *Paladin*.

At last the cruisers' ordeal was ended. 424 men had been lost, among them a number of the South African contingent of eighty-six aboard *Dorsetshire*.

When *Dorsetshire* and *Cornwall* sank Force A was about seventy miles away to the SSW on a course for the rendezvous at a speed through the placid sea of eighteen knots. Both before and after the sinking the day had been marked by a considerable number of misleading signals. As Admiral Fletcher commented after the Battle of the Coral Sea 'there is a hell of a lot of groping around'. Somerville was groping.

From daylight four Fulmars from *Indomitable* covered sectors 215 miles to the eastward of Force A – with no result except the sighting of one enemy seaplane. Between 0700 and 1100 Colombo relayed messages to Force A giving the opinion that Kondo's battle squadron was 'marking time' only 120 miles south of Dondra Head.

At 1330 *Dorsetshire*'s aircraft sighting report was relayed, albeit in mutilated form, then just before 1600 an aircraft reported sighting wreckage in a position which coincided with Agar's at 1330.

Somerville despatched a destroyer to investigate. Then soon after 1700 an aircraft reported five unidentified ships only thirty miles from the wreckage steering *south*-west – towards Force A. Fearful for the safety of the destroyer, Somerville recalled her and turned his Force to the southward to keep his distance until nightfall.

Rear Admiral Boyd aboard *Indomitable* assessing the situation at 1817 placed the enemy on a course of *north*-west in a position about 140 miles to the north of Force A and he reckoned the enemy force comprised two carriers and three other vessels.

Working on Boyd's assessment, Somerville shaped a course for the north-west to keep within striking distance of the enemy during the night, flying search aircraft throughout the hours of darkness in the hope of locating the enemy and launching a torpedo attack. But to no avail. Nagumo's Striking Force was steaming away from Somerville: they were hundreds of miles apart and increasing the distance by the hour.

At about 1600 just as an aircraft sighted the cruisers' wreckage, another aircraft from one of Boyd's carriers was sighted by Nagumo's Striking Force: Nagumo suspected the presence of a British carrier force and he considered it prudent to turn his Force to the south-east. Throughout the 6–8 April he kept beyond a 500-mile circle from Dondra Head.

At daylight on the 6th Force B joined Force A and the assembled fleet set course to the eastward. Somerville believed Nagumo might attack Addu Atoll, code named Port T. In fact the use of the Atoll as a Fleet base was a well kept secret. Nagumo had no idea of its existence. Somerville, unaware of Nagumo's ignorance on this point, believed that the Japanese force intended to attack and made dispositions accordingly, still with the objective of making a night torpedo attack on Nagumo.

At 1115 course of the Fleet was altered to seek survivors from the sunken cruisers. At 1300 *Enterprise, Paladin* and *Panther* were detached to scout ahead of the Fleet and, as we have seen, they effected the rescue.

This period of the naval operations was marked by two powerful fleets manoeuvring a few hundred miles apart, one fleet seeking a daylight battle where its vast superiority in carrier bomber aircraft would prove decisive and the other fleet prepared to engage only in a night battle where its superiority in gunfire (forty 15-inch guns against twenty-four 14-inch) might give it victory. Somerville and

Nagumo were sparring like two heavyweight boxers, seeking an advantage before risking all on a knockout punch.

Somerville, accordingly kept clear of Addu Atoll until after daylight on the 7th and in fact it was 1100 on the 8th when the Fleet finally entered the anchorage. That afternoon Somerville called a conference of his flag and commanding officers aboard *Warspite*.

Meanwhile, ashore in Colombo Admiral Layton, now aware of Admiral Ozawa's Malaya Force in the Bay of Bengal in addition to the forces south of Ceylon had signalled the Admiralty warning them of the prospect of the 'immediate annihilation' of the Eastern Fleet. The Admiralty replied giving Somerville complete discretion to withdraw his old battleships to East Africa if he considered them a liability.

At the conference aboard the flagship Somerville explained how he was convinced of the undesirability of operating his battle fleet which lacked speed, endurance and AA gunpower in Ceylon waters in the face of such superior Japanese naval and air power. Accordingly he decided to send the battle squadron to Kilindini in East Africa to assume convoy protection duties. He, himself, with Force A would retire to Bombay as a deterrent against Japanese raids into the western Indian Ocean.

These grave decisions were approved by the Admiralty and the Cabinet whose thoughts during the past few days had followed almost identical lines.

This same day – 8 April – other threatening events were looming. Nagumo had not yet finished with the British Eastern Fleet.

The British hospital ship *Vita** was ordered to sail from Trincomalee on 8 April to embark the injured survivors from *Dorsetshire* and *Cornwall*. That same day orders were sent to other ships in Trincomalee. At 1500 a Catalina aircraft reported an enemy force of three battleships and one aircraft carrier east of Ceylon steering almost due north. This was part of Nagumo's Striking Force. He was preparing for another strike.

Vice Admiral Sir Geoffrey Arbuthnot, Commander-in-Chief

*On Easter Monday 1941 *Vita* was severely damaged by German dive bombers outside Tobruk. 430 wounded Australian and British soldiers were transferred to HMAS *Waterhen* and *Vendetta*. *Vita* survived and was patched up sufficiently for her to reach Bombay for repairs. On Easter Monday one year later she was in Trincomalee.

East Indies, believed an air strike against Trincomalee was imminent. Following the success of the dispersal tactics at Colombo, he instructed the harbour of Trincomalee to be cleared. *Hermes*, with only one damaged aircraft aboard, the Australian destroyer *Vampire*, the minelayer *Teviot Bank*, the Royal Fleet auxiliary *Pearleaf* (5911 tons), *Athelstone* (5571 tons), the corvette *Hollyhock* and tanker *British Sergeant* (5868 tons) all left that night, keeping close inshore with orders to be at least forty miles south of Trincomalee by dawn on the 9th. A southward dispersal was ordered because northwards more than twenty ships already congested the Palk Strait between Ceylon and India, offering an inviting target, after fleeing from Colombo.

By daylight on the 9th Nagumo's Striking Force had reached a flying off position for an attack on Trincomalee. A few hours earlier Admiral Willis with Force B had left Addu Atoll for Kilindini and now, as Somerville in *Warspite* with his Force A carriers left for Bombay, Nagumo's carriers launched a powerful force of ninety-one bombers and thirty-eight fighters.

The first sighting of Nagumo's Force was by a Catalina at 1500 on the 8th* which gave rise to the evacuation of Trincomalee harbour. Another Catalina sighted the Force soon after daylight on the 9th but its signal was cut off abruptly before it could complete the report. But by then the die was cast. Enemy aircraft were on their way. They appeared on the British radar screens, ninety miles away approaching from the eastward. At 0720 the large formations were visible in the clear blue sky at a height of about 15,000 feet.

Leader of the strike was Commander Fuchida, and he reported entering a barrage of fire at 0725 as his aircraft led the attack on the dockyard installations and the airfield at China Bay where, Fuchida claimed, he saw aircraft lined up on the apron of the field. These must have been aircraft which were operationally unfit because by the start of the air raid all the fighters had been scrambled and were airborne. They totalled seventeen Hurricanes and six Fulmars. Fierce dog fights developed in which the Japanese fighter pilots displayed a marked superiority in skill – and in sheer numbers. Eight Hurricanes and one Fulmar were shot down.

Fuchida directed some of the bombers against the shipping still

*Arbuthnot quotes a position of 9 degrees 18′N, 84 degrees 40′E about 240 miles east of Trincomalee at 1500: Somerville quotes 6 degrees 10′N, 85 degrees 49′E, about 480 miles ENE at 1517.

remaining in the harbour, one of the world's largest natural anchorages, fringed with palms and dotted about with tree-clad islets. The 7200-ton monitor *Erebus* was damaged during the attack. The merchant ship *Sagaing*, 7958 tons, was set ablaze by direct hits but was successfully beached.

While the flames still raged and smoke of the raid still smothered the dockyard and airfield, Fuchida called off the raid, leaving some of the un-attacked shipping in the harbour for the second wave dive bombers which were to follow. He radioed *Akagi* to this effect and set course for his carrier.

Then came a repetition of the Colombo incident – a radio signal of a sighting by a Japanese pilot – of a destroyer and a carrier! *Hermes*, of course, was the carrier. She had been sighted by a reconnaissance float plane. It was a little after 0855 when Captain Tamotsu Takama on the bridge of his battleship *Haruna* received the signal from his float plane reporting the sighting of *Hermes* and *Vampire*. He informed Nagumo who quickly authorised the second wave force of Lieutenant-Commander Egusa's aircraft to change his target from Trincomalee to the carrier.

By the time that Fuchida had landed on *Akagi*, Egusa's force was well on its way. Fuchida's planes were quickly re-fuelled and re-armed, many with torpedoes, in case of need as a second wave attack to finish off the carrier.

'Suddenly *Akagi*'s loudspeakers blared AA action!' Fuchida later recorded.* 'Almost simultaneously there was the stunning noise of bomb explosions, and six white columns of water rose off the ship's bows, four to starboard, and two to port. Looking up I saw a formation of six Wellington† bombers passing over at 4000 feet. They had somehow caught our combat air patrol flat-footed, though not for long.'

The nine Blenheim bombers of No. 11 Squadron – all the available serviceable bombers on the island – had taken off at 0840 to strike at Nagumo's Carrier Striking Force which was reported to comprise three battleships and four or five carriers.

The Blenheims were the first squadron of bombers to penetrate the Nagumo fighter patrols and deliver an organised attack upon the Force. Although they managed to catch the fighter patrols on the hop and release their bomb loads, the Zero fighters were soon

**Midway* by Fuchida and Okumiya, page 62.

†They were Blenheims, not Wellingtons and there were nine of them, not six.

among them. No direct hits were scored by the Blenheims and out of the nine which set out only four returned – all of them damaged.

Heading for *Hermes* was Lieutenant-Commander Egusa and his dive bombers: with the skill born of rigorous training and combat experience they were to enjoy a considerably higher measure of success than the Blenheims.

CHAPTER 10

Loss of the British Carrier

CAPTAIN RICHARD F. J. Onslow aboard the bridge on the island of the 10,850-ton carrier *Hermes* knew his ship had been sighted. The morning sky was Ceylonese blue with an extreme visibility. The bows of the attendant destroyer *Vampire* of the ancient V and W class of 1917 gently cut through the blue sea, providing a picture of sheer delight. *Vampire* was a veteran Australian ship, supplier to besieged Tobruk and survivor of the holocaust in the Gulf of Siam when Force Z was despatched in minutes.

Onslow had no illusions of his ship's mortal peril when he sighted the float plane. He had no fighter cover, none of his own aircraft were aboard to provide defence except for one unserviceable Swordfish. No vessel can feel so naked and vulnerable as a carrier devoid of aircraft when under threat of impending air attack.

Hermes had gone to dawn action stations at 0520. Paymaster Commander McNeil-Smith recalls:*

> I put on a pair of shorts, my blue action overalls, sandals as it was too hot for shoes, my uniform cap and identity disc . . . my torch, inflatable life belt, flash-proof gloves . . . and mask. For two months the temperature in my cabin where I mostly worked and slept varied between 88 degrees and 94 degrees. It took ten minutes to get from my cabin to my action station, having to pass through and open and shut four water-tight doors and up two ladders, along the battery . . . up a wooden ladder overhanging the sea to the Flight Deck and into the Cypher Office in the island abaft the bridge. We did not secure as usual at daylight but remained at Action Stations.

The carrier was still at action stations when the pilot of the float plane made his sighting report. The report was in clear and within minutes Colombo had intercepted the signal, translated it and

*Paymaster Commander (S) E. F. McNeil-Smith, *Papers* including a *Report* on sinking of HMS *Hermes*.

relayed warnings to *Hermes* and *Vampire*. They were then in a position 7 degrees 26′N, 81 degrees 52′E, about sixty-five miles south of Trincomalee and only five miles off the coast when the message was received. About seven miles to the south-east lay the *Athelstone* with the corvette *Hollyhock* ahead, while the *British Sergeant* was over the horizon to the north. Here, too, the sea was smooth, sky clear, weather fine and visibility extreme.

On translation of the *Haruna* plane's signal, *Hermes* and the accompanying ships were ordered to return to Trincomalee at full speed – *Hermes* could manage twenty-four knots – and signals were despatched to alert fighters at China Bay and Ratmalana. But owing to communications failures these signals were not received at the airfields until too late for effective action with the result that the ships had no umbrella of fighters to give protection.

Aboard Nagumo's carriers there was, as we have already seen, intense activity in getting Egusa's force of aircraft airborne. At 0945 the flying-off of his squadron began until a force of eighty bombers and nine fighters was aloft.* At about 1030, off Batticoloa Light, the north-bound *Hermes* met the south-bound hospital ship *Vita* and at that moment the port bridge lookout on the carrier sighted dots of aircraft low on the horizon. Egusa's squadrons had arrived.

Egusa noted that there was no fighter protection nor were there any aircraft on the carrier's deck. *Hermes* had also been heard asking Trincomalee repeatedly if fighters had been despatched. *Hermes*, as seen by Egusa, was a sitting duck.

The attacks upon the carrier and the destroyer began at 1035. The scale of the attack was so overwhelming and the defence resources so meagre that it was only a matter of time before the ships were destroyed. Mercifully, *Vita* went unmolested.

Egusa launched his dive bombers from a height of about 10,000 feet and they fell upon their prey at an angle of about 65 degrees. *Hermes* was struck immediately and within the next few minutes was struck by perhaps forty 250-kg bombs at the rate of one every few seconds.

McNeil-Smith recorded the event: 'The attack was carried out relentlessly, like a highly organised deck display. The aircraft peeled off in threes diving straight down on the ship out of the sun.' McNeil-Smith came out from the Cypher Office on to the Flight

*On the face of it, the composition of this force seems unbalanced, but the evidence supports the accuracy of the figures.

Deck stunned by the shock of exploding bombs and gunfire: he moved along the port side of the island holding tight because of the list which had already developed. He heard a plane, looked up and saw the bomb released.

It struck and I was enveloped in flames but managed to stumble and fall across to the port side and into the sea: in the flames I tried to shield my face with my flash gloves . . . As I entered the sea the flight deck . . . was touching it. The next thing I knew was that I felt cool and fresh and was swimming in the warm sea, in the hot sun, almost on the equator. I did not know that my right shoulder had a gaping wound from a bomb splinter, clogged with oil fuel and that my head, face, back, knees, elbows and feet were badly burned . . .

My life belt kept me up well and I lay and watched the ship go down . . . there were about 400 of us left in the sea which was black with thick oil fuel and strewn with wreckage and corpses. I . . . began to weaken when to my great relief I saw the oily face of Surgeon Lieutenant James A. Smart RNVR who sent two unhurt sailors to tow me on a grating to a Carley Float. Smart had been shipwrecked twice before and had made a canvas wallet to fit round his chest and from this he took a syringe and gave me morphia. Some of the ratings on the raft – particularly Leading Stoker Powys and Writer McNeill, both South Africans – kept the sun off me with a piece of cloth and covered the shoulder wound. Dr Smart swam from raft to raft comforting the dying and wounded.

McNeil-Smith remained in the sea for about four hours before a boat from the *Vita* rescued him.

Hermes had taken about forty direct hits and in twenty minutes from the first aircraft sighting she was a terrible wreck, stopped, listing heavily to port with the flight deck awash, with a solitary foremost gun still firing pointlessly into the sky. Suddenly the heel increased and *Hermes* rolled right over and sank. She was the only British aircraft carrier in World War II to be sunk by air attack.

Vampire took a little longer to succumb. She fought with customary Australian courage. Two near misses astern shook her World War I plates badly, and a third shot past the bridge, cleared the whaler in its davits and exploded alongside. The eruption of water washed the port oerlikon gun crew clear out of the gun mounting, the phone number being brought up short by the lead to his head set.

The next bomb was a direct hit in A boiler room. *Vampire* was brought to a standstill. A stick of three or four more bombs created more major damage. Potatoes rained down like shrapnel when the vegetable locker was struck. The destroyer took on a list to starboard and the rudder jammed hard over. In a moment the bow section fell away but the after section remained afloat until 1102. Then a magazine exploded and the stern was shattered to pieces. The last part of the ship to be seen amid the smoke and spray was the rudder, propellers and the tattered remains of her white ensign. Before she sank Commander W. T. A. Moran ordered abandon ship and Carley floats and rafts were cast overboard.

Vita was quickly upon the scene of the *Hermes*'s survivors who now lay scattered over three or four square miles of the sea. Lifeboats and a motor boat began the long task of rescuing the hundreds of men swimming or clinging to rafts. The motor boat with a lifeboat in tow was sent to pick up *Vampire*'s survivors because as Captain Sinclair of the *Vita* reported later* he had to keep his hospital ship idle in the water because 'so many of the *Hermes* survivors were still . . . alongside the ship and round my propellers'. The only losses from *Vampire* were Commander Moran himself and seven ratings.

Captain Onslow with eighteen officers and 288 ratings of *Hermes* were also lost. *Vita* collected 590 survivors from both ships and delivered them to Colombo at 2200 the next day. A few more survivors were picked up by local craft and a handful of swimmers managed to struggle ashore.

Simultaneous with the sinking of these ships, six dive bombers sought out the tanker *British Sergeant* as their target. She was about twelve miles to the north of the carrier. She was struck many times and eventually foundered off Elephant Point two-and-a-half hours later: her crew landed safely in boats.

Even now Nagumo had not finished with his mauling of the Royal Navy. Another force of his bombers – nine in number – located the corvette *Hollyhock* and the *Athelstone* about thirty miles south of Batticoloa Light – so close to safety – and sank both vessels in a display of ruthless and accurate bombing. Fifty-three men went down with their corvette.

Thus, at last, ended Nagumo's destructive voyage in the Indian Ocean. His success was achieved with seeming nonchalance, like the shrugging of his shoulders. While he was dealing this last blow

*Quoted in *Valiant Voyaging* by H. St. G. Saunders, 1948, page 133.

his compatriot, Vice-Admiral Ozawa, with his Malaya Force was wreaking havoc near by in the Bay of Bengal.

On 1 April when Nagumo and Somerville were embarked on their elaborate game of blind man's buff, Vice Admiral Ozawa and his Malaya Force of one light carrier, five heavy cruisers and screening destroyers left Mergui. In the channel between the Nicobars and the Andamans the force manoeuvred at leisure trying to 'lose' twenty-four hours in order to synchronise its movements with Nagumo's operations.

On 4 April Ozawa entered the Bay of Bengal and headed north-west to the coast of India. By 1730 – just before dusk – on the following day, Ozawa split his force into three, two of the detachments heading towards India's ports of Vizagapatam and Coconada, the other steaming due north. The damage and destruction these detachments wrought is comparable in severity and losses with the heavy loss of ships and men in Convoy PQ 17.

The high loss of ships was due to the decision to clear the east Indian ports of shipping, a decision which, in the circumstances, was undoubtedly correct. As there were no escorts available the ships were despatched in small, make-shift, unescorted convoys, clustering together as if numbers alone gave protection. The ships were all routed close inshore.

During the period in question fifty-five merchant ships were ordered to sea from India's east coast ports: thirty-five of them reached their destination; twenty of them were sunk by Ozawa's Force, most of them within a few hours of each other on 6 April. Even more ships were sunk by Japanese submarines both in the Bay of Bengal and in the seas to the west of India and Ceylon.*

Two of the ships lost in the Bay of Bengal were the 7726-ton *Dardanus* and the 5281-ton *Gandara* proceeding in an unescorted convoy. Captain English, master of the *Dardanus*, sailed his ship in ballast from Calcutta on 2 April. Soon after passing Vizagapatam on Easter Sunday the ship was attacked by two carrier planes from *Ryujo*. One bomb struck the vessel and completely disabled her engines. Captain English ordered the ship to be abandoned but some minutes later while the boats were still being got away she was attacked again. Her guns again engaged the raiders but they proved ineffective. She took another hit. As the ship remained

*For full details see Appendix C.

afloat Captain English and some of his crew returned aboard to try to save the ship, despite the heavily flooded stokehold and engine room.

Salvation then appeared in the form of the *Gandara* who took the damaged *Dardanus* in tow and headed for Madras. But at 0730 on the 6th a Japanese float plane appeared and bombed both ships. Thirty minutes later three of Ozawa's heavy cruisers came upon the damaged ships from astern and began shelling them. They became like practice targets, were hit repeatedly and soon both had to be abandoned. The cruisers hove off to the north in search of more victims and left the ships to sink. But, stoutly, they remained afloat until a light cruiser came upon them and despatched both with more shells and torpedoes while their crews witnessed the destruction of their ships from the lifeboats.

At the time that *Dardanus* was spotted by the seaplanes and attacked – at 0730 – a convoy of six ships in three columns two days steaming behind her, was also located by a seaplane. Within minutes of being spotted heavy shells began falling among the ships from warships looming over the horizon. One of the convoy was the 7621-ton *Autolycus*, who had only part-loaded a general cargo in Calcutta on 4 April when she was ordered away to Madras. The *Autolycus* was the first of the convoy to be hit and it soon became evident that she was doomed. Ship was abandoned and the vessel sank at 0900. Two days later, the master, three other Europeans and twelve Chinese crew safely made a landfall.

The arrival of so many survivors along this part of the Indian coast and the sinking of so many ships gave rise to much alarm ashore. When *Ryujo*'s planes made bombing raids on Cocanada and Vizagapatam on the 6th – the first bombs to land on Indian soil – panic spread wildly and both towns were practically cleared. Madras caught the panic fear and the wailing of air raid sirens was enough to create a heavy exodus into the interior.

Vice Admiral Ozawa re-concentrated his forces on 7 April and shaped course for Singapore. He had not only sunk a great deal of shipping, but so disrupted sea traffic that the normally busy port of Calcutta and other east coast ports were brought to a virtual standstill for the next three weeks.

Before we turn our attention away from the naval operations in the Indian Ocean to the greater events to take place in the South-West Pacific let us summarise the naval events of the next few days.

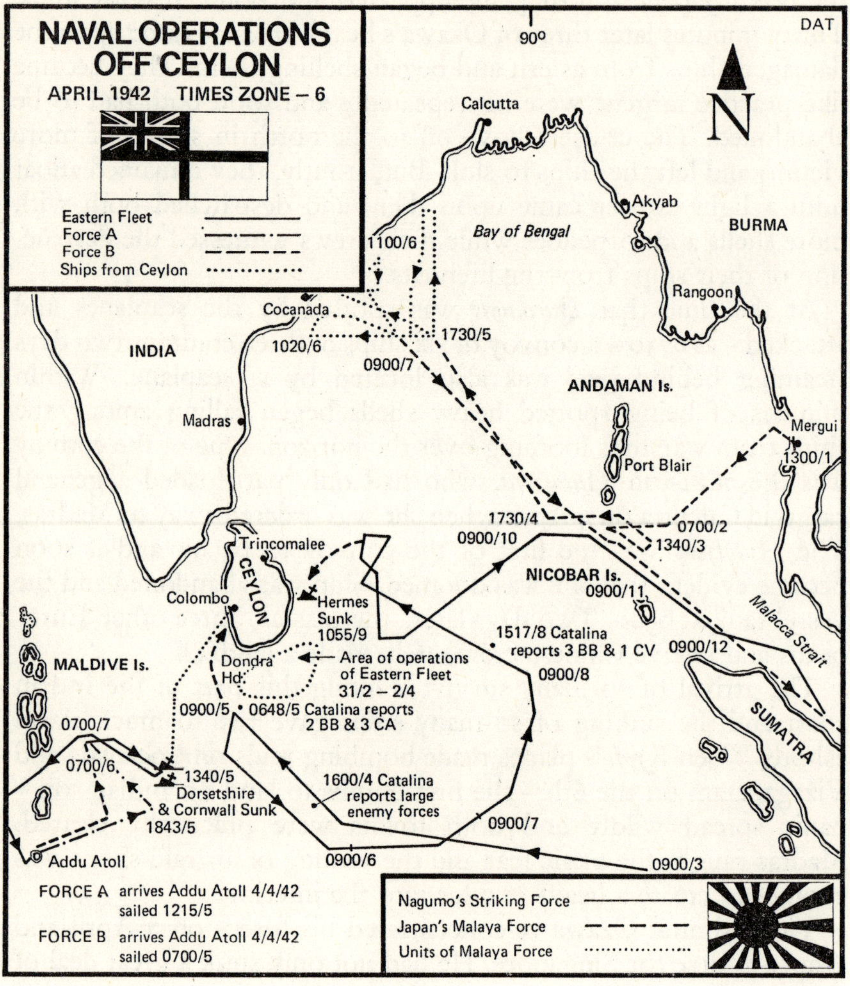
NAVAL OPERATIONS OFF CEYLON
APRIL 1942 TIMES ZONE – 6
Eastern Fleet
Force A
Force B
Ships from Ceylon
DAT
90°
N
Calcutta
Akyab
BURMA
Bay of Bengal
1100/6
Rangoon
Cocanada
1730/5
1020/6
0900/7
INDIA
ANDAMAN Is.
Madras
Mergui
1300/1
Port Blair
1730/4
0700/2
0900/10
1340/3
Trincomalee
NICOBAR Is.
0900/11
CEYLON
Colombo
Hermes Sunk 1055/9
Malacca Strait
1517/8 Catalina reports 3 BB & 1 CV
0900/12
MALDIVE Is.
Dondra Hd.
Area of operations of Eastern Fleet 31/2 – 2/4
0900/8
0900/5
0648/5 Catalina reports 2 BB & 3 CA
SUMATRA
0700/7
0700/6.
1340/5
Dorsetshire & Cornwall Sunk
1600/4 Catalina reports large enemy forces
1843/5
0900/7
Addu Atoll
0900/6
0900/3
FORCE A arrives Addu Atoll 4/4/42 sailed 1215/5
FORCE B arrives Addu Atoll 4/4/42 sailed 0700/5
Nagumo's Striking Force
Japan's Malaya Force
Units of Malaya Force

Paradoxically, the result of the Ceylon raid was the creation of a naval vacuum. As Admiral Willis with his Force B withdrew west to Kilindini and a disconsolate Somerville with Force A to Bombay, a trio of exultant admirals, Nagumo, Kondo and Ozawa headed east for the Pacific. Unknown to the Allies the foray into the Indian Ocean was finished. It was never to be repeated. Far from being a threat of invasion for Ceylon and India the operation marked the limit of Japan's naval excursions westward.

With the completion of the destructive strike against Trincomalee, Nagumo had notched up yet another major triumph, crowned this time with the sinking of a carrier. As soon as the recovery of the scores of Egusa's aircraft had been completed aboard Nagumo's carriers, the Striking Forces retired southerly and then easterly for Singapore and the homeland. He was retiring behind the perimeter of Japan's outer defences, never to venture beyond it again towards the west.

But nothing of this was known to Wavell, Somerville and the Chiefs of Staff in London. To them 'this was India's most dangerous hour; our Eastern Fleet was powerless to protect Ceylon or Eastern India: our air strength was negligible'.*

Somerville, of course, was criticised for the losses of the cruisers and *Hermes*. The Prime Minister expressed the view that the admiral had imprudently dispersed his forces but the First Sea Lord, Admiral Sir Dudley Pound and the First Lord of the Admiralty, Mr A. V. Alexander, defended him well enough for the Prime Minister to announce to the House of Commons 'I cannot make any statement about the strength of the forces at Admiral Somerville's disposal or of the reasons which led him to make the dispositions of his fleet, for which he was responsible. Nothing in these dispositions or in the consequences which followed from them have in any way weakened the confidence of the Admiralty in his judgement.'†

On 13 and 14 April Wavell conferred with Somerville in Bombay and was gravely disturbed at the admiral's assertion that he could not prevent an invasion of southern India and Ceylon. On the 19th Wavell took passage in *Warspite* to Colombo to confer with Admiral Layton. Somerville had more time to convince Wavell of the desperate straits of the naval situation and to add that in May what naval units there were in the Indian Ocean would be engaged

**Despatch* by Field Marshal Earl Wavell, 17 September 1946.

†Statement to the House of Commons 13 April 1942.

in the approaching occupation of Madagascar (Operation Ironclad). Hope in the longer term was extended to Wavell on the passage by a signal from the Prime Minister relating the steps being taken by the government, in particular the building up of a fleet for the Indian Ocean strong enough to repel any detachment of their main fleet that the Japanese could afford to detach. In eight to ten weeks Admiral Somerville should have three fast capital ships and three large carriers. This would be made possible by American transference of a US battleship to the Home Fleet at Scapa Flow. In the meantime, Winston Churchill pointed a warning finger: the defence of Ceylon was paramount; its loss would make all these efforts futile.

Wavell was unimpressed by all these promises of jam tomorrow. His cynicism was well-founded for Operation Ironclad did intervene, then a Malta convoy threatened to take major units out of Somerville's fleet and finally Australia asked for the return of some of her troops from Ceylon. Wavell exploded: 'The War Cabinet must really make up their minds whether or not they propose to defend India and Ceylon seriously.' But by this time all danger had passed and India and Ceylon were never to be threatened by sea again. And, of course, the War Cabinet were compelled to consider global strategy whereas Wavell only had his command to consider, and as events turned out the War Cabinet's judgements were proved right. India – and all the other commands – not only survived – they triumphed in the end.

CHAPTER 11

Preparations for Operation MO

ON 13 APRIL Nagumo's five carriers and Kondo's battleships steamed through the Malacca Straits, passed Singapore and entered the South China Sea. Course was then set NNE towards Bako in the Pescadores en route to the homeland. Already the preliminary and complex moves for the next operation were being formulated like a gigantic game of chess by the naval staff aboard the Combined Headquarters in *Yamato*.

Ahead of Nagumo's carriers was Vice Admiral Ozawa with his light carrier *Ryujo*, supporting cruisers and destroyers. They had put in to Singapore on 11 April. *Ryujo* joined Nagumo for the first leg of the homeward passage then detached and put in to Camranh Bay on the 16th. Two days later – as Colonel Doolittle's bombers were taking off from the carrier *Hornet* for the historic raid on Tokyo – Admiral Nagumo's Force arrived off the Pescadores in the Formosa Strait, due west of what is now Taiwan. The 5th Carrier Squadron, *Zuikaku* and *Shokaku*, were detached from Nagumo and ordered in to Bako to re-fuel and provision.

Akagi, Hiryu, Soryu and most of the cruisers and destroyers of the screening force continued on their way to the homeland but they soon received orders to divert and search for the US carrier force that had launched the Tokyo raiders: the force had been reported by Japanese picket boats stationed in northern waters. The search was called off at 2200 on 20 April and the carriers were ordered to proceed to their home ports. *Akagi*, the world's most destructive warship, with Nagumo, Japan's most respected Force commander, on the bridge and a jubilant ship's company, arrived at Kure on the 22nd.

Nagumo took to his homeland a record of unparalleled success. He had good reason to feel proud. In a period of four and a half months he had operated with effect and authority across 120 degrees of longitude – *one-third of the way around the world* – from Hawaii to Ceylon. He had steamed nearly 50,000 miles: he had sunk five battleships,* one carrier, two heavy cruisers, seven destroyers: he had damaged several more capital ships, destroyed tens of thousands of tons of auxiliaries and merchant ships; he had conducted devastating strikes against port installations at Pearl Harbor, Rabaul, Amboina, Darwin, Tjilatjap, Colombo and Trincomalee: hundreds of Allied aircraft had been shot from the sky or destroyed on the ground. And the cost to Nagumo was negligible. Not one ship of his Striking Force had been sunk or even damaged. As the United States Strategic Bombing Survey commented:† 'Indeed, the Force was seldom sighted and never effectively attacked.' The only sacrifice had been in aircraft and air crew, but even these losses were not considerable. It is true that when the Force struck at Ceylon they encountered for the first time opposition of some consequence: 'they met bone' as Winston Churchill commented. And damaging though their losses had been it would be absurd to describe them as anything more than annoying.

However, what the Ceylon raid did achieve was possibly a month of distraction for the Nagumo Force. There is no denying that Admiral Yamamoto's strategic thinking had been correct: no Pacific war would be won until the US Pacific Fleet had been destroyed. The Pearl Harbor Attack had gone some way towards that objective. A second strike should, of course, have been made, but equally important, sorties to the *east* to seek out and destroy the remnants of the US Pacific Fleet – especially the carriers – was the right strategy. In the event, Nagumo was sent south and west, earning the hard-pressed US Navy a respite. Nearly the whole of March and part of April was wasted by the Japanese in costly cat and mouse games with an impotent British Eastern Fleet while the US Navy laboured with customary skill and swiftness to overcome its initial setbacks. Seen in this perspective the Indian Ocean foray was a strategic blunder that was to cost Japan dear. As if in acknowledgment of this and in an effort to rectify the position, all attention was now concentrated on the east.

*See footnote to page 16

†United States Strategic Bombing Survey, Naval Analysis Division, *The Campaigns of the Pacific War*, page 31.

March and April in the Japanese camp were days of planning, argument and counter argument, mainly centred on the choice of south or east as the direction of the next thrust: in simplified terms, it became a choice of attacking and invading the island of Midway or of straddling Pacific lines of communication and isolating Australia.

Admiral Yamamoto considered the prime condition of any plan should be to force the US Pacific Fleet to do battle. Advocates of the 'isolate Australia' view believed their plan would accomplish this. Acrimonious argument bubbled like a hot-pot, but Yamamoto was adamant: he regarded as a portent of the future the US carrier raids of the past few weeks against the Marshalls, Wake and Marcus Islands and New Guinea.

Yamamoto's Midway plan, seeking a final reckoning with the US Pacific Fleet, was expounded by Commander Yasuji Watanabe to the Imperial Headquarters in Tokyo, where he arrived on 2 April from the battleship *Yamato* in Hiroshima Bay. The plan aimed at securing Midway and the Western Aleutians. It had as its first stage the operation to capture Port Moresby with the ultimate objective of establishing an outer defence perimeter linking Kiska in the Aleutians, Midway, Wake, the Marshall and Gilbert Islands, Samoa, Fiji and New Caledonia.

Bitter opposition to the plan was put by Commander Mitsushiro, Senior Air Staff Officer at Imperial HQ. The discussions were protracted and heated. On 5 April Vice Admiral Ito and Rear Admiral Fukudome representing the Naval General Staff argued with Watanabe to such a degree that the Commander broke off discussions to telephone Combined Fleet HQ aboard *Yamato*, requesting instructions as to the stand he should take. He resumed his seat at the table and stated Yamamoto's unequivocal standpoint:*

> In the last analysis the success or failure of our entire strategy in the Pacific will be determined by whether or not we succeed in destroying the US Pacific Fleet, more particularly, its carrier task forces . . . We believe that by launching the proposed operation against Midway we can succeed in drawing out the enemy's carrier strength and destroying it in decisive battle.

*Quoted by Fuchida and Okumiya in *Midway*, page 76. Co-author Commander Masatake Okumiya was present at the Imperial HQ as an observer at the time of the discussions.

Fukudome acknowledged defeat and proposed the adoption of the Midway plan. Ito nodded silent agreement.

Curiously, unknown to anyone, the fate of Nagumo's Striking Force had been sealed: and, equally curiously, Nagumo had no say at all in his Force's participation in the Midway operation. He was still on his way to Kure. In the meantime, the haggling over the details of the plan continued unabated, but a few days later – on 18 April – most argument ended and disunity evaporated. At noon on that day Doolittle's B25 bombers flew over Tokyo.

When the Doolittle raid was launched Nagumo, as we have seen, was approaching the homeland with his Carrier Force. Vice Admiral Kondo with his Second Fleet had entered Yokosuka the day before. He was ordered to sea immediately to take command of all surface units including Vice Admiral S. Takusu's First Fleet to flush out the *Hornet* force.

Nagumo's carriers were passing through the Bashi Strait at the southern end of Formosa, today's Taiwan, when the picket boat sighting report came through and activated Tactical Method No. 3, a set plan of action for the defence of the homeland. Nagumo's Force had a part to play and the Force shaped course for the estimated enemy position. Top speed was ordered and the carriers again became hives of activity as aircraft were hoisted from their hangars to the flight deck and lined up in readiness for action. Commanders Genda and Fuchida hurriedly made their plans and even while they were engrossed in their work news came through of bombing raids on Tokyo, Yokahama, Kawasaki and Yokosuka, followed later by reports of raids on other towns.

These reports came as a baffling shock to those aboard *Agaki*, baffled not only by the raid on Tokyo but by the widespread enemy action throughout the homeland. It was soon realised that *Akagi* was too far away to establish contact with the US task force and at 2200 on the 20th the attempted interception was called off. Nagumo's Force changed course for its boisterous homecoming.

The Doolittle raid, so small, which achieved so little in terms of military damage, in fact had accomplished so much. One of its principal results was the universal acceptance of the Midway plan. Even the most vociferous opponents of Midway and advocates of the southward thrust could not now dispute the threat from the east and the need to destroy the US carriers. Captain Toshikazu

Ohmae subsequently referred to the raid under interrogation:* 'Though in itself not very destructive, caused considerable discussion and confirmed the need for eastward expansion to acquire bases to protect the home islands; the mainland.'

It is not the purpose of this book to relate the story of the Battle of Midway, thus we shall not follow the fortunes of Vice Admiral Nagumo and his flagship *Akagi.* She, the *Kaga, Hiryu* and *Soryu* were all to be sunk in the battle off Midway early in June 1942. We shall follow in detail the events which led directly to another confrontation – in the Battle of the Coral Sea – which was the outcome of the Japanese Operation MO and which involved the two carriers of the 5th Carrier Squadron, *Zuikaku* and *Shokaku* and their flag officer Rear Admiral Chuichi Hara.

Between 1 and 20 April a small Japanese force comprising the seaplane carrier *Chitose* (11,023 tons), the light cruiser *Kinu* (5170 tons), four destroyers and four patrol boats, consolidated the Japanese positions to the rear of New Guinea, occupying numerous islands and ports as a prelude to another major offensive.

The new major offensive was Operation MO. Its prime objective was the capture and occupation of Tulagi on Florida Island and of Port Moresby in Papua, with the aim of establishing air bases from which to attack Australia, and the capture of Nauru and Ocean Islands.

The Japanese were anxious about the build up of Allied forces in Australia. They estimated – with accuracy – that the number of first line US aircraft was 200, and while they suspected the presence of a US naval task force they considered it 'not large'. They also believed that a British force was operating in the area and thought it comprised 'a light cruiser, two or three heavy cruisers and one battleship'.† This was probably Task Force 44 with the US heavy cruiser wrongly identified as a capital ship.

The Japanese were not far wrong in their assessment of the Allied forces operating in the Coral Sea area. The strength of these Allied forces gave rise to no real anxiety: the Japanese, with

*USSBS 192 Nav No. 43 *Japanese Naval Planning.* Ohmae 'is probably the most intelligent and well-informed Japanese naval officer that has been interrogated by this section'.

†ATIS Document 18665F (WDI 56) *Operation MO.*

customary efficiency, were assembling forces adequate to combat any likely Allied strength. These forces were as follows:

OPERATION MO
JAPANESE NAVAL FORCES

Overall Naval Commander: Vice Admiral Shigeyoshi Inouye, Commander-in-Chief Fourth Fleet, aboard his flagship, the light cruiser *Kashima* at Rabaul.

GROUP 1: TULAGI INVASION FORCE: Rear Admiral Kiyohide Shima aboard the minelayer *Okinoshima*. One transport, *Asuman Maru*. Destroyers *Kikutsuki* and *Yuzuki*. Two submarine chasers and five minesweepers.

GROUP 2: PORT MORESBY SUPPORT FORCE: Rear Admiral Kuninori Marushige flying his flag in the light cruiser *Tenryu* with sister ship *Tatsuta* forming the 18th Cruiser Squadron. The seaplane carrier *Kamikawa Maru* and three gunboats. The objective of this force was to set up a second seaplane base at Misima Island off New Guinea's easternmost point as a preliminary to the invasion of Port Moresby.

GROUP 3: PORT MORESBY INVASION FORCE: Rear Admiral Sadamichi Kajioka, flying his flag in the light cruiser *Yubari* with the destroyers *Oite, Asanagi, Mutsuki, Mochitsuki, Uzuki* and *Yayoi*. The minelayer *Tsugaru* and five minesweepers. A total of eleven transports were under the command of Rear Admiral Koso Abe. This Force's mission was to round the eastern tip of New Guinea and storm Port Moresby.

GROUP 4: PORT MORESBY COVERING FORCE: Rear Admiral Aritomo Goto in his flagship *Aoba* with the heavy cruisers *Kinugasa, Kako* and *Furutaka*, the destroyer *Sazanami* and the light aircraft carrier *Shoho*. Orders were to stand off Port Moresby to protect the invasion force.

GROUP 5: CARRIER STRIKING FORCE: Vice Admiral Takeo Takagi in his flagship the heavy cruiser *Myoko*, accompanied by *Haguro* and the destroyers *Ariake, Yugure, Shiratsuyu, Shigure, Ushio* and *Akebono*. The carrier power in this Force comprised Rear Admiral Chuichi Hara's flagship *Zuikaku* and her sister ship *Shokaku*.

GROUP 6: SUBMARINE ATTACK FORCE: Captain Ishizaki commanded the submarines which comprised *RO 33* and *RO 34* who were given instructions to 'destroy enemy fleet' and *I 21, I 22, I 24, I 28* and *I 29* were assigned patrol positions and ordered to lie in wait.

GROUP 7: LAND-BASED 25TH AIR FLOTILLA: Rear Admiral Sadoyoshi Yamada commanded about 160 land-based naval aircraft stationed at

Rabaul, Shortland and Tulagi, all within range of Port Moresby. The Flotilla acted as a naval-air support force.

It was Vice Admiral Inouye who, with marginally more powerful forces, had commanded the assault upon Rabaul three months earlier. He was equally confident of success in Operation MO. His plans had the merit of simplicity. Tulagi was the first objective and was planned to be occupied on 3 May. This would enable the establishment of a seaplane base with a commanding position for patrolling the Coral Sea. The Allies would have to rely upon Port Moresby and Noumea for operating their reconnaissance planes and both these bases were far distant and entailed long patrols. The Port Moresby Invasion Force was scheduled to leave Rabaul on 4 May, the day after the occupation of Tulagi, and would start storming the objective on the 7th.

It was expected the US forces in the Coral Sea would intervene to obstruct the Japanese intentions: in such an event it was proposed that two enveloping movements, like a boxer's simultaneous left and right hook, would trap the Americans: Goto's Port Moresby Invasion Covering Force coming in from the north-west, to the west of the Solomons, would provide the right hook; Takagi's Carrier Task Force sweeping round to the east of the Solomons and into the Coral Sea from the south-east could well provide a knock-out left hook. Thereafter, the Japanese carriers would attack Australian bases and the Tulagi Invasion Force would occupy the islands of Odan and Nauru.

However, there was one major flaw in an otherwise faultless plan: the Americans were privy to it. If they were not aware of all the details at least the information to hand enabled the Americans to make an assessment of the Japanese forces as follows: three carriers, *Zuikaku*, *Shokaku* and *Ryukaku* (actually *Shoho*: early reports of the Coral Sea battle carry this mistake), five heavy cruisers, four light cruisers, twelve destroyers and a submarine force. In actuality the forces comprised two fleet carriers, one light carrier, four heavy and six light cruisers and fourteen destroyers.

Opposed to these Japanese forces, the Americans were able to marshal two fleet carriers, seven heavy and one light cruisers (one of each being Australian), thirteen destroyers and some auxiliaries.

ALLIED FORCES

TASK FORCE 17

Commander: Rear Admiral F. Jack Fletcher in *Yorktown*

TG 17.2 ATTACK GROUP Rear Admiral Thomas C. Kinkaid (Comcrudiv 6)

Minneapolis	Captain Frank J. Lowry
New Orleans	Captain Howard H. Good

Rear Admiral William W. Smith (TF Cruiser Commander)

Astoria	Captain Francis W. Scanland
Chester	Captain Thomas M. Shock
Portland	Captain Benjamin Perlman

Destroyer Screen: Captain Alexander R. Early (Comdesron 1)

Phelps	Lieutenant-Commander Edward L. Beck
Dewey	Lieutenant-Commander C. F. Chillingworth
Farragut	Commander George P. Hunter
Aylwin	Lieutenant-Commander Robert H. Rogers
Monaghan	Lieutenant-Commander William P. Burford

TG 17.3 SUPPORT GROUP Rear Admiral J. G. Crace R.N.

HMAS *Australia*	Captain H. B. Farncomb RAN
Chicago	Captain Howard D. Bode
HMAS *Hobart*	Captain H. L. Howden RAN

Destroyer Screen: Captain Francis X. McInerney (Comdesdiv 9)

Perkins	Lieutenant-Commander Walter C. Ford
Walke	Lieutenant-Commander Thomas E. Fraser

TG 17.5 CARRIER GROUP Rear Admiral Aubrey W. Fitch in *Lexington*.

Yorktown	Captain Elliot Buckmaster
	Air Group: Lieutenant-Commander Oscar Pederson

VF 42 20 F4F–3 Wildcats Lt-Cdr Charles R. Fenton
VB 5 19 SBD–2–3 Dauntlesses Lt Wallace C. Short
VS 5 19 SBD–2–3 Dauntlesses Lt-Cdr William O. Burch
VT 5 13 TBD–1 Devastators Lt-Cdr Joe Taylor

Lexington	Captain Frederick C. Sherman
	Air Group: Commander William B. Ault

VF 2 22 F4F–3 Wildcats Lt-Cdr Paul H. Ramsey
VB 2 18 SDB–2–3 Dauntlesses Lt-Cdr Weldon L. Hamilton
VS 2 18 SDB–2–3 Dauntlesses Lt-Cdr Robert E. Dixon
VT 2 12 TBD–1 Devastators Lt-Cdr James H. Brett

Destroyer Screen: Captain Gilbert C. Hoover (Comdesron 2)

Morris	Commander H. B. Jarrett
Anderson	Lieutenant-Commander J. K. B. Ginder
Hammann	Commander Arnold E. True
Russell	Lieutenant-Commander Glen R. Hartwig

TG 17.6 FUELLING GROUP: Captain John S. Phillips

Oiler	*Neosho*	Captain Phillips
Oiler	*Tippecanoe*	Commander A. Macondray
DD	*Sims*	Lieutenant-Commander Wilford M. Hyman
DD	*Worden*	Lieutenant-Commander William G. Pogue

TG 17.9 SEARCH GROUP: Commander George H. De Baun
Tender *Tangier* at Noumea with twelve PBY – 5 (Catalinas)

Notes:
(a) Allied Air Forces in the South West Pacific Area (General Douglas MacArthur) under the command of Lieutenant-General George H. Brett, totalled 482 aircraft of all types. Technically these were available for the support of Allied naval operations in the Coral Sea, but as in all such inter-service co-operative ventures the outcome fell far short of hopes.
(b) The Eastern Australia Submarine Group comprising eleven submarines stationed on the depot ship *Griffin* at Brisbane were also available in the area.

The Coral Sea was given its name in 1831 by Captain Mathew Flinders of the Royal Navy. It is perhaps one of the most beautiful stretches of water in the world brushed by the fresh south-easterly trade winds which ruffle the transparent sea into white caps: it is the same breeze which dissipates the tropical heat to a year-round temperature both tolerable and pleasant. There is no such thing as winter in the Coral Sea. Brightly coloured coral reefs ring the jungle-clad islands which fringe the sea to the north and east while on its western boundary the 1500 mile Great Barrier Reef allows the Coral Sea swell to crash itself to white foaming destruction in a display of rare maritime beauty. Peace, natural beauty, the warmth and iridescence of a tranquil sea, all these were to be defiled by the carnage, fuel oil, wreckage and bomb bursts of the first great naval battle between aircraft carriers.

The opening moves in the battle took place in the early days of April. Admiral Nimitz began deploying his Task Forces in a series of complex moves preceded on 3 April by the key naval appointment of Rear Admiral Aubrey Fitch as flag officer aboard USS *Lexington*, a ship which he had commanded in 1936. The fifty-eight-year-old officer had qualified as a naval aviator in 1930 and subsequently commanded the seaplane tender *Wright* and the ill-fated *Langley*. Many years later – in 1940 – he became Commander

Carrier Division One with his flag in *Saratoga*. His appointment to *Lexington* strengthened a powerful team headed by Captain Frederick C. (Ted) Sherman. 'Lady Lex', as the carrier was affectionately known by her crew, left Pearl Harbor with her screening units on 16 April. Several days later Fitch was ordered to rendezvous with Rear Admiral Fletcher in *Yorktown* at 'Point Buttercup', 16 degrees S, 161 degrees 45′E, 320 miles south of San Cristobel Island in the Solomons on 1 May.

Rear Admiral Frank Jack Fletcher, the distinguished fifty-six-year-old officer who had taken part in the Marshall–Gilbert Island operations of February and the Salamaua–Lae operations in March, commanded Task Force 17 operating out of Noumea. On 14 April the Task Force was ordered to Tongatabu for replenishment and preparation for the expected operations in the Coral Sea.

Nimitz was hard put to assemble more forces for the battle which he now expected to take place on 3 May. Admiral Halsey's Task Force with *Enterprise* and *Hornet* arrived in Pearl Harbor on 25 April from the successful Doolittle Raid: it would be impossible to get the Task Force re-provisioned and into the Coral Sea in time for the predicted deadline – unless the Japanese delayed their plans and arrived some days late.

Vice Admiral Herbert F. Leary, Commander of the South West Pacific Forces (which was constituted on 22 April and absorbed the previous Anzac Force) contributed a small squadron – Task Force 44 – commanded by Rear Admiral John G. Crace RN. At the time that Nimitz was marshalling the Allied forces, Task Force 44 was dispersed. The three Australian cruisers *Australia* (flagship), *Hobart* and *Canberra* were at Sydney, but the latter was under refit and was unavailable for operations: USS *Chicago* and the destroyer *Perkins* were at Noumea. These two US ships were ordered to escort the oiler *Tippecanoe* and to join Fletcher on 1 May. Crace and his two cruisers were to rendezvous with the admiral on 4 May, collecting the US destroyer *Whipple* en route.

By noon on 29 April Nimitz had completed his dispositions and orders. Fletcher, who was given tactical command over his force and over the forces of Fitch and Crace,* received orders to 'operate in the Coral Sea commencing 1 May'.

*Crace was senior to Fletcher but the Combined Chiefs of Staff had agreed that the senior US naval officer commanding a carrier task force would exercise tactical command of combined units regardless of relative rank.

But Fletcher did not exercise tactical command over two important forces. The first, and the most important, was the Allied air forces under MacArthur's overall command which carried out 'air reconnaissance of the general area'. The second force was Captain Ralph Christie's submarine group based on Brisbane whose boats patrolled the coastal waters of Papua, the Louisiades and the Bismarcks.

Fletcher made his intentions clear to his combined forces in an order dated 1 May, the day of his rendezvous in the Coral Sea. Their aim, he signalled, was to 'destroy enemy ships, shipping and aircraft at favourable opportunities in order to assist in checking further advance by enemy in New Guinea–Solomons area'.*

The union of the Forces took place as planned. Rear Admiral Fitch with his *Lexington* Task Force joined Rear Admiral Fletcher's *Yorktown* Task Force at 0615 on 1 May in a position 16 degrees 16′S, 162 degrees 20′E.

Fletcher immediately set about re-fuelling his ships from the oiler *Neosho* and he directed Fitch to join *Chicago* and *Perkins* who were now joining company to re-fuel from their oiler, *Tippecanoe*. The American preparations for battle would soon be complete.

The Japanese naval units made the first of their preliminary moves towards battle on 29 April, the very day that Nimitz had completed his plans. On this day Rear Admiral Shima's invasion force for Tulagi left Rabaul and Rear Admiral Marushige's Port Moresby Support Force departed Truk. Shima headed south-east through the Solomon Sea until south-east of Woodlark Island, then altered course almost due east and finally made another change to north-east to Tulagi. On 2 May – D Day minus 1 – Tulagi was subjected to six air raids: on this day the tiny RAAF contingent and a few AIF troops were withdrawn.

On 3 May the Japanese landed at Tulagi off Florida Island to a bloodless victory.

By this date Vice Admiral Takagi with his Carrier Striking Force was well on his way to the Coral Sea to deliver the Japanese left hook to Fletcher's concentrated forces, having left Truk on 31 April.

On this day, too, the Port Moresby Invasion Force was just leaving Rabaul while hundreds of miles away down south Rear

*ComTaskFor 17 Secret Operation Order No. 2–42 of 1 May 1942.

Admiral Crace with *Australia* and *Hobart* was two days out from Sydney and heading for a rendezvous with Fletcher. Warships from many nations were moving inexorably towards battle.

Throughout 1 and 2 May Fletcher's forces re-fuelled from the two oilers. But more importantly all the US ships were put at incredible risk by both Fletcher and Fitch in the ensuing series of movements: the wonder is that they both came out of the episode unscathed. But – at long last – luck was going for the Americans.

The re-fuelling appears to have been a leisurely affair. While it was proceeding Fletcher was receiving some intelligence from MacArthur's HQ about the enemy shipping movements. But he was anxious to get his own pilots' reports and got increasingly frustrated by the time taken to re-fuel. At 1800 on the 2nd, on completion of fuelling of his own Task Force – *Yorktown, Astoria, Chester, Portland* and six destroyers – he set course for the west at slow speed leaving Fitch to finish his fuelling then to re-join Fletcher at daylight on the 4th in latitude 15 degrees S, longitude 157 degrees E, 400 miles south-west of Tulagi. At this time Takagi had reached his farthest south, 460 miles from Fletcher and was about to shape course for the last leg of his passage to Tulagi. Rear Admirals Goto and Marushige with their covering and support forces were hovering far to the north-west like guardian angels for Shima's Tulagi force.

At 1310 on the 3rd Fitch in *Lexington* completed re-fuelling, about twenty-four hours ahead of the original time schedule, and headed for the next morning's rendezvous. There now followed a series of incidents of alarming proportions. Quite rightly Fitch did not break radio silence to inform Fletcher of the early completion of his Force's fuelling, but incredibly he made no effort to advise his senior officer by aircraft, a natural enough precaution in the circumstances. It might have been a costly omission.

Thus, at the time Fitch completed fuelling at 1310 on 3 May, the US forces were split: Fletcher was about a hundred miles away, not knowing where Fitch was, knowing little of the enemy's movements. It was a situation fraught with danger.

Later that day – at 1900 – Fletcher's patience was rewarded: he received intelligence which made him change his plans immediately. Two of MacArthur's aircraft sighted some of the Tulagi invasion forces – two transports in the harbour and five or six warships in the roads near by. 'This was just the kind of report we had been waiting two months to receive.'* But Fletcher, with only one carrier and without support from Fitch, was at risk. Furthermore, he was confronted with unforeseen developments: the sighting of seaplanes at Tulagi presented an additional risk to Allied forces in the Coral Sea. Another factor was a huge, wide belt of bad weather which stretched across the Coral Sea between his force and Tulagi, a condition which would provide excellent cover for his own ships but could well impede his pilots.

Believing Fitch in *Lexington* still to be re-fuelling, Fletcher now saw the precarious position in which he found his *Yorktown* force, unsupported and compelled to strike with *Yorktown*'s aircraft alone. The alternative of not carrying out a strike would be almost certain discovery by the seaplane patrols. Fletcher resolved to strike. He acted swiftly. He detached *Neosho* with the destroyer *Russell* as escort to join Rear Admirals Fitch and Crace at 0800 on 4 May: that force was then to proceed to a new rendezvous with the *Yorktown* force in latitude 15 degrees S, 160 degrees E, about 300 miles south of Guadalcanal, at daylight on 5 May.

Fletcher determined to strike what he believed to be an important blow at the enemy shipping. At 2030 Task Force 17 altered course to north at a speed of twenty-four knots which was soon increased to twenty-seven. The first phase in the Battle of the Coral Sea was about to begin.

Fletcher maintained his northerly course throughout the night, reaching a position about 100 miles south-west of Guadalcanal at 0700 on 4 May. It was at about this time that *Neosho* and *Russell* joined Fitch who now, rather belatedly, learnt of Fletcher's intentions.

At 0900 Rear Admiral Crace with *Australia, Hobart* and *Whipple* also joined Fitch after an uneventful passage from Sydney. Thus at a crucial time the two main US task forces were about 250 miles apart, unable to support each other in case of need, and with Fitch now adopting a south-easterly course, the distance apart was increasing every minute.

*Fletcher's *Report*.

CHAPTER 12

Overkill at Tulagi

AT 0701 ON 4 May *Yorktown* launched the first aircraft to take part in the series of disjointed events which jointly became the Battle of the Coral Sea, the first naval battle in which the main contestants never sighted each other. It was also the first ever carrier-versus-carrier naval battle. Carriers once and for all established their superiority over the battleship as the capital ship of the navy. Naval warfare had taken a dramatic and startling turn at Pearl Harbor: it was emphasised in the Gulf of Siam: here in the Coral Sea carriers carried the story a stage further.

Fletcher had sped north through the 300-mile-wide belt of bad weather under thick black clouds with the thirty-mile-an-hour squally trade winds lashing across the decks from the starboard quarter.

By 0600 Fletcher had arrived at the pre-arranged point about 100 miles south-west of Guadalcanal where his aircraft would be launched to attack Tulagi. During the next hour, starting a little before sunrise, Captain Buckmaster turned *Yorktown* into wind and launched her aircraft, eleven Douglas Devastator torpedo bombers, twenty-eight Douglas Dauntless dive bombers and six Grumman Wildcat fighters, though the latter were to give air cover over the carriers. Eighteen other fighters were kept aboard in reserve. The unescorted torpedo and dive bombers flew through the dark weather, practically flying blind towards Tulagi Island. They emerged from the gloom of the clouds soon after 0800 to a bright clear sky, accurately on the approach to Tulagi. Each squadron, as was customary in those days, was to attack independently.

Lieutenant-Commander Burch in command of flight VS 5 of the Dauntless dive bombers was the first to arrive over the target. He led his flight in a wide arc over the area in order to identify targets and at 0815 the bombers dived to attack. Five minutes later the eleven Devastator torpedo bombers of flight VT 5 led by Lieu-

Admiral Sir James Somerville, Commander-in-Chief British Eastern Fleet, in flying kit aboard HMS *Formidable*, 1942.

Rear Admiral Frank (Jack) Fletcher USN, Commander of Task Force 17.

Rear Admiral Aubrey C. Fitch USN assumed tactical command of air operations during the main phase of the Coral Sea action.

Rear Admiral Crace's Task Group 17.3 mistaken for a Japanese squadron under high level attack by US bombers during the Battle of the Coral Sea, May 1942. Photograph located in Admiral Crace's War Diary

tenant-Commander J. Taylor arrived from seaward on the last leg of their approach at sea level.

Lieutenant Short, leading flight VB 5 of Dauntless dive bombers made the final attack. The enemy had been caught by surprise, unprepared for the strike, and though his reaction was swift and loud, the AA gunfire was largely ineffectual and wildly erratic. All the US planes survived the attack.

The explosions of shells, bombs, torpedoes and machine guns, the general convulsive atmosphere of battle, the obscuring smoke and flames and the excitement of youth in violent combat all contributed to a gross over-estimation of success. In fact the successes were minimal: the destroyer *Kikutsuki* was near missed, severely damaged and beached, later to become a total loss: the converted minesweeper *Tama Maru* was struck, blew up and sank and Minesweeper No. 1 and No. 2 were also sunk: the destroyer *Yuzuki* and sundry smaller vessels were damaged.

Only one of the torpedoes had struck home. Not one of Lieutenant Short's flight had scored a direct hit. The Japanese casualties were eighty-seven killed and 124 wounded.*

All US aircraft had landed-on by 0930. Not one had so much as a bullet hole or a shrapnel scratch.

While the crews were being de-briefed Rear Admiral Fletcher and his Air Group Commander, Lieutenant-Commander Pederson, pondered the next move. They decided upon a second strike. In the meantime *Yorktown*'s crew had worked furiously hard to re-arm and re-fuel the aircraft and when the order came to launch the second strike, eleven torpedo bombers and twenty-seven dive bombers were waiting with engines turning over. They all flew off without incident and arrived over Tulagi to a barrage of AA fire. Again, the Devastators showed poor marksmanship, not one torpedo striking home. The dive bombers near-missed a patrol boat, inflicting damage and sank two moored seaplanes. Only one Devastator was lost in the attack, all other aircraft safely landing-on *Yorktown* where the crews again claimed 'sensational' successes. The returning crews also claimed sighting three more seaplanes at the island of Makambo.

Fletcher and Pederson doubted the totality of their air crews' claims but they were concerned over the remaining seaplanes.

*Japanese Document 18665F (WD 156)

Accordingly, they ordered a third, limited, raid. Four Wildcat fighter aircraft were flown off and headed for Makambo to destroy the seaplanes. With commendable precision they emerged from the clouds right over the seaplane moorings. In a few minutes the seaplanes were smashed and burning.

Then the destroyer *Yuzuki* was sighted retiring from the area. She was strafed repeatedly suffering many casualties including the death of her captain. Two of the Wildcats were damaged in these attacks and made forced landings on the south coast of Guadalcanal. Both pilots were lucky to survive and even more fortunate to be rescued by the destroyer *Hammann* the following night.

Incredibly Fletcher ordered yet another strike against Tulagi. He despatched another twenty-one Dauntless dive bombers at 1400 to annihilate anything that resembled a target. This amounted to only four landing craft all of which were sunk. By 1702 all aircraft had been safely recovered aboard *Yorktown*.

The US pilots' claims for all the raids, when scaled down by the de-briefing officers, amounted to two destroyers, one cargo ship and four gunboats sunk: one light cruiser beached and sunk: one destroyer, one heavy cruiser or aircraft tender severely damaged: one cargo ship damaged: various small craft destroyed and five float planes also destroyed.*

But Fletcher was under no illusion. Despite the gross exaggeration of the pilots' claims and the excessive number of strikes launched against Tulagi, he believed the attacks to have been singularly unrewarding in relation to the scale of the attacks. He confessed so to Nimitz who replied to Fletcher in generous terms: 'This operation is indisputably disappointing in the quality of the results achieved, particularly in view of the cost in ammunition and equipment. It shows the need for training in the dropping of bombs and torpedoes whenever possible.' The expenditure of ammunition, in fact, totalled twenty-two torpedoes, seventy-six 1,000-lb bombs and about 83,000 rounds of machine gun bullets.

But Nimitz overlooked an important aspect of the Tulagi affair: in itself it had provided the pilots with a valuable experience which was to be put to good use in the next few days, and later still at Midway. Another, more immediate and important aspect had not

*For a graphic eye-witness description of *Yorktown*'s adventures in the Coral Sea see Stanley Johnson's *Queen of the Flat-Tops*, an interesting, albeit, inaccurate contemporary document.

escaped Nimitz nor Fletcher: the attacks had confirmed to the Japanese the presence of at least one US carrier in the northern waters of the Coral Sea. Their search craft would be out in earnest now to locate *Yorktown*.

Fletcher, for all his belief in the exaggeration of his pilots' claims still believed there was a mopping up task around Tulagi. He signalled Admiral W. W. Smith to nominate two cruisers to 'go into Savo Island and clean up the cripples the following dawn'. *Astoria* and *Chester* were appointed, but Fletcher had second thoughts and cancelled the order. It was a fortunate decision for an army reconnaissance plane sighted a Japanese naval force to the south of Bougainville comprising a carrier and two heavy cruisers. They were *Shoho* and two of Rear Admiral Goto's heavy cruisers. Smith's two cruisers would have been vulnerable had they been sighted and attacked by *Shoho*'s aircraft.

As soon as *Yorktown* had recovered all her aircraft on the afternoon of 4 May, Task Force 17 set off south-east and south, less *Hammann* and *Perkins* who were detached to search for the missing Wildcat pilots. *Hammann*, as we have read, recovered them, but *Perkins* who also searched for a missing bomber's crew failed to locate the men. The destroyers re-joined the force shortly before Fletcher made the rendezvous with Rear Admirals Fitch and Crace at 0816 on 5 May, 320 miles south of Guadalcanal. It was a happy reunion.

At this time the nearest Japanese force was four hundred miles away to the NNE and the Japanese plan for a left and right hook envelopment seemed far-fetched. This nearest force was Vice Admiral Takagi's Carrier Striking Force with Hara's two carriers *Zuikaku* and *Shokaku* and with Takagi's own flagship *Myoko*, accompanied by *Haguro*. This Carrier Striking Force was on its way to deliver the Japanese left hook, steaming south-east at twenty-five knots giving the island of Malaita a wide berth before rounding San Cristobel Island and entering the Coral Sea.

Rear Admiral Goto with his Port Moresby Invasion Covering Force of light cruisers and the light carrier *Shoho* were five hundred miles away to the north-west of Fletcher in a position south of Bougainville where the force was to re-fuel before covering the Port Moresby operation.

About 150 miles farther to the south-west was Rear Admiral Marushige's Port Moresby Support Force steaming south-west for the island of Misima where a temporary seaplane base was to be established with the seaplane carrier *Kamikawa Maru*. Marushige was then to retire to the north-west to a position between the tip of New Guinea and Woodlark Island.

Two more Japanese forces concern us: the Port Moresby Invasion Force, commanded by Rear Admiral Kajioka, had left Rabaul at 1800 on the 4th, headed south and was now in a position about 150 miles into the Solomon Sea barely having started its passage on the long journey to Port Moresby. Heading to rendezvous with Kajioka was Rear Admiral Shima with the small force of minor vessels which had comprised the Tulagi Invasion Force, most of whom had escaped destruction by *Yorktown*'s bombers.

All these forces, engaged in complex, ever-changing moves, were aware of the presence of the other: and each was aware of the presence of an enemy force, though neither Japanese nor American knew the exact strength nor position of the other. The Japanese came very near to discovering these missing elements in the vast jigsaw puzzle when a four-engined seaplane from Rabaul's 25th Air Flotilla sighted the Allied force but was shot down by a *Yorktown* Wildcat before it could get away a report. When the seaplane failed to return to Rabaul Admiral Inouye assumed it to have been shot down but he had no idea of when or where. Had the *Yorktown* pilot been less vigilant, had the patrol seaplane got away a signal then Inouye would have been able to fit vital pieces into the complicated jigsaw, and he would have rejoiced at the forces under his command being nicely positioned for execution of the pre-arranged plan to catch the Allied force between two fires – a measureless advantage, denied him by a young pilot.

The three forces under Fletcher's command spent the whole of 5 May and part of the 6th in re-fuelling from *Neosho*, keeping within visual signalling distance of each other, and now steaming at a leisurely speed. Early on the morning of the 6th Fletcher integrated the two carrier forces and Crace's Task Force 44 into one unified command, designated Task Force 17. It presented a splendid sight – *Yorktown*, *Lexington*, seven 8-inch gun cruisers, one 6-inch cruiser and eleven destroyers. The mood aboard ships was buoyant and matched the tropical weather: the cold front had passed and a stiff trade wind rolled the cumulous clouds across the sky, minimising the heat of the sun: life aboard the American and Australian ships was light-hearted and sparkling, such is the effect of a victory at sea, as the Tulagi affair was regarded.

Part of the organisation of the newly constituted Task Force 17 was Fletcher's intention to delegate command during air operations to Rear Admiral Fitch whose experience in carriers was considerable. Fletcher was inexperienced in carrier operations; but for reasons known only to himself Fletcher did not acquaint Fitch of this intention until immediately before the action of 8 May, two days later. He seemed intent upon retaining command until convinced that battle had been truly joined, a sensible enough intention – had he given Fitch prior notice.

Throughout the whole of 6 May Fletcher was assailed by a great number of reports from C-in-C US Pacific Fleet and Commander South West Pacific Forces which 'placed a large number of enemy ships in the area between New Guinea, New Britain and Solomon Islands'. Fletcher later bemoaned his confusion in his *Report*. 'Practically every type of ship was reported and it was fairly definitely established that three Japanese aircraft carriers were in the area. The forces were scattered and there was no common direction of movement. Courses varied from 100 degrees clockwise to 342 degrees. A battleship and a carrier . . . were reported hove to or moving slowly north.' It was a confusing day for Fletcher.

He encountered another source of confusion and irritation on 6 May. The demarcation line between the South Pacific and the South West Pacific Commands passed north to south through the Coral Sea. The western three-quarters of the Coral Sea was under the aegis of the Commander-in-Chief South West Pacific whose area was supposed to be searched by land-based aircraft from Australia. It was physically impossible for them to do so. As Fletcher was operating in this area he was compelled to supplement this inadequacy by providing his own aircraft patrols to safeguard his Task Force.

The fragmentary information fed back to *Yorktown* by these navy patrols and by all the other sources began to form a fairly reliable picture by the late afternoon of the 6th – at least of the north-west. It became evident that the Japanese Forces were moving against Port Moresby, through the Jomard Passage, setting up en route a seaplane base in the Louisiades – either at Deboyne or Misima Island. This appreciation was confirmed by COMSOUWESPAC who gave the date of 7 May as the likely date for making the Jomard Passage and the 8th as D Day for the attack on Port Moresby.

It was late this same afternoon – on the 6th – that Takagi's Carrier Striking Force and Fletcher's Task Force 17 passed each other at a distance of only seventy miles, each blissfully unaware of the other's presence. It is incredible that battle was not joined that evening. It is also incomprehensible that both forces failed to discover the other. A combination of factors contributed to this failure. For his part, Takagi, for reasons which have never been explained, neglected to fly off long distance patrols during this period, a precaution which common prudence demanded. At this stage of the opposing forces' movements, the first to sight the other would have had an inestimable advantage: Takagi's neglect to keep reconnaissance planes airborne denied him this advantage of first strike. Fletcher maintained a continuous reconnaissance from the air but it is possible that clouds concealed Takagi's movements. This is substantiated by *Zuikaku* who recorded the clearly audible sounds of US aircraft flying in the heavy overcast above Takagi's ships during the afternoon.

It was when Takagi changed course in a position 13 degrees 20′ S, 157 degrees 40′E that the forces were only seventy miles apart. The change of course took Takagi's Force to the north at slow speed while he re-fuelled.

Fletcher completed his Task Force's re-fuelling at about 1800 on the 6th and an hour-and-a-half later the Force had adopted a course of NW heading for a launching position for his aircraft in readiness for a dawn attack on the 7th against the Japanese forces due in the Jomard Passage. This position was 310 miles south-east of Deboyne Island. The launch, of course, would be subject to the sighting of the enemy forces.

The oiler *Neosho*, now practically empty and of no further use to Fletcher, was detached south with the destroyer *Sims* as escort to a rendezvous named 'Rye' in position 16 degrees S, 158 degrees E by 1810 on 7 May.

All these moves were bringing the opposing forces inevitably to a clash of arms: it was only a question of time before the clash occurred. It was clear to Japanese, Americans and Australians in the Coral Sea that this encounter would come on 7 May. But before we leave Wednesday the 6th mention must be made of one more tragic episode in the annals of US military history: 6 May was the day of surrender of General Wainwright's courageous defending troops in the Philippines.

The change from the Corregidor surrender to the subsequent events in the Pacific war, starting in the Coral Sea in the next two days, was startling, dramatic and significant. A Churchillian phrase, taken out of context is appropriate: 'This is not the end. It is not even the beginning of the end. But it is, perhaps, the end of the beginning.'* Corregidor and the Coral Sea, perhaps, marked the end of the beginning for the Allies in the Pacific.

*Winston Churchill at the Lord Mayor's Luncheon at the Mansion House, London, 10 November 1942 after the Desert victory in North Africa.

CHAPTER 13

Coral Sea: Strike and Counter-Strike

AT DAYLIGHT ON Thursday 7 May the naval situation in the north Coral Sea can be summarised as follows:

1. Task Force 17, comprising *Yorktown, Lexington,* heavy cruisers *Astoria, Chester, Minneapolis, New Orleans, Portland,* destroyers *Hammann, Anderson, Morris, Phelps, Dewey, Aylwin, Monaghan* and *Russell,* as we have seen, was in a flying-off position 310 miles south-east of Deboyne Island.
2. Rear Admiral Crace was detached at 0650 with Task Group 17.3 comprising cruisers *Australia, Chicago* and *Hobart* with destroyers *Perkins, Walke* and *Farragut* to proceed ahead of Task Force 17 towards the Jomard Passage to destroy enemy ships passing through the Passage to Port Moresby.
3. Oiler *Neosho* and escort *Sims* were steaming south, still a few miles short of their rendezvous position 'Rye' where they were due later that afternoon.
4. Oiler *Tippecanoe* and escort *Worden* had already cleared the zone.
5. Vice Admiral Takagi's Carrier Striking Force of carriers *Zuikaku* and *Shokaku* with heavy cruisers *Myoko* and *Haguro* and six destroyers, having steamed north away from Fletcher during the night reversed course two hours after midnight and was now roughly abeam of Rossell Island, still heading south.
6. Rear Admiral Goto's Covering Force comprising the heavy cruisers *Aoba, Kinugasa, Kako* and *Furutaka,* the light carrier *Shoho* and a destroyer, had taken up a waiting position ninety miles north-east of Deboyne Island to give cover to the invasion force.
7. Rear Admiral Kajioka's Port Moresby Invasion Force now approaching the Jomard Passage, forging south-east.
8. Rear Admiral Marushige's Support Force of light cruisers *Tenryu* and *Tatsuta,* having set up a seaplane base at Deboyne Island was steaming

south-east before withdrawing north-west towards the D'Entrecasteaux Islands.

At dawn on 7 May Admiral Takagi was a worried man. He had no exact knowledge of the position of the Allied forces: his carrier commander, Rear Admiral Hara in *Zuikaku*, recommended a search to the southward to protect the Carrier Striking Force on its port quarter when it turned west to provide cover for the Port Moresby Invasion Force. Takagi accepted Hara's proposal and at 0600 the reconnaissance aircraft flew off. Hara confessed after the war that he 'was quite pleased with himself at the time . . . for his planes located what they reported as the United States carrier force at the eastern edge of the search sector . . . In the end it did not prove to be a fortunate decision.'* It was much less fortunate for the ships companies of *Neosho* and *Sims*.

The oiler, with *Sims* steaming one mile ahead sighted two aircraft about ten miles away towards the end of the morning watch. They were two of Hara's planes. At 0736 they wrongly reported sighting a carrier and a cruiser, yet another error of recognition with dreadful consequences to both the Japanese and the Americans. Hara accepted the sighting report at its face value and ordered a full scale strike. Course was altered and speed increased to close the enemy. One aircraft was flown off quickly to relieve the reconnaissance aircraft: it arrived over the US ships at 0900 and dropped a single bomb which missed.

Aboard *Zuikaku* and *Shokaku* strenuous efforts resulted in flying off the first group of fourteen Kate bombers at about 0810, quickly followed by another ten. These were followed in quick succession by eighteen Zero fighters and thirty-six Val dive bombers under the command of Commander Kakuichi Takahashi.

When all these aircraft were airborne and committed, Hara received more information. Since daylight – a few hours earlier – the Japanese had made a concerted and widespread effort to locate the Allied forces. Reconnaissance aircraft had been despatched from carriers and cruisers at sea, from Rabaul, Deboyne, Shortland and Tulagi, sectoring the northern waters of the Coral Sea in an almost frantic effort to locate the enemy first and help clear the way for the Port Moresby Invasion Force. The effort was rewarded at 0840

*S. E. Morison quoting from the 'Truk Report' (see Appendix A under 'Supplemental Report . . .') in his Vol IV, page 34. The most important contributor to this Report was Admiral Hara.

by the pilot of the cruiser *Kinugasa*'s seaplane who reported one carrier and about ten other vessels. But he got his co-ordinates mixed and it took Rabaul some time to interpret the signal, re-encode it and transmit it. By the time the signal reached Hara his strike aircraft were committed to their major strike against an oiler and a small destroyer. The commitment was irrevocable. And Hara, himself, was now vulnerable.

Commander Takahashi reached the reported position at 0935 to find an empty expanse of sea. He ordered his aircraft to fan out to search the area. One of his searching planes reported sighting a tanker and a destroyer. But no carrier was sighted and in the absence of better targets Takahashi ordered his aircraft to attack *Neosho* and *Sims*.

Both the US ships were at action stations when the first Japanese attack developed at 0945. The first wave of fourteen low level bombers scored no hits. The next attack by ten Kate bombers developed at about 1030 and was directed at the destroyer. By skilful manoeuvring the destroyer managed to avoid every bomb. At about noon Commander Takahashire-appeared on the scene with his group of thirty-six Val dive bombers. The group split into three and attacked from the stern of the oiler with *Sims* now close on her port quarter to give closer protection.

It was the destroyer who took the brunt of the attack. Within seconds of this new attack *Sims* was struck by three 250kg bombs, two of which pierced her thin plating and exploded in the engine room with devastating effect, creating many casualties and bringing the ship to a standstill. Within minutes she broke her back amidships and began to settle stern first. The crew began to abandon her for she was clearly doomed, and as if to emphasise the fact, a violent explosion erupted, lifting the broken ship bodily ten to fifteen feet before she settled and sank.

Depth charges then exploded, survivors reported; but it is incredible to think these had not been set to safe during the early hours of the day. One of the survivors was Chief Signalman R. J. Dicken: he managed to get aboard a single lifeboat and pulled stunned men from the sea. Just fifteen others survived.

As Dicken clutched men from the sea, Takahashi's dive bombers directed their attacks upon the oiler, *Neosho*. Within minutes seven direct hits were scored and another eight bombs exploded close alongside. One aircraft committed a kamikaze act – whether by accident or design is unknown – exploding astern and creating a large and damaging fire.

The commanding officer, Captain Phillips, gave orders to prepare to abandon ship, an order which was mistaken by many who probably failed to hear the word 'prepare' in the heat and alarm of battle. Many sailors leapt overboard, others cast life rafts adrift and launched two lifeboats. In response to orders some men clambered back aboard, but others drowned and yet more remained on the rafts.

Neosho's empty tanks provided her with sufficient buoyancy to withstand all the bomb hits and near misses that Takahashi's dive bombers had directed at her. Then occurred another error which had unfortunate consequences and was to cost many American lives. The navigator took a sight reading from the sun and plotted it as latitude 16 degrees 25′S, longitude 157 degrees 31′E. Captain Phillips later disclosed that the correct position was 16 degrees 09′S, 158 degrees 03′E. It was a costly error.

At the risk of losing chronological sequence, it is convenient here to pursue the story of *Neosho* and *Sims* to the bitter end.

Captain Phillips mentally bludgeoned the hundred or so crew remaining aboard *Neosho* into a sense of discipline, got the fires extinguished, plugged the leaks and tended the wounded. Distress signals were transmitted in clear giving the wrong position. Despite manful efforts by damage control parties the oiler refused to answer the rudder; she drifted like a reefed barquentine west-north-westerly at the mercy of the trade winds for four days.

Catalina PBY seaplanes were despatched from Noumea in extensive searches for the oiler but to no avail: they were, of course, searching the wrong area. Two days after the crippling, Admiral Leary sent the destroyer *Henley* to locate the oiler at all costs. Again, the wrong area was searched systematically and fruitlessly. On 11 May a Catalina chanced upon *Neosho* still drifting helplessly before the wind. *Henley* hastened to the rescue and arrived upon the scene late that afternoon and rescued 123 men. Buoyant, indefatigable, *Neosho* had to be sunk by *Henley*'s torpedoes. She was a stoutly built ship.

The rescuing destroyer then started to search for the members of the oiler's crew who had precipitately abandoned ship on 7 May, but she broke off the search at nightfall on the 12th to head for

Brisbane in order to seek better medical attention for the wounded survivors aboard.

By now Captain Phillips had plotted his ship's position at the time of her crippling and discovered the plotting error. Leary despatched the destroyer *Helm* to take up the search. On 17 May, ten days after the attack, she found a raft with four men, barely alive, and one destined to die, the sole survivors of sixty-eight men on four rafts who had prematurely abandoned *Neosho*. It was a tragic end to a rare episode of indiscipline.

The heavy loss of life from the oiler and her destroyer escort had compensations for other US forces: their deaths had not been totally in vain. For while Commander Takahashi's powerful force of dive bombers was engaged in the *Neosho* and *Sims* episode, Fletcher's Task Force 17 went unmolested.

The *Neosho* incident was a costly strike for Hara who was denied the priceless advantage of an early strike at Task Force 17. It is to Admiral Fletcher's Task Force that we must now turn our attention in order to resume chronological sequence.

Rear Admiral Jack Fletcher had been giving a great deal of thought to the developing situation in the early hours of the morning watch of 7 May. He was faced with two problems: he was required to intercept the invasion convoy, for which purpose his Task Force had been steaming north-west for thirty-six hours: he was also aware that to pursue a north-westerly course would draw him away from the covering force known to contain one carrier. A huge question mark hung over the precise position of the Japanese Carrier Striking Force. To launch a strike against the covering force and possibly having to take on the Striking Force as well was a daunting prospect. Paramount, he judged, was the need to intercept the Port Moresby invasion convoy. Fletcher accordingly made a bold – a gambler's – decision. He split his forces. At 0608, nearly forty minutes before sunrise, he ordered Crace:

> Proceed at daylight with your Group *Australia, Chicago, Hobart, Perkins* and *Walke* to destroy enemy ships reported passing through Jomard Passage and threatening Port Moresby. Conserve fuel. Fuel destroyers from cruisers. Retire to Townsville when necessary to fuel. Kinkaid detailing one destroyer [*Farragut*] to augment your force. Break radio silence at your discretion to inform COMSOUWESPACFORCE of your movements. For information my estimate of minimum number of units be-

tween Bougainville Island and Louisiade Archipelago is six cruisers, one aircraft carrier, one seaplane carrier, fifteen destroyers, seventeen transports and merchant ships, three submarines and some auxiliaries. Most units appear to be concentrated about Deboyne Island. One report indicates some units proceeding Jomard Passage. Our carriers will no doubt attack today and we are proceeding to destroy enemy units which may pass through Jomard.

By dividing his forces in this fashion Fletcher deprived his Task Force of the AA screen of two heavy cruisers, one light cruiser and three destroyers, a serious weakening of his fire power. Fletcher later excused this extraordinary decision on the basis that he expected a carrier battle during the day and in the event of his carriers being put out of action, Crace's group would still be available to thwart the invasion. This view seems to overlook the fact that if Takagi could dispose of Fletcher's carriers – made easier for him by the absence of Crace's ships – Crace's ships, without the benefit of air defence, would later fall easy prey to the Japanese bombers. As it turned out it was purely providential that Crace's ships survived the air attacks directed at them later in the day.

Conversely, if Fletcher should emerge victor of the expected carrier battle that day, then the Japanese invasion convoy would be at the mercy of the Allied Task Force. Many will think Fletcher had gambler's luck in the Coral Sea: others may think it was about time, too.

At 0650 Crace proceeded to comply with Fletcher's order at a speed of twenty-five knots to arrive off the Jomard Passage at 1400 to give him five hours of daylight. Without his own aircraft he would have to rely on shore- and carrier-based aircraft for intelligence.

Evidence that US Army aircraft were operating in the area came at 0940 and at 1008 and again at 1440 when Crace's group spotted a Curtis SOC, a Marauder and a Dauntless. During the day Crace received reports of *Neosho* being bombed and later a message was intercepted from a Task Force 17 aircraft to the effect 'We got the carrier good' a reference Crace took to mean a successful attack on the covering force carrier in the Misima vicinity, believed at the time to be *Ryukaku*. Crace reasoned that 'it lessened considerably the air threat to Task Group 17.3.'* But Crace's reasoning was premature. At 1423, by which time his force was in its planned

*Crace's *Report* 'Operations in the North Coral Sea – 5 to 11 May 1942.'

position SSW of the Jomard Passage, aircraft were sighted and a few minutes later *Chicago, Hobart* and some destroyers engaged eleven aircraft with a barrage of fierce and concentrated AA gunfire and drove them off.

The force was now in an anti-aircraft formation with *Hobart* and *Chicago* eight cables on the port and starboard quarters of the admiral and a destroyer six cables ahead of each cruiser. Crace's group had, in fact, been sighted by a float monoplane as early as 0810: the series of air attacks now about to be launched against his force were at the direct order of Rear Admiral Yamada, commander of the 25th Air Flotilla, at Rabaul.

The reconnaissance signal reported a force consisting of at least one battleship but no carriers. Yamada judged it represented a major threat to the invasion force and resolved to attack it.

The first attack, as we have seen, was repulsed with ease. The second developed at 1506 when twelve twin-engined Mitsubishi Nell bombers approached the force from ahead to deliver a torpedo attack. A fierce barrage met them and they suffered immediate casualties. Four were shot down before they got within range. All told eight torpedoes were loosed, some at too great a range, with the aircraft then continuing at low level to strafe the ships with gun and cannon fire. But four pilots pressed home their attacks more courageously, selecting *Chicago* as their target. The cruiser narrowly missed disaster when one of the torpedoes passed directly under her. She avoided the others by skilful ship handling. One pilot paid the price of courage and his aircraft crashed in flames.

Australia, too, came in for attention. Three torpedoes were directed at her. 'The day was calm and sunny and the sea very blue so that the tracks were very easily seen.'* Crace recorded:† 'Two tracks on starboard side missed by twenty feet or so and I could have sworn we couldn't escape them. Farncomb [the commanding officer] used the wheel well' and these two and a third torpedo were avoided. All aboard had hardly stopped congratulating themselves before another force of nineteen bombers‡ appeared from astern,

*Letter from Rear Admiral Crace to Vice Admiral Sir Guy Royle, 1st Naval Member, Australian Naval Board, 12 May 1942.

†Crace's *War Diary* entry 7 May 1942.

‡*Chicago* reported twenty-six bombers: Crace's *War Diary* states twenty-two and Crace's *Report* nineteen. Captain T. Mayazaki, under interrogation by the United

up sun, at a height of about 14,000 feet. Despite the barrage of AA fire the bombers maintained close formation. Crace estimated that about twenty 500 lb bombs and several smaller were dropped in a pattern with a spread of five hundred yards. Captain Farncomb ordered *Australia*'s wheel hard over to starboard just as the bombs were released and the pattern missed close to port. In his letter of 12 May to Royle, Crace wrote: '*Australia* was completely blotted out by splashes higher than the masthead . . . we were all soaked to the skin on the compass platform and even the masthead lookout was drenched!'

A few minutes later three more high level bombers appeared and dropped bombs which exploded harmlessly between *Perkins* and *Farragut*. It was subsequently discovered that these aircraft were US Army B 17s' from Townsville.

Crace complained about this incident to Leary who planned to improve the Army's ship recognition, but the Army Air Command denied any guilt and prohibited any further discussion.

Crace's Task Group 17.3 had survived the day's attacks* but by sunset no enemy surface vessel had been sighted. However, Crace had intercepted reports indicating twenty to thirty ships previously in the Misima Island area, were now moving to the north-west, and it appeared likely to him that the intended attack on Port Moresby had been postponed.

The Japanese were convinced that they had scored another major triumph in their attacks on Task Group 17.3. They claimed to have sunk an *Augusta* class cruiser and a *California* class battleship and to have torpedoed another battleship like HMS *Warspite*. In fact, Crace's group suffered only minor superficial damage from shrapnel and the heavy US cruiser suffered a few casualties.

Throughout the day Crace was devoid of knowledge about Fletcher's movements: 'I had received no information,' he recorded later, 'from the Commander Task Force 17, regarding his position, his intentions or what had been achieved during the day.' It was a

*Okumiya only learned of the outcome of this phase of the battle after the war. He was astonished when he 'learned that not a single Japanese torpedo or bomb had struck any of the ships!' *Zero!* page 110.

States Strategic Bombing Survey, stated: 'we sent twelve twin-engined attack planes (Betty's) accompanied by twenty fighters from Rabaul. These planes made a torpedo attack upon your cruiser force. We received incomplete reports because *only two torpedo planes returned*. We did not lose any fighters, however.' USSBS Nav No. 97.

regrettable failure in communications, but Fletcher had many things on his mind.

After detaching Crace's Task Group 17.3 at 0650 on the 7th, Rear Admiral Fletcher altered course to the northward with his force now comprising *Yorktown*, *Lexington*, five cruisers and nine destroyers. It soon encountered bad weather with a rough sea whipped by strong south-east trade winds. Before dawn Fletcher had already launched several reconnaissance aircraft into a totally overcast sky and he impatiently awaited pilots' reports.

He was still without precise knowledge of the whereabouts of the Japanese forces known to total three carriers and many screening cruisers and destroyers possibly somewhere to the north of his position. He knew that Japanese reconnaissance planes would be out searching for his forces and, in fact, almost simultaneous with the launching of Fletcher's aircraft others were flying off *Shoho*. The first of these many young pilots to sight the enemy would give his admiral a commanding advantage.

The first significant sighting was made by a *Yorktown* pilot at 0815 who reported 'two carriers and four heavy cruisers' in a position 10 degrees 03'S, 152 degrees 27'E, which on the plot showed the force to be 225 miles to the northward of Task Force 17.

Fletcher was elated. He naturally assumed that it was Takagi's Carrier Striking Force which had been sighted. He increased speed towards the enemy eager to attack and ordered a full scale strike.

Rear Admiral Fitch began launching aircraft from *Lexington* at 0925 at a point about 160 miles south-east of the reported position. The air group comprised twenty-five bombers, twelve torpedo bombers and ten fighters with Commander Ault, the Air Group Commander with three more bombers.

Yorktown's aircraft began flying off thirty minutes later and completed at about 1030. Her group consisted of twenty-five bombers, ten torpedo bombers and eight fighters. Her Air Group Commander remained aboard the carrier as fighter director officer. Forty-seven aircraft were kept in reserve. By 1030 a total of ninety-three US aircraft were airborne and heading north-west.

When the *Yorktown*'s scouting pilot returned aboard and he was interrogated it was discovered 'that an error had been made in using the contact pad and that the pilot had not sighted any carriers'. It was evident that a serious error had occurred. Fletcher was disconsolate. The corrected signal should have read: 'two heavy cruisers and four destroyers.' The force against which Fletcher had committed all his strength was not Takagi's Carrier Striking Force at all: it was not even Goto's *Shoho* force. It was Marushige's two old light cruisers screened by four gunboats!

Vice Admiral Takagi was in an identical predicament. He too had committed his strength to striking at *Neosho* and *Sims* believing – like his adversary – that he was attacking a carrier.

Fletcher was also unaware of other movements of great significance though perhaps no one could appreciate it at the time. Task Force 17 had been under surveillance since 0830 that day, the trailing aircraft reporting direct to Rabaul. Crace's Task Group 17.3 had also been sighted early in the day and the combination of these two forces frightened Vice Admiral Inouye, overall commander of the Port Moresby invasion forces. Anxious for their safety, he resolved to order the Port Moresby Invasion Force to turn away instead of passing through the Jomard Passage. This order was made at 0900 on the 7th, and in its own small way it was historical. It marked the nearest that any Japanese naval force ever got to Port Moresby, and for the first time since 7 December 1941 a Japanese invasion force had been repelled.

Fletcher, ignorant of this action, let alone its historical import, was beset by grave anxieties which suddenly lifted as his luck changed once more.

Lieutenant-Commander W. L. Hamilton, commanding *Lexington*'s flight VB 2 in his Douglas Dauntless bomber flew over Tagula Island at 1015 and had time to note the sea, the green of the island and the breakers combing over the coral reefs like whipped cream. When he reached the reported position there was nothing to be seen. But the visibility was extreme with a cloudless, blue sky. With his binoculars Hamilton spotted a number of thin white hairs on the sea at a distance of about forty miles to the east on the starboard beam. Closer inspection revealed that they were the wakes of Japanese ships. He radioed to the other flights in order to guide them to the ships and when he was close enough to identify the vessels he clearly saw the sun reflected from a light coloured flight deck. 'I see one flat top bastard,' he radioed jubilantly.

The Japanese force was, in fact, Rear Admiral Goto's and

the carrier was *Shoho*, though at the time she was identified as *Ryukaku* and contemporary reports carry that name. The sighting was fortuitous for the Americans. Fletcher had been let off the hook.

Lieutenant-Commander Robert Dixon, commanding VS 2 flight, led the attack with his Dauntless at about 1105. He began his dive from about 12,000 feet and concentrated on the carrier through his telescopic sight, watching the planes on the flight deck and another hoisting in the elevator while the carrier made a sharp turn into wind to try to get her planes airborne.

Dixon's was the first bomb to strike home, landing squarely on the flight deck and preventing the landing of any aircraft. Ensign P. F. Neely was next and his 500 lb bomb burst close alongside to port, flinging two aircraft into the sea. Third came Ensign Smith with a direct hit on the carrier's starboard battery, hurling another three aircraft overboard. The fourth dive bomber, piloted by Ensign J. A. Leppla was forced into errors by tenacious Zero fighters: he was badly damaged and crashed into the stern of a cruiser. More and more bombers dived upon the carrier scoring many hits.

Lieutenant-Commander Hamilton was the first to score a direct hit with a 1,000 lb bomb, twice the weight of the others. He pushed over into his dive at 12,000 feet and made a perfect approach. His bomb landed on the flight deck just abaft amidships. The entire after part of the flight deck was ablaze and pouring out black smoke. The rest of Hamilton's flight followed him.

The dive bombing attacks were coordinated with the Devastator torpedo attacks led by Lieutenant-Commander Brett in an almost text-book situation.

By 1125 *Yorktown*'s air group was on the scene and added to the devastation aboard *Shoho* which now lay stopped with internal explosions adding to her damage, burning and sinking. She had been struck by thirteen bombs and seven torpedoes. The order to abandon ship was given at 1131 and four minutes later she sank in a position 10 degrees 29′S, 152 degrees 55′E. The destroyer *Sazanami* managed to rescue 100 men from the sea: most of the carrier's aircraft went down with her.

While this battle raged north of the Louisiade Archipelago ships of Fletcher's Task Force 17 were tuned in to the aircraft frequency and relayed the almost unintelligible snatches of pilots' battle conversations and repartee when suddenly Lieutenant-Commander

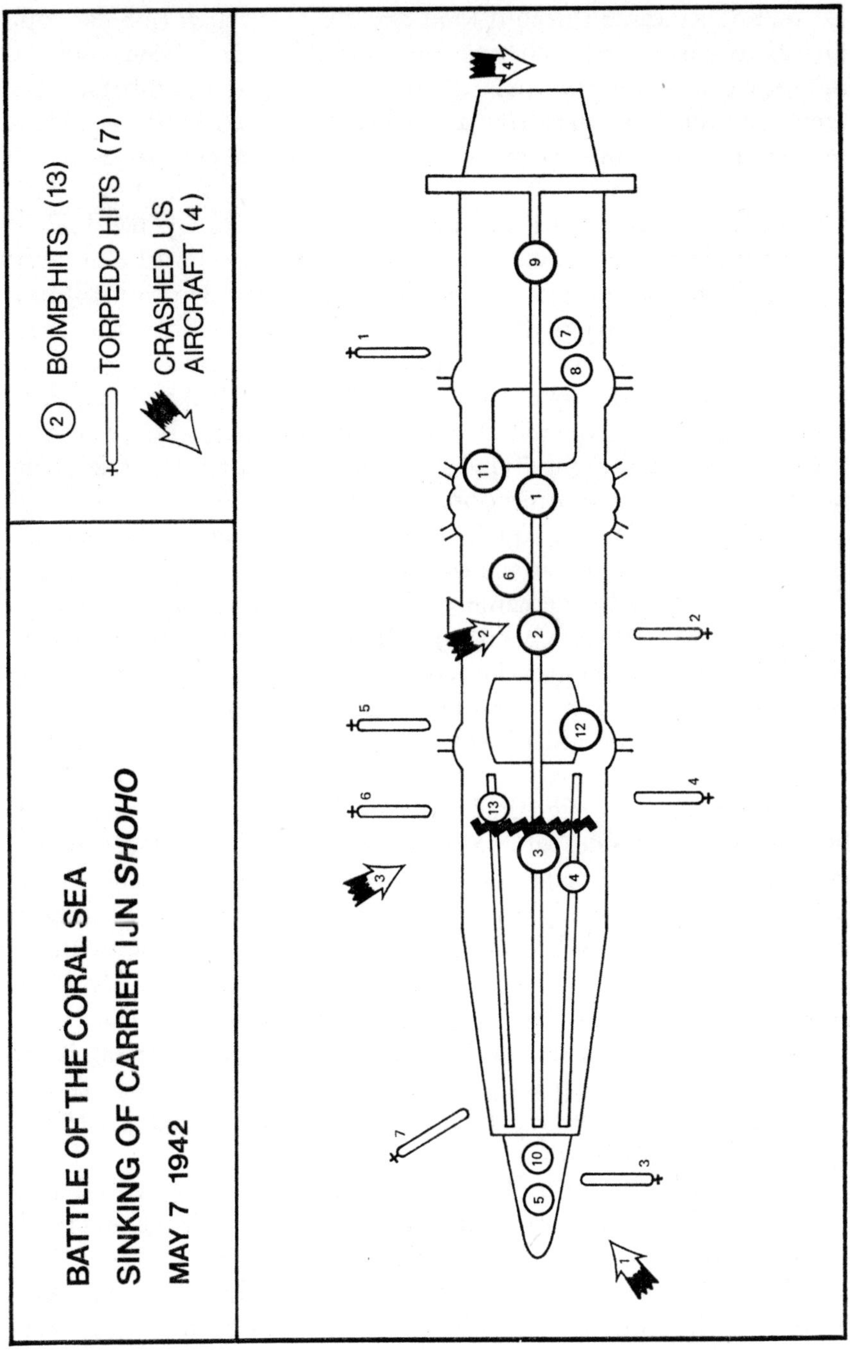
BATTLE OF THE CORAL SEA
SINKING OF CARRIER IJN SHOHO
MAY 7 1942
BOMB HITS (13)
TORPEDO HITS (7)
CRASHED US AIRCRAFT (4)

Dixon's voice came through loud and clear: 'Scratch one flat top. Dixon to carrier. Scratch one flat top.' *Shoho* had been sunk at minimal cost – for the loss of just four torpedo bombers. The remaining ninety of the strike aircraft had returned to their carriers by 1335 to boisterous receptions from their ships' companies.

Fletcher was encouraged to launch another strike against *Shoho*'s accompanying four heavy cruisers and the second strike aircraft were made ready by 1450, but prudence prevailed. He had still not located Takagi's carriers *Zuikaku* and *Shokaku* yet he knew that they must be aware of his own position: to launch a second strike against the cruisers would prevent him from attacking Takagi's carriers should they be discovered that afternoon. Fletcher held the aircraft in check awaiting the vital sighting report, a report which was not forthcoming that afternoon.

Vice Admiral Takagi, equally disconsolate as Fletcher because he had launched an all-out attack on an oiler and a destroyer, was now faced with precisely the same problems as his opposite number, whether or not to launch his aircraft on a second strike that day with the fatigue of his crews to consider, with the danger of having to recover the aircraft after nightfall, an evolution in which the Americans with the aid of radar were more competent than the Japanese. Takagi resolved to accept the risk. 'Can you launch a night air attack?' he signalled Hara in *Zuikaku*. Hara replied that he was prepared to despatch a restricted force of twenty-seven aircraft and he was ordered to do so.

Hara instructed his flight commanders to select pilots with night flying experience or with good night vision. The chosen crews knew the double danger they faced – the enemy and the dark. By 1630 all was ready and the aircraft began flying off. Commander Takahashi led a force of twelve Aichi Val dive bombers and fifteen Kate torpedo bombers. Their targets – *Yorktown* and *Lexington* – were a long flight away. It would be 1800 before they would reach the carriers, with nightfall only minutes away.

It was a dreadful flight. The weather worsened, thick cloud and rain squalls made navigation difficult and when the force emerged from the gloom over the target area, there were no ships to be seen. A brief search revealed nothing. The fatigued pilots were ordered to jettison their bombs and torpedoes to help conserve their fuel and to making landing-on possible. Takahashi organised the aircraft into three groups which then headed for their carriers. Their course took them almost over the top of Task Force 17 and they encountered the last of the day's combat patrols. Wildcat fighters fell upon the enemy planes shooting down eight Kates and one Val for the loss of two of their own aircraft.

At about 1900 some extraordinary incidents occurred. Three Japanese pilots searching for their carrier and almost at the limit of their endurance dimly spotted a carrier, switched on indicator lights and flashed recognition signals. The carrier was *Yorktown* and all her aircraft had been recovered sometime before: the night flyers were taken for what they were – Japanese. In an attempt at deception the flight deck landing lights were switched on and signals flashed to the aircraft: meaningless though they must have been to the pilots, they were accepted by the pilots as friendly and a sense of security must have been engendered: the approach for landing was made. As the first aircraft passed close by *Yorktown*, a gunner opened fire and the three Japanese, realising the enormity of their error, opened throttles and roared off into the night.

Minutes later another three aircraft made the identical mistake. The first aircraft was struck repeatedly by AA fire as she came in to land and crashed in flames: the other two swerved off and flew to safety.

Further tragedy was in store for the Japanese aircrews. Without radar and direction finding equipment they were dependent upon accuracy of navigation. Further, the pilots were denied the use of radio transmission for the radio operators of Task Force 17 were jamming their frequencies.

When in due course Rear Admiral Hara heard the drone of approaching aircraft he took it to be his returning bombers. He ordered searchlights to be exposed to aid the pilots. Seventeen aircraft pilots, now in desperate straits through lack of fuel, fatigued to the point of exhaustion and desperation, unable to see other aircraft in the darkness, jostled each other in a state of near panic to land aboard *Zuikaku*. Some ran out of fuel before they could make an approach. Others crashed on landing. Of the original twenty-seven planes flown off for the night strike, by 2100 only six had returned safely. It had been a calamitous incident.

The night's events were not yet over. As the Japanese pilots who had attempted to land on *Yorktown* flew away, they were tracked by radar in an effort to locate their carrier. *Lexington*'s radar – wrongly as it turned out – also followed the aircraft and placed the enemy carrier only thirty miles to the east, but when this information was passed to Fletcher he did not believe it. But he did consider detaching a force of cruisers and destroyers to make a search and strike against the enemy carrier force; however, good sense prevailed and the Task Force was kept intact. 'All things considered,' Fletcher wrote in his *Report*, 'the best plan seemed to be to keep our force concentrated and prepare for a battle with enemy carriers next morning.' It was a wise decision.

Away in Rabaul another night attack by surface vessels was contemplated. Overall commander of the Japanese forces, Vice Admiral Inouye, ordered an attack, thought better of it and cancelled it during this evening of dreadful turmoil and indecision for the Japanese. He ordered Goto's cruisers and Kajioka's destroyers to leave their transports, rendezvous off Rossel Island and attack the Allied forces, but he failed to specify whether Fletcher's or Crace's. Then, just before midnight, he cancelled the order, directed that the Port Moresby invasion be delayed two days, that two of Goto's cruisers should join Takagi's Striking Force and that Goto's remaining ships should close the invasion transports. Retreat is hardly too strong a word to use to describe the plans that occupied Inouye's thoughts that night.

Takagi, brooding unhappily at the humiliation of the abortive strike by *Zuikaku*'s aircraft, discussed with his staff aboard his flagship, *Myoko*, the possibility of mounting a night attack by his cruisers and destroyers. He and Hara were anxious to regain lost face or prestige, but the plan bore the hint of desperation: how such a strike could be seriously entertained when Takagi had only two heavy cruisers and six destroyers screening the two carriers is difficult to understand. The argument was settled for Takagi and Hara when they received a signal from Rear Admiral Abe who requested air cover at dawn the next day for his invasion transports now retiring north, away from the Jomard Passage. The signal was timely. It reminded Takagi where his duty lay. At about 2200 Takagi led *Zuikaku*, *Shokaku*, *Myoko*, *Haguro* and his six destroyers to the north.

At that time Task Force 17 was only ninety-five miles away to the west. At midnight Takagi was still heading north and Fletcher was drawing farther away to the south-westward. Each was ignorant of the other's intentions that night.

The clash of their giant carriers, it seemed, would never come. But come it did: Friday was the day of destiny.

CHAPTER 14

Clash of the Carriers

THE NAVAL SITUATION in the north Coral Sea at 0600 on 8 May was much less complicated than the day before even though the climax was fast approaching. We need only concern ourselves now with three forces, those of Rear Admiral Fletcher (Task Force 17), Vice Admiral Takagi (Carrier Striking Force) and Rear Admiral Crace (Task Group 17.3). The remaining Japanese units were now in retirement and took no part in the naval operations on this Friday morning.

The relative positions of these forces at 0600 were as follows:

1. Rear Admiral Crace's Task Group 17.3 was still patrolling 220 miles south-east of Port Moresby but was now running short of fuel in *Hobart* and the destroyers. Crace was still without information from Task Force 17.
2. Rear Admiral Fletcher's Task Force 17 was 350 miles away to the east-south-east in perfect yachting weather with a clear sky and a light south-easterly trade wind.
3. Vice Admiral Takagi's Carrier Striking Force was 180 miles north-north-east of Task Force 17 with the advantage of thick cloud cover.

Rear Admiral Crace continued patrolling off the Jomard Passage guarding the exit like a cat at a mousehole. He contained his anger at being denied information of his senior officer's movements. Throughout the whole of 8 and 9 May, during which period the destroyers were fuelled and *Hobart* with *Walke* were detached for Brisbane at sunset on the 9th, the only information gleaned by Task Group 17.3 was overheard snatches of conversation on the Fighter Direction wavelength and out-dated signals from COMSOUWESPAC which were less than helpful.

By 1900 on the 9th Crace reasoned that Fletcher would have retired from the battle zone and that the enemy had definitely given up its southward thrust through the Jomard Passage. At 0100 on 10 May in the absence of any direct orders or information Crace led

Task Group 17.3 from the complexities of operations in the waters of the Coral Sea to the relative peace and sanity of Australia. Crace's Chase in the Battle of the Coral Sea had played a vital part in blunting the spear of Japan's southward thrust.

Takagi's Carrier Striking Force reached the position Rear Admiral Hara specified – 100 miles south-east of Rossel Island – by 0600 having held its northerly course throughout the night. It was the point at which Hara wanted to fly off his reconnaissance planes from *Zuikaku* and *Shokaku*. Several aircraft took off into the gloom of the early morning overcast to cover an arc of search extending from 145 to 235 degrees with a radius of 200 miles. Takagi knew that Task Force 17 was within this sector.

Hara got his strike aircraft airborne with orders to proceed along the axis of the search arc. This was an unusual tactic at that time, but an effective one. In the event of a sighting report the strike squadrons would be diverted to the position of the contact. This tactic had the merit of saving valuable time, but the element of risk was high.

Commander Kakuichi Takahashi, the executioner of *Neosho* and *Sims*, led the strike aircraft which comprised thirty-three Val dive bombers, eighteen Kate torpedo bombers and eighteen Zero fighters.

The first sighting of Task Force 17 was made by Warrant Officer Kenzo Kanno piloting a Kate. His message was received aboard *Shokaku* at 0833 and it gave an accurate report of the composition of Task Force 17. *Shokaku* relayed it to Takahashi who altered course to intercept. Kanno was approaching the very end of his time on patrol: he remained in contact as long as possible before his fuel limit was reached and he headed back for his carrier. He was thirty minutes on the homeward leg when he encountered Takahashi's squadrons which he considered were not on an interception course. Then occurred one of those rare examples of selflessness when Kanno, for reasons which go unrecorded, directed Takahashi's squadrons on to a correct course and then led them directly to the US Task Force. In doing so Kanno passed his own point of no return. He headed back to his carrier but was never heard of again.

Yorktown and *Lexington* had not been idle during this period of intense Japanese activity. Almost identical activity was taking place aboard the US carriers. Because of the uncertainty of the enemy positions Fletcher ordered a 360 degree search at dawn. Eighteen Dauntlesses flew off at sunrise – about 0625 – into a beautiful sky which remained clear around Task Force 17 throughout the day.

At 0833 a radio operator aboard *Lexington* intercepted Warrant Officer Kanno's message to *Shokaku*. It was hurriedly translated. Fletcher then knew that his Task Force had been sighted and its composition, position, course and speed had been correctly signalled to the enemy. Takagi now possessed a measureless advantage. Fletcher, on the other hand, could do nothing but await his own search aircrafts' reports and the passing minutes must have seemed endless. But only five minutes after the intercepted Kanno message, Ensign J. G. Smith, a pilot from *Lexington*, signalled the position, composition, course and speed of Takagi's Carrier Striking Force.

The young pilot was conscientious. He had actually discovered Takagi's force at 0815 but had delayed transmission of his message until he was certain of his facts. In the event, some of the facts he quoted were inaccurate. He stated that the force comprised two carriers, four heavy cruisers and several destroyers and he gave a chart position of 120 miles bearing 006 degrees from a reference point Zed. *Lexington* plotted this as 11 degrees 51'S, 156 degrees 40'E, true bearing 028 degrees, 175 miles from Task Force 17. In fact the enemy force was another forty-five miles to the north. It might have been a disastrous mistake.

It was fortunate that Lieutenant-Commander Robert E. Dixon, who helped sink *Shoho*, was on hand to rectify the error. On receipt of the sighting report he altered course from his adjoining search sector to assist Smith in maintaining contact, but on arrival at the given position at 0900 neither the Japanese forces nor Smith were to be seen. Dixon initiated his own personal search and located the enemy at 0930, heading south at twenty-five knots. He signalled this vital information to Fletcher then maintained contact by adroit use of cloud cover until 1045 when fuel stocks forced him to break off contact and head for his carrier.

Meanwhile, Smith's inaccurate sighting report had activated all the resources of the two US fleet carriers. On the strength of the report Fletcher ordered the strike aircraft away from *Yorktown* and *Lexington*. At 0907 Fletcher issued the order for Commander Air,

Rear Admiral Aubrey Fitch to assume tactical command, a decision made remarkable by its timing rather than its content.

Yorktown flew off twenty-four Dauntless bombers, nine Devastator torpedo bombers and eight Wildcat fighters. They assembled in formation before setting off north-east at 0915.

By 0925 *Lexington*'s force had also assembled and set course for the enemy: it comprised twenty-two Dauntless dive bombers, twelve Devastators and nine Wildcat fighters. The total force airborne was eighty-four.

Flying on a reciprocal course and destined to pass within close range of the US forces* were Takahashi's squadrons, totalling sixty-nine aircraft. The first carrier-versus-carrier battle in naval history was about to erupt.

While the air groups of four fleet carriers sped through the thick cloud belt separating the enemy fleets, Rear Admiral Fletcher signalled a message to General MacArthur's headquarters at 1000 giving his own position, that of the enemy and requested the assistance of military aircraft in attacking the Japanese forces. This help did not materialise and the subsequent battle was fought entirely between carrier-borne aircraft.

Although it was the Japanese planes which were airborne first, the American planes from *Yorktown* adopted a higher cruising speed and it was they who made the first sighting of the enemy: the Dauntless dive bombers, led by Lieutenant-Commander William O. Burch, made the sighting soon after 1030. The aircraft sighted the ships through a break in the clouds which disclosed two groups of ships about eight to ten miles apart. The cloud effect was to have a significant bearing on this phase of the battle: it was to give virtual immunity to Rear Admiral Hara's *Zuikaku* while *Shokaku* was left to bear the brunt of the US attacks.

Lieutenant-Commander Burch signalled his sighting and adopted a holding operation, circling the enemy ships until the US air groups assembled. A few minutes before 1100 the *Yorktown* flyers began the first US carrier-borne aircraft attack upon a Japanese fleet carrier. It was a disappointing initiation.

Lieutenant-Commander Joe Taylor gave the signal to attack at 1057. *Shokaku* was the target. She was now the only carrier visible:

*Despite contemporary reports to the contrary, these opposing air squadrons did not sight each other.

Zuikaku, Hara's flagship, had disappeared from view into a rain squall. *Shokaku* now became subjected to a four minute ordeal as thirty-three aircraft from *Yorktown* unleashed bombs and torpedoes at her.

Taylor led flight VT 5 of nine Devastator torpedo bombers. They dived towards the warships to adopt the low level attitude for launching torpedoes. Flight VF 42 comprising 6 Wildcat fighters followed to afford protection from the Japanese Zeros. A few minutes later, in order to coordinate their attacks, the Dauntless dive bombers peeled off in succession from a height of 15,000 feet.

The defending Zero fighters swept down upon the Devastators which also faced a furious fusillade of fire. The Wildcats engaged the Zeros and a series of high speed individual dog-fights ensued.

Taylor's flight approached *Shokaku* bravely but a combination of factors made the attack abortive. All nine torpedoes were launched from a good, low level, but the range was too great; the torpedoes themselves were notoriously defective: they were too slow, poor at depth-keeping and were not even guaranteed to explode even if they hit their target. In this, the first concerted aerial torpedo strike against a fleet carrier, not one torpedo struck home. Nevertheless, the coordination of the dive bombing and torpedo attack reaped a reward and the Devastators could claim – justifiably – that their diversionary effect contributed to the success of the dive bombers.

These were led by Lieutenant-Commander Burch. He dived through the AA fire and released his bomb below 2000 feet. He was followed by twenty-three more Dauntlesses. Ensign J. H. Jorgenson saw Burch's 1000 lb bomb land flush on *Shokaku*'s flight deck on the starboard side for'ard of the island. The bombs rained down from the diving bombers, throwing up huge columns of stained sea water as some bombs exploded relatively harmlessly near by. Jorgenson's aircraft was hit by AA fire and he suffered a leg wound: he managed to retire from the scene of battle towards *Yorktown*, ditched at 1248 and was pulled aboard a destroyer at 1252.

Another heavy bomb struck *Shokaku* well aft and wrecked the aircraft engine repair compartment. This bomb hit and that of Burch's created extensive damage and put an end, albeit temporarily, to flying operations. Huge fires were started amidships and aft and thick, billowing, black and white smoke enveloped the after part of the carrier. The screening destroyers and cruisers maintained a continuous barrage of AA fire.

When Hara's *Zuikaku* emerged from the rain squall it was to see his second carrier burning furiously and evidently in dire straits.

After only four minutes of bombardment, the *Yorktown* flyers cleared the scene. They, and Hara as he emerged from the squall and the *Lexington* pilots who now began to appear, all must have thought *Shokaku* a doomed vessel. 'Burning furiously' was the phrase Hara used later when interrogated. But unknown to Hara and to *Shokaku* the damaged carrier was about to be assaulted by another strong force of strike aircraft. Little would anyone have believed that *Shokaku* would emerge from *Lexington*'s attacks almost unscathed.

Lexington's fortunes seemed ill-starred that day. Her aircraft were launched successfully from 0840 onwards and assembled aloft; by 0925 all groups headed for the enemy's reported position. The first set-back occurred when three Wildcats escorting the eighteen Dauntlesses lost contact with their charges in the clouds and failing to locate them, returned to *Lexington*.

The eighteen dive bombers of this flight, led by Lieutenant-Commander W. L. Hamilton, themselves encountered misfortune. After reaching the enemy's reported position and finding no trace of Japanese ships, a search was instigated, but without result. Another minor factor now contributed to their overall failure: all the Dauntlesses had not been fuelled to capacity, each was about thirty gallons short and when their fuel gauges registered half empty Hamilton had no option but to abandon the mission and head for *Lexington*.

The torpedo bombers fared better, though they too endured ordeals even before confronting the enemy. One Devastator developed engine trouble and returned to its carrier. The eleven remaining Devastators, under the command of Lieutenant-Commander Brett, also failed to locate the enemy, but Brett ordered a box search and much fuel was consumed flying through thick cloud and squally rain before the enemy was discovered at about 1130.

The *Lexington* strike force had now been reduced to six Wildcat fighters from flight VF 2, the eleven Devastators of Brett's flight and just four Dauntless dive bombers from flight VS 2, commanded by Commander Ault. This combined force had joined forces during the search for the enemy and was now at an altitude of about 6000 feet when the Japanese carrier and screening ships were sighted through a break in the clouds. It was *Shokaku* again, still burning after the *Yorktown* attacks. *Zuikaku* again remained hidden to view in the mist and low clouds.

The torpedo bombers started a spiralling dive, protected by the six Wildcats which were immediately pounced on by patrolling Zeros and three were promptly shot down.

Commander Ault's dive bombers coordinated their attacks with Brett's eleven torpedo bombers, but the weather made flying conditions difficult. Thick cloud from 2000–6000 feet obliterated much of the scene and made the approach of all aircraft hazardous.

Brett's torpedo bombers came down to about seventy-five feet and fanned out to present as many targets as possible to the defending gunners who soon put up a heavy barrage. Ensign N. A. Sterrie, one of Brett's pilots, recalled after the raid that *Shokaku* went into a tight turn as he approached to drop his 'fish' on her starboard quarter at a range of only 500 yards. At the time he was being subjected to heavy AA fire and attack from a Zero.

Commander Ault pressed home his attack through the barrage of fire. His aircraft was struck and crashed into the sea. Both Ault and his rear gunner were killed. Ault's was the only torpedo bomber to be lost in this raid despite the intensity of the AA fire. But *Lexington*'s Devastators scored no hits at all, although the pilots claimed a total of five hits during this attack. A Japanese officer later recalled derisively, when interrogated about US torpedoes, 'We could turn and run away from them.'*

While the torpedo attacks were being pressed home, Brett led his four dive bombers in a steep dive towards the blazing and smoking carrier. They encountered practically no AA fire, most of which was being directed at Ault's aircraft. The only hit was scored by Lieutenant John Powers whose attack fell little short of a kamikaze suicide mission. With the zest and enthusiasm of youth Powers had often spoken of his determination to bomb a carrier. This action was his moment of truth. He made the strike but it cost him his life. He was well aware that to dive below about 700 feet in the recovery from a dive, the blast of a 1000 lb bomb would be fatal to the aircraft. Eye witnesses estimate that he dived well below even 500 feet. This ensured a direct hit upon *Shokaku* but the

******Interrogation of Japanese Officials*, I 54.

explosion of his bomb destroyed his own aircraft which crashed into the sea killing both Powers and his observer. Powers was posthumously awarded the US Congressional Medal of Honour.

Powers's bomb hit was the sum total of *Lexington*'s success against *Shokaku* – just one bomb hit from an original strike force of forty-three aircraft. The *Lexington* air strike had lasted just four minutes. When the last of the US aircraft had left the scene, *Shokaku* was still burning from her three bomb hits. But these fires were soon got under control. She had suffered no torpedo hits and had not been holed below the waterline. But the internal damage she sustained was substantial. At 1300 – only one-and-a-half hours after the third bomb struck her – she set course for the homeland, almost capsizing on the way.* She had suffered 108 men killed and another forty wounded.

Zuikaku's part in this phase of the battle is shrouded in mystery. During both raids, as we have seen, she had been concealed by the weather. Rear Admiral Hara subsequently stated to interrogating US officers after the war that his flagship was not attacked on either occasion. Captain Y. Watanabe recorded during his interrogation that '*Zuikaku* received minor damages and many people were killed'. Captain Yamaoto recalled that *Zuikaku* was attacked by torpedo and dive bombers but was not hit. It is likely that both captains were faulty in their recollection: the evidence supports the view that *Zuikaku* did not come under attack and remained unscathed.

Vice Admiral Takagi aboard his *Myoko* flagship was happy enough to permit Hara to detach the damaged *Shokaku* to the homeland because, by the early afternoon, Takagi and Hara genuinely believed that their carriers' strike aircraft had sunk one large carrier which had been identified as the *Saratoga* and one medium carrier either *Enterprise* or *Yorktown*. The mood aboard *Zuikaku* was exuberant. The Imperial Japanese Navy, it was already being claimed, had scored yet another incredible victory.

Let us now pause to examine this claim and return to Task Force 17 riding out its part in the battle under the clear blue skies over the Coral Sea.

**Interrogation of Japanese Officials*, I 68. Captain Watanabe inspected *Shokaku* for the C-in-C Combined Fleet.

CHAPTER 15

Attack on the American Carriers

Yorktown AND *Lexington* were bathed in unwelcome sunshine which reflected brightly from the high acreage of their huge flight decks. The heat of the morning was tempered by the eighteen-knot south-easterly trade wind which also gently roughened the sea.

Rear Admiral Aubrey Fitch, now in tactical command of the US carriers, stood on the bridge of *Lexington* with the ship's commanding officer Captain 'Ted' Sherman: alongside was Commander Seligman, the executive officer; Commander Winthrop Terry, the communications officer; Commander Herbert Duckworth, Ship's Air Officer; Lieutenant-Commander Edward Eldridge, Ship's Air Staff; Commander R. Dudley, the navigator. They all knew that battle was imminent. Sherman predicted – on the strength of enemy carrier radio activity during the forenoon – that the enemy strike would occur at about 1100. In preparation for the attack Condition Red – readiness for battle – had already been ordered, watertight doors were closed and dogged, hatches bolted down, the ship divided into many hundred watertight compartments. The ship's company had gone to general quarters; air staff in *Lexington* were conducting fighter direction for the defence of both carriers, controlling combat air patrols and anti-submarine patrol aircraft. Fitch had ordered Task Force 17 to alter course to 028 degrees – towards the enemy – in order to reduce the distance for his returning aircraft. The mood of expectancy aboard both *Yorktown* and *Lexington* was at a high pitch. Hundreds of eyes squinted skywards for the first sight of enemy aircraft known to be winging towards Task Force 17.

But organisationally all was not well aboard *Lexington*. The Wildcat fighters launched for patrol earlier in the morning were now, on the brink of battle, dangerously low in fuel. And a reserve

IJN *Shoho* under dive bombing and torpedo bombing attack during an early phase in the Battle of the Coral Sea on 7th May 1942.

Lieutenant John Powers USN of USS *Lexington* was killed by his own bomb blast when diving low to ensure a hit on the Japanese fleet carrier *Shokaku*. 8th May 1942.

ieutenant-Commander Robert Dixon, leader of *Lexington*'s dive bomber flight which sank the carrier *Shoho* and helped damage *Shokaku* during the Coral Sea battle. Photograph taken in 1943.

One of the last gigantic explosions aboard Rear Admiral Fitch's flagship *Lexington* during the final phase an
retirement of the Battle of the Coral Sea. Her abandonment was so orderly that only one life was lost.

flight of twenty-three Dauntless dive bombers was still aboard *Lexington*. Fitch made the wise decision to launch these aircraft, fully fuelled, guns ammunitioned but minus their bombs: they could act as scouting aircraft and at a pinch they could double as fighters rather than be uselessly destroyed on the flight deck in the event of their carrier being attacked. When the anticipated Japanese raid developed these aircraft were aloft and served a useful purpose. Of the Wildcats, only eight were over the carriers when needed, and they had such depleted stocks of fuel that they were unable to intercept and fight the enemy. Captain Sherman later disagreed that the fighter defence organisation of the carriers was at fault but the evidence of this muddle and failure is unarguable.*

The first sign of the enemy was a four-engined Kawanishi Mavis patrol seaplane. It was intercepted by a patrolling US aircraft and it plunged seaward in flames leaving a dark spiral of smoke in the sky.

Moments later, at 1055, the radar operator aboard *Lexington* announced a contact of a large number of echoes bearing north-east, distant seventy miles. The carriers altered course to 125 degrees to head into wind, other ships conforming, increasing speed to twenty-five knots then later to thirty so that launching could begin of the nine Wildcat fighters which had only recently landed-on and re-fuelled. When these nine were airborne, they joined the eight *Yorktown* Wildcats already aloft but low in fuel. Thus a total of seventeen US fighters patrolled to defend the carriers of Task Force 17, some at low altitude to intercept any torpedo bombers, others at high altitude but low on fuel and still more striving to gain advantageous altitudes. The air defence of the carriers took on the appearance of a makeshift force of twenty-three ill-employed, slow Dauntlesses doubling as fighters, eight low-fuelled Wildcats and another nine hastily scrambled Wildcats which were unable to reach a sufficient height to make successful interception of the enemy bombers. The fighter air defence of *Yorktown* and *Lexington* was yet another mistake in what Morison was impelled to refer to as the Battle of Naval Errors.†

It is not known how many of the strike force of sixty-nine aircraft launched from *Zuikaku* and *Shokaku* actually participated in the

**Combat Command: The American Aircraft Carriers in The Pacific War*, Admiral Frederick C. Sherman, Dutton, 1950.

†S. E. Morison's *History*, Vol IV, page 34.

attack, but its composition of eighteen fighters, thirty-three Val dive bombers and eighteen Kate torpedo bombers was well balanced and formidable.

Even as the brown smoke trail of the destroyed Kawanishi Mavis float plane still dirtied the blue sky, reports began to reach *Lexington*'s air control centre of the approach of this force of Japanese aircraft. This was the moment to relish. It was as if all their months of training, of striking at land targets and shipping throughout the west Pacific were but the overture for these Japanese pilots and air crews; bombing, gunning, strafing, wreaking havoc: but nothing, nothing at all, in all that they had achieved during those weeks and months compared with the ultimate in their aspirations of attacking a US fleet carrier. And here, on 8 May, their flight decks glistening in the sun, lay not one but two fleet carriers. The Japanese flyers were keyed to a high pitch of efficiency: they wore their treasured 'belly-bands': they had the true Bushido spirit and in the manner of their Samurai ancestors they sought immortality in battle.

The first of the scouting pilot's reports was radioed to *Lexington*'s air control centre: 'Big force of enemy aircraft coming in from right ahead: they are sixty miles away.' This was quickly followed by a more accurate message from Lieutenant-Commander Paul Ramsey: 'Enemy planes 17,000 feet, four groups of nine each. Two groups dive bombers . . . and Zero fighters in escort. I'm at 14,000 feet twelve miles north-east of you and climbing hard. They are going awfully fast.' Then he added significantly, 'Doubt if I can catch them.' Another report gave warning of torpedo bombers 'spilling out of clouds eight miles out. They are 6,000 feet in a steep dive.'*

Lexington was about two miles ahead and fine on the starboard bow of *Yorktown* with the screening cruisers and destroyers concentrating in a protective circle about them: it was a sound, defensive deployment which stood the test of battle in the next twenty or so convulsive minutes. The defending cruisers were the first to open AA fire, though the opening shots of this phase of the battle were probably fired by some of the luckless Dauntless dive bombers which intercepted some of their opposite numbers and shot them down, before they themselves were set upon and destroyed by Zeros. With the US air defence in disarray even before battle was joined it soon developed into a duel between US anti-aircraft gunnery and the Japanese aircraft, handled with skill and courage

Queen of the Flat-Tops by Stanley Johnson, Dutton, 1942.

and utter determination. They approached down sun – dive bombers and torpedo bombers – taking full advantage of the fine weather conditions afforded them, in a series of separate groups.

The torpedo bombers made their approach in three small groups at levels between fifty and 200 feet. Two of these groups selected *Lexington* as their target and the third attacked *Yorktown.*

The *Lexington's* assailants made their approach from both sides, a standard practice employed to split the AA gunfire. An early success for the gunners was a direct hit upon one Kate torpedo bomber as it neared its launching position. The aircraft disappeared in a spectacular display as its fuel and torpedo exploded in a ball of fire and flame. But this did not deter the other pilots who forged through the barrage of fire, shell bursts, shrapnel and smoke which smudged the sky, to ranges below 1000 yards before releasing their torpedoes.

Captain Sherman conned the huge carrier as well he could in the standard manner of turning his ship's bows or stern towards the advancing torpedoes, but carriers are unhandy vessels, not adept at this manoeuvre, better executed by destroyers or light cruisers. Furthermore, the concerted attack by the two groups of aircraft was well executed, so designed that a turn to starboard would make the ship vulnerable to the port side attack and vice versa. At one stage the tell-tale trails of torpedoes were seen to run parallel, one down either side of the ship. No less than eleven* torpedoes were reported as either missing their target or being dodged by the lumbering carrier before the courage and skill of the Japanese pilots took their toll of the ship's massive bulk.

The first torpedo to strike home exploded on the port bow at 1120 and it was quickly followed by another also on the port side – amidships. The leader of these torpedo bombers, Lieutenant-Commander Shimazaki described his part in the battle two weeks later to Commander Okumiya in these words:†

*Most reports repeat this figure which simply will not stand up to analysis. At most only eighteen torpedo bombers could have taken part in the attacks on *both* carriers. If eleven torpedoes missed *Lexington,* and two struck home, making thirteen in all, to which must be added the torpedo destroyed when the Kate bomber was blown to pieces, this disposes of fourteen out of the possible eighteen. Thus only four more torpedoes are unaccounted for and as we shall see later, more than four torpedo bombers attacked *Yorktown.*

†Quoted in *Zero! The Story of the Japanese Navy Air Force 1937–1945* by M. Okumiya and J. Horikoshi with M. Caidin, Cassell, 1957, page 114. Shimazaki was a veteran group commander with combat experience in China since 1937.

Never in all my years in combat have I even imagined a battle like that! When we attacked the enemy carriers we ran into a virtual wall of anti-aircraft fire; the carriers and their supporting ships blackened the sky with exploding shells and tracers. It seemed impossible that we could survive our bombing and torpedo runs through such incredible defences. Our Zeros and enemy Wildcats spun, dived and climbed in the midst of our formations. Burning and shattered planes of both sides plunged from the skies. Amidst this fantastic 'rainfall' of anti-aircraft and spinning planes, I dived almost to the water's surface and sent my torpedo into the *Saratoga*-type carrier. I had to fly directly above the waves to escape the enemy shells and tracers. In fact, when I turned away from the carrier, I was so low that I almost struck the bow of the ship, for I was flying below the level of the flight deck. I could see the crewmen on the ship staring at my plane as it rushed by. I don't know that I could ever go through such horrible moments again.

The torpedo attack was barely three minutes old when another danger loomed for *Lexington*. The Val dive bombers, approaching Task Force 17 at a height of 17,000 feet, dived in two groups, one taking *Yorktown* as its target and the other *Lexington*. The Vals peeled out of formation unmolested by fighters and with most AA gunfire being directed at the torpedo bombers. They made almost unimpeded dives upon their targets. Those attacking *Lexington* pulled out at about 2400 feet before releasing their bombs and levelling out at about 1500 feet. Bombs should have struck Fitch's flagship with machine-like repetition. The wonder is that in the event the accuracy of their bombing was so lamentable. But hits were scored. The first one, probably a 250-kg bomb, exploded on the port side of the main deck well for'ard, wrecking a battery of three 5-inch guns, killing the guns' crews and exploding the ready use ammunition locker. Another bomb, thought to be a 500-kg one, exploded on the superstructure adjoining the funnel, killing many men on the catwalk. Another two bombs near-missed close alongside, exploding with tremendous concussive force producing a mining effect, rupturing and denting the hull plating.

A macabre wailing note was struck in the midst of the ear-shattering cacophony of the battle when a bomb passed between the island and the funnel – a thirty-foot gap – and exploded in the sea; on its way it activated the ship's siren.

During the few minutes that *Lexington* was being subjected to her torpedo and dive bombing attacks, *Yorktown* also suffered her share of attention. In her case the Japanese marksmanship was even more deplorable.

The first three torpedoes launched at her were released at about 1118 almost simultaneously. All three missed. Another four* are reported to have been launched at the carrier but not one struck home. Captain Buckmaster was able to manoeuvre his carrier more easily than could Captain Sherman handle his carrier for *Yorktown*'s turning circle was only 1840 yards compared with *Lexington*'s 3300 yards. This manoeuvrability, coupled with the fact that the torpedo attack was delivered from one side only, contributed to the Japanese pilots' failure.

Buckmaster's conning of his carrier also helped disconcert the dive bomber pilots. Of the many bombs directed at her only one scored a direct hit, although two more caused slight damage when they exploded close alongside. The one direct hit caused severe damage and many casualties. A large bomb struck the flight deck only a few yards inboard of the island and penetrated through to the fourth deck where it exploded with dreadful effect killing thirty-seven men, seriously wounding another thirty-three and causing serious fires. Damage control parties immediately buckled to, controlled the fires and cleared the debris. Flying operations were not impaired.

The battle lapsed for some minutes. Silence enveloped the scene which gave the appearance of confusion with the two fleet carriers disgorging billowing smoke from their wounds; their wakes and those of the screening cruisers and destroyers weaving odd patterns over the aquamarine sea; the sky a mass of pock-marked shell bursts with trails of smoke from burning aircraft.

Then almost as suddenly as the silence had descended, so it was shattered by the appearance of a lone Kate torpedo bomber which came in low towards *Yorktown* and launched its torpedo. Buckmaster altered course towards and the torpedo sped by more than fifty yards away. The Kate skimmed over the sea followed by gunshot and bullets as it flew off to the north. The time was 1140. Calm settled again. The battle was over. But there was still drama to follow.

*See earlier footnote about expenditure of torpedoes. It is almost indisputable that a total of eight torpedoes were directed at *Yorktown*, the last of which was launched singly later.

CHAPTER 16

Loss of the USS *Lexington*

IF AT MIDDAY on 8 May a line could have been drawn and a profit and loss account of the various engagements comprising the Battle of the Coral Sea have been rendered Admirals Fletcher and Fitch would have been well content with the findings. They would have been celebrating a victory of some appreciable significance, the main element of which was the thwarting and turning back of a Japanese invasion force, added to which was the sinking of a light carrier, one destroyer, three minesweepers, sundry smaller harbour craft and the serious damaging of a fleet carrier. For their part, the US admirals had lost one destroyer, one oiler and had had their two fleet carriers damaged, though not apparently very seriously: not, for example, sufficiently to impair flying operations. But the full story of this battle had not been told by midday. The final chapter was still to be written.

As the last, lone Japanese torpedo bomber scudded away from the US carriers at a minute or so after 1140 Task Force 17 was in some disarray. The unpredictable changes of course of the two carriers while under attack had created problems for the commanding officers of the screening cruisers and destroyers, all of whom, without instructions, instinctively grouped themselves about the two carrier flagships to afford a concentration of defensive AA gunfire.

It was not known to the US admirals that this last, lone torpedo bomber, was in fact the last of the raiders; in the ensuing respite everyone aboard the two US carriers looked about them to take stock of their predicament.

Yorktown was not in bad shape at all. Captain Buckmaster received damage control reports of the effect of the single bomb hit to his ship. The fire was soon confined to the damaged compartments and was got under control: the damage to the flight deck was confined to an area close to the island which did not impede the flying off and landing-on of aircraft. Within minutes *Yorktown* was back in business.

Captain Sherman had more to contend with in *Lexington*. The huge carrier was listing 7 degrees to port due to flooding through the torpedo damaged hull. Commander (E) H. Junkers had three of his sixteen boilers flooded and out of commission. Sick berth attendants collected the dead, dying and wounded, the shocked and burned, and mustered them in the hospital two decks below up for'ard. Two of the dead were Commander Walter Gilmore, the paymaster commander, and Commander Wadsworth Trojakowski, the dental surgeon. Both had been killed by the blast from one bomb which also ripped cabin bulkheads apart as if made of tinfoil.

Chaplain Markle, who had unsuccessfully tried to revive his best friend Gilmore, described some of the horror to Stanley Johnson.*

I arrived on the main deck – two below the flight deck – to find dust and smoke drifting through the passageways coming from farther aft. In the passageway amidships I found four men who were nearly naked . . . they were horribly burned. A Filipino cook . . . assisted me to get the men on to the cots in the passageway and take off the remainder of their clothes, give them a drink of water and a morphia injection. A hospital corpsman . . . treated their burns with tannic acid jelly and took over their care. Men kept coming in from the 5-inch gun galleries, sometimes alone, others with the help of comrades. We had about twelve men on the cots and during a brief lull I went to the gun galleries to see what had happened. There I saw several bodies: they seemed to have been frozen or charred into grotesque statues.

Commander H. R. 'Pop' Healy, senior damage control officer, commanded many hundred men who toiled fiercely; the three major fires were brought under control; the damaged flight deck was cleared and made ready for flying operations and efforts were being made to repair the damaged plane lifts; oil ballast was being pumped from port to starboard to off-set the ship's list; and sea floodwater was being pumped from the boiler-rooms. Within an hour of the departure of that lone torpedo bomber pilot *Lexington* began to look more like the dowager 'Lady Lex' she was affectionately called by her crew. Aircraft from the morning strike against *Zuikaku* and *Shokaku* were now arriving over the Task Force and recovery operations were in hand. To the pilots up above, *Lexington*

***Queen of the Flat-Tops* by Stanley Johnson.

looked shipshape except for the bomb damage on the 5-inch for'ard gun battery.

Commander Healy telephoned his damage control report to Captain Sherman with a touch of Sam Goldwynism. Had he lived he might have had cause to regret his light-heartedness, but he only had a few minutes left and for Commander Healy there was no time to regret. 'We've got the torpedo damage temporarily shored up, the fires are out and soon will have the ship back on an even keel. But I would suggest, sir, that if you have to take any more torpedoes, you take 'em on the starboard side.'*

Barely had he made this report than a thunderous blast jolted the great ship with a convulsive force far greater than the earlier bomb explosions. The blast seemed to emanate from the Central Control Station area where Commander Healy and many others were killed outright. A violent blast of what seemed like streams of flame and a myriad sparks seared through compartments and passageways, tore watertight doors open, blasted through bulkheads, ripped hatches and doors off their hinges and filled passageways for hundreds of feet with thick, choking smoke and fumes; decks above and below were opened up by the frightening explosion.

Twenty minutes after that first great shuddering explosion, before damage control parties had even begun to grapple with all the complex problems created by the explosion, another blast ripped through the ship, adding to the damage and death.

Pumps throughout the ship were rendered useless when the water mains were shattered and fire fighting became impossible. When longer hoses had been coupled together to link water source and pump and fire, the fires had engulfed the electrical mains, plunging the ship into darkness and cutting off all power to the pumps. No sooner was one problem solved than trouble flared elsewhere as minor explosions continued to rumble through the carrier. It began to look as if the damage control parties might not be able to cope.

But up top all looked deceptively fine. Recovery of the strike aircraft from the clear blue sky continued with customary efficiency while *Lexington* steamed on an even keel at twenty-five knots. The sea remained unruffled by the drama being enacted in what was now becoming a significant phase in the Battle of the Coral Sea – the fight to save Rear Admiral Fitch's flagship.

*Stanley Johnson in *Chicago Tribune* 17 June 1942.

It soon became evident to the engineers that the cause of the initial internal explosion was due to the ignition of highly volatile vapours escaping from damaged hundred octane fuel tanks, ruptured by one of the torpedo hits. The blast itself then contributed to the subsequent series of explosions because of the further rupturing of fuel tanks, increasing seepage of their contents, the collecting of gases into inaccessible compartments, all helping to stoke the fires. Each blast worsened the situation; piece by piece the ship was being successively damaged, link by link the chain of communication was beginning to fail. The column of thick black smoke began to take on the appearance of a pall of death.

On the bridge the breakdown in communications posed grave problems. When the telephone switchboard was destroyed in the first great internal blast, a team of messengers had to communicate with compartments where speaking tubes were not connected. When the electric mains were consumed by fires, steering was put out of control and the change was made to auxiliary steering. Remote though it was, it proved satisfactory until eventually it needed scores of men in a line extending aft, four decks below, a distance of probably 450 feet, to transmit the helm orders to the quarter-master. *Lexington* remained with the Task Force, but her course was now erratic: 'Lady Lex' seemed a drunken lady.

By 1345 flight operations aboard her had to be cancelled as smoke billowed across the flight deck in impenetrable thickness. Emergency power and light enabled the crew to cope as best they could with the increasing gravity of the situation but by 1430 the conditions between decks had deteriorated to such an extent that Captain Sherman approved the decision to withdraw damage control parties from compartments where fires could no longer be fought. The parties were withdrawn and the compartments sealed where possible by watertight doors in the hopes of containing the fires.

The hospital became uninhabitable and patients had already been shifted as fumes, smoke and fires drove them from one place to another, ending up on the for'ard flight deck, with aircraft dollies doubling as patients' trollies.

At 1445 events took another stunning turn for the worse when once more the giant carrier shook from stem to stern as a major internal explosion caused serious damage, including wrecking the ventilation system feeding the engine-room and boiler-rooms.

Temperatures rose alarmingly as air stopped circulating and working conditions became unbearable. A start was made in evacuating the engine-room. The great carrier's speed was reduced.

At 1510 Fletcher resumed tactical command and minutes later Captain Sherman signalled the admiral requesting assistance for cruisers and destroyers in fighting fires. A little later *Yorktown* was asked to recover the remainder of *Lexington*'s aircraft, a total of nineteen being subsequently recovered safely. At the same time Sherman asked for rescue vessels to stand by. The writing was on the wall.

The destroyer *Morris* was ordered alongside and her hoses were manned but her efforts were unavailing for the fires raging aboard the huge carrier were now incapable of being extinguished: their hold was complete: the smoke was engulfing the ship for the whole of her length and the heat being generated throughout the ship threatened to explode in one giant eruption like the majestic *Hood* in the Atlantic or the battleship *Barham* in the Mediterranean. Sherman later reported,* 'By this time the fire was beyond control. Additional explosions were occurring; it was reported that the warheads on the hangar deck had been at a temperature of 140 degrees (60 degrees C); ready bomb storage was in the vicinity of the fire and I considered there was danger of the ship blowing up at any minute.'

The Senior Medical Officer, Commander A. J. White, was a casualty himself having received a broken ankle and shoulder injuries during one of the early internal explosions, but he continued to supervise his department and the transfer of 150 wounded into the boats.

Sherman asked the navigator, Commander Dudley, for the distance to the nearest land and to shape a course for the nearest point of Australia. He also gave orders for the wounded to be got into the ship's whalers. Sherman did not underestimate the danger. Twenty 1000-lb bombs, many smaller ones and forty-eight torpedo warheads were still aboard the carrier in addition to the normal magazines of shells and stores of aviation fuel. Pilots, aircrew and other flying personnel were ordered down life lines from the carrier to the destroyer alongside.

At 1600 Captain Sherman gave the order to evacuate the engine-room of all remaining personnel. The order to draw the fires and

***Lexington Action Report.*

abandon the engine-room was passed to Lieutenant-Commander M. Coffin, in charge of the watch. He turned off the oil feed lines and opened the cocks to allow steam to escape from the boilers. Up top the din was terrific as steam from sixteen boilers screamed through the funnel adding to the general scene of confusion and unreality.

Lexington lost way, and gradually came to a stop. It was 1630. Sherman ordered preparations for abandoning ship. Commander Seligman ordered all men up from below. Life lines were cast over the side to stream in the sea. Rafts were cut adrift.

At 1507 Rear Admiral Fitch called out to Captain Sherman: 'Well, Ted, let's get the men off.' The Captain agreed and the order to abandon ship was given. It was an efficient and orderly abandonment.

Rear Admiral Kinkaid in the cruiser *Minneapolis* was given charge of the rescue operations. He ordered the destroyers *Morris, Anderson* and *Hammann* to recover the men from the sea. Aboard the carrier men lined up to await their turn to descend the life lines. As they waited gallons of ice cream from the ship's service store was distributed in plentiful helpings. Shells from the ready use lockers were being jettisoned overboard. Other items of armoury such as gun barrels were being lowered to a destroyer. Sherman's spaniel, Wags, was collected by Ensign Martin and safely lowered to a destroyer.

Rarely can there have been such an orderly abandonment with minimal loss of life and absence of fear or panic. This was specially creditable considering that more than six hundred of the *Lexington*'s ship's company were making their first sea cruise: the marines aboard set a particularly fine example of discipline.

While this abandonment proceeded, Admiral Fitch transferred his flag to *Minneapolis*. Last to leave the ship was Captain Sherman. Before he left her he made a final inspection of all accessible parts of the ship with his executive officer, Commander Seligman, to satisfy himself that no wounded remained aboard. Even as they made their rounds an explosion nearly killed them, but they emerged from the smoke and flame, dirtied but unhurt.

The last three men to leave *Lexington*, a corporal of marines, Seligman and Sherman, descended on a life line hand over hand. While still fifty feet above the water another violent explosion blasted the Executive Officer and the Commanding Officer from the rope. They landed in the warm sea and were hauled ignominiously aboard a whaler none the worse for their experience.

The explosion that blew them into the sea was the final act of violence in the drama of the sinking carrier. A blinding flash lept with awful suddenness through the ruptured flight deck amidships and through the billowing smoke as the hoard of bombs and torpedo warheads exploded. Chunks of flight deck, hull plating, débris of unknown origin, all soared through the air and showered into the sea.

Dusk descended but the giant was reluctant to go. Internal explosions of a minor character were occurring almost every few minutes.

Rear Admiral Fletcher gave the order for the destroyer *Phelps* to sink the battered and abandoned carrier with torpedoes. Four were fired from a range of about 1500 yards. 'Lady Lex' finally settled with rumblings of regret and sank in 2400 fathoms of the Coral Sea. Men who had served aboard her for years openly wept at the sight. Her final position was 15 degrees 12′ S, 155 degrees 27′ E. She had taken with her 216 men killed in combat. But more significantly, 2735 men were rescued.

CHAPTER 17

Retirement from the Coral Sea

THE END OF *Lexington* was not the end of this story. Indeed, we must go back to the early afternoon of 8 May to follow the Japanese commanders' reactions to the morning's strikes. It will be recalled that the damaged *Shokaku* had been released at 1300. Vice Admiral Takagi had no reservations in detaching this carrier. He and Hara genuinely believed that their aircraft had sunk the two American fleet carriers and for this reason the subsequent Japanese actions appear inconsistent and their strange decisions difficult to understand.

One could well ask what now prevented Admiral Inouye from ordering the Port Moresby Invasion Force to turn about and resume course for its original objective. What opposition was there left? Inouye was overjoyed that the two American carriers had been sunk and the rest of the Task Force dispersed in disarray. He was jubilant at the successes against Crace's Task Group 17.3 and believed it to have been badly mauled. The Jomard Passage to his knowledge must therefore have been clear and the air devoid of Fletcher's aircraft. A golden opportunity appeared to be within Inouye's grasp. Resolution, courage and a firm decision, none of these qualities was lacking in the Japanese naval commanders during these early months of the Pacific war: yet now Inouye displayed caution. In the eyes of Admiral Yamamoto he did worse. He pursued a course of retreat. Earlier in the day he had taken the decision to formally postpone the invasion and now at 1800 he ordered Takagi to retire with *Zuikaku* to Truk. All Japanese forces were now in retirement.

Inouye's reasoning was faulty. He feared, with little justification, for the safety of his invasion transports at the hands of the bomber squadrons of the US Army Air Force and the RAAF, arguing that since *Shoho* was sunk, *Shokaku* detached and *Zuikaku* retiring to Truk for overhaul of her battle-scarred aircraft, the transports would be denied air cover.

Admiral Yamamoto, C-in-C of the Combined Fleet, did not share Inouye's conclusions and deplored his caution. His order to Inouye at midnight on 8 May weighed in the balance the state of Takagi's ships, augmented by Goto's and the probable over-estimation of the Japanese pilots' claims; Yamamoto made this quite clear and implied criticism and reprimand in his signal: 'Annihilate' the enemy forces, he instructed Inouye.

But by midnight all hope of re-establishing contact had gone, and Inouye must have known this. Nevertheless, he ordered poor Takagi to take *Zuikaku*, to turn south-east and intercept the remainder of Fletcher's fleeing ships. At 0200 on 9 May Takagi turned about to comply. It was, of course, a forlorn mission.

Goto, who must have been distraught at the series of conflicting orders he had been expected to execute these past few days, was instructed to join Takagi and this he proceeded to do. The two forces joined at noon on the 10th but only an hour later Takagi gave up the hopeless pursuit and headed northward. The next day Takagi received firm orders to quit the area.

One final Japanese movement needs chronicling. On 10 May, the day Takagi finally gave up the pursuit, Rear Admiral Shima with his invasion force destined for Ocean and Nauru islands departed from Rabaul and the next day US submarine *S 42* torpedoed his flagship, the minelayer *Okinoshima*. On the 15th this invasion, too, was called off when Admiral Halsey's Task Force comprising the carriers *Enterprise* and *Hornet* with screening cruisers and destroyers were sighted steaming fast for the Coral Sea. But by then the Battle of the Coral Sea was over.

Some days earlier – on 8 May after *Lexington* had sunk and the rescue operations had been completed – Rear Admiral Fletcher ordered Task Force 17 to withdraw, a decision approved by Admiral Nimitz, who at one stage entertained ordering Fletcher to strike again at Takagi, but was restrained by his staff who considered it unreasonable to hazard *Yorktown* with the impending Battle of Midway known to be only a short time away.

Accordingly, Task Force 17 headed southward and at dawn on 9 May course was altered to take the force out of the Coral Sea. By

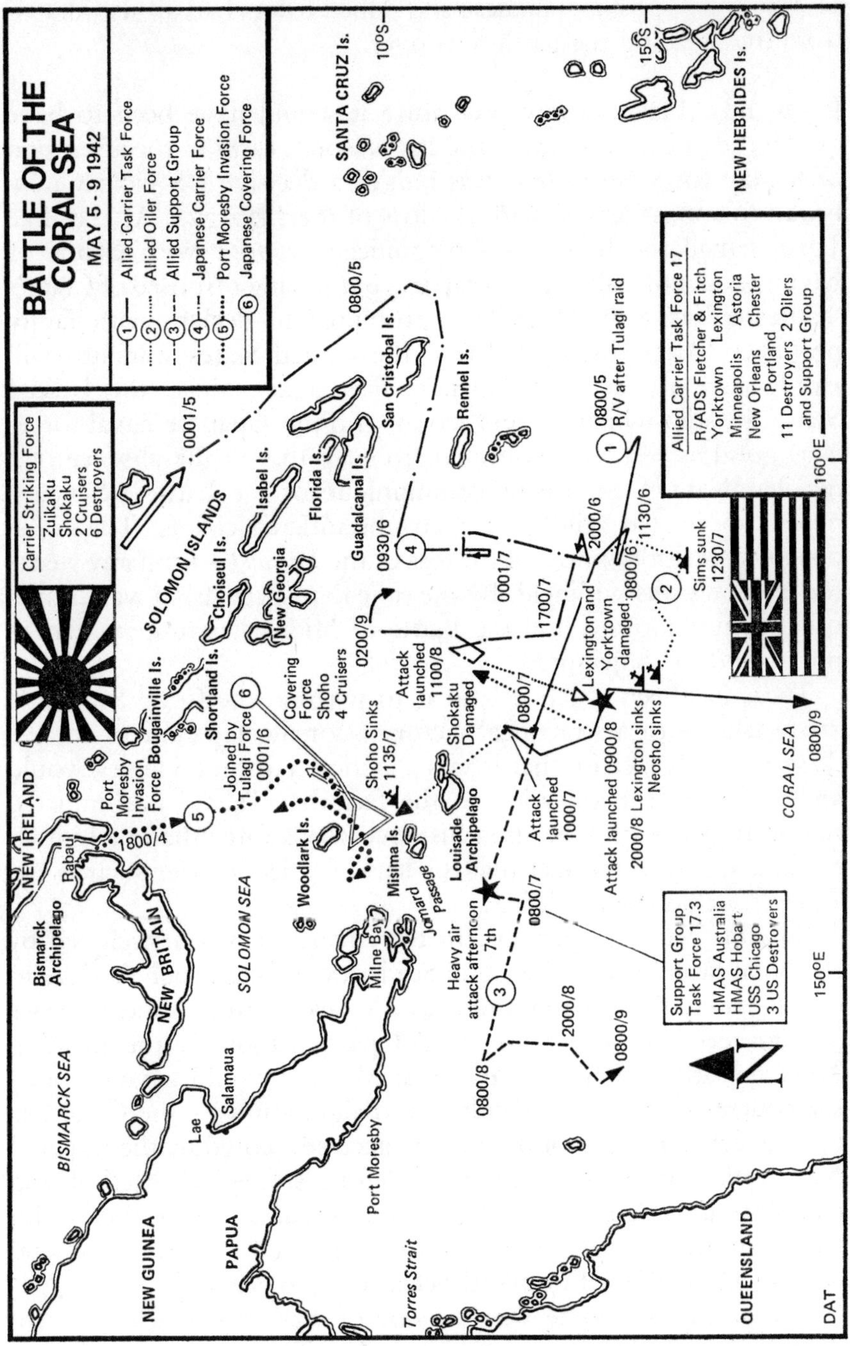

BATTLE OF THE CORAL SEA
MAY 5 - 9 1942
1 Allied Carrier Task Force
2 Allied Oiler Force
3 Allied Support Group
4 Japanese Carrier Force
5 Port Moresby Invasion Force
6 Japanese Covering Force
Carrier Striking Force
Zuikaku
Shokaku
2 Cruisers
6 Destroyers
Allied Carrier Task Force 17
R/ADS Fletcher & Fitch
Yorktown Lexington
Minneapolis Astoria
New Orleans Chester
Portland
11 Destroyers 2 Oilers
and Support Group
Support Group
Task Force 17.3
HMAS Australia
HMAS Hobart
USS Chicago
3 US Destroyers
BISMARCK SEA
SOLOMON SEA
CORAL SEA
NEW GUINEA
PAPUA
QUEENSLAND
NEW BRITAIN
NEW IRELAND
Bismarck Archipelago
SOLOMON ISLANDS
SANTA CRUZ Is.
NEW HEBRIDES Is.
Rabaul
Lae
Salamaua
Port Moresby
Torres Strait
Milne Bay
Jomard Passage
Misima Is.
Louisade Archipelago
Woodlark Is.
Bougainville Is.
Shortland Is.
Choiseul Is.
New Georgia
Isabel Is.
Florida Is.
Guadalcanal Is.
San Cristobal Is.
Rennel Is.
Port Moresby Invasion Force
1800/4
Joined by Tulagi Force 0001/6
Covering Force Shoho 4 Cruisers
Shoho Sinks 1135/7
Shokaku Damaged
Attack launched 1100/8
0200/9
0930/6
0001/5
0800/5
0001/7
1700/7
0800/7
Attack launched 1000/7
Attack launched 0900/8
2000/8 Lexington sinks
Neosho sinks
Lexington and Yorktown damaged
0800/6
2000/6
1130/6
0800/5 R/V after Tulagi raid
Sims sunk 1230/7
Heavy air attack afternoon 7th
0800/8
2000/8
0800/9
10°S
15°S
150°E
160°E
DAT

11 May the opposing Japanese and Allied forces had all withdrawn from the area and the battle was over.

It can now be seen how premature it would have been to have drawn the line on the profit and loss account early in the afternoon of 8 May for what at first was judged a decisive US victory now began to appear less so with the loss of the *Lexington*. At the time Japan hailed the battle as a magnificent victory with claims of having sunk not only the two carriers but having disposed of Crace's 'battleship' as well. Hitler was prompted to declare with faulty prophecy 'After this new defeat, the United States warships will hardly dare to face the Japanese fleet again, since any United States warship which accepts action with the Japanese naval forces is as good as lost.' It is only fair to state that in the absence of a detailed Navy Department communiqué of the battle US newspapers speculated wildly with unsubstantiated claims. The newspapers were not to know of the loss of the *Lexington* for many weeks for the news was withheld. By the time that speculation was ending other events loomed and the Battle of Midway's stunning results put an end to conjecture.

There has been much debate as to whether the Coral Sea battle was a tactical or a strategical victory – for the Japanese or for the Americans. The claim that it was a tactical Japanese victory would appear to have justification in the fact that Takagi had inflicted relatively heavier losses upon his adversary's force than he himself sustained, and in the fact that the loss of a fleet carrier such as the *Lexington* is in itself a defeat.

But this claim is specious. In the balance, it is out-weighed by two vital facts: firstly, the Coral Sea battle inflicted such damage to one Japanese fleet carrier and heavy losses in aircraft and aircrews to another that both were denied participation in the pending Midway battle. Their appearance at Midway would have changed the course of events. Secondly – and significantly – the Coral Sea battle marked the end of the run of successes scored by the Imperial Navy's fleet carriers. Thereafter, defeat, strategical, tactical and complete attended the Japanese navy's carrier operations with barely another victory of any consequence and brought to an end its enviable record of no naval defeat for 350 years.

The battle's outcome was not one of war's most delusive products – a half victory and a half defeat. The important, the real victory – hidden to all protagonists at the time – was not to be counted in the number of ships sunk nor in the number of aircraft shot from the skies over the placid Coral Sea: it was the denial of passage to the Port Moresby invasion forces. Therein lay the victory. And it was a crucial one.

APPENDIX A

Sources and Bibliography

Since the implementation of the thirty-year rule making public the records and documents of World War II, the researcher's greatest problem is one of sheer volume of paperwork. Many wartime enterprises were two- and three-service operations involving the naval researcher additionally in air force and army records. Furthermore, many of these operations involved one or more Allied service, entailing even more research. Finally, in order to approach nearer the balanced view to which every historian aspires, the enemy sources must also be delved into. It makes research a daunting prospect.

ALBION, Robert G, and CONNERY, Robert H. *Forrestal And The Navy*, 1962.

BARKER, A. J. *Midway*. The Pan/Ballantine History of World War II, 1970.

BATESON, Charles. *The War With Japan: A Concise History,* Barrie & Rockliff, 1968.

BERGAMINI, David. *Japan's Imperial Conspiracy*, Heinemann, 1971.

BLIVEN, Bruce. *From Pearl Harbor to Okinawa*, Random House.

BRERETON, Lewis H. *The Brereton Diaries 3 October 1941–8 May 1945*, William Morrow, 1946.

BRICE, Martin H. *The Royal Navy and the Sino-Japanese Incident 1937–1941*, Ian Allan, 1973.

BROWN, David. *Carrier Operations in World War II*, Vol I, The Royal Navy, and Vol II The Pacific Navies, Ian Allan, 1974.

BROWNE, Courtney. *Tojo: The Last Banzai*, Angus and Robertson, 1967.

BULLOCK, Cecil. *Etajima: The Dartmouth of Japan*, Sampson Low, Marston & Co, 1942.

BUTOW, Robert J. C. *Tojo and the Coming of the War*, Princeton University Press, 1961.

BYWATER, Hector C. *Seapower in the Pacific*, Houghton Mifflin, 1921.

CAIDIN, Martin, with OKUMIYA, M. and HORIKOSHI, J. *Zero! The Story of the Japanese Navy Air Force*, Cassell, 1957.

CAIDIN, Martin. *Zero Fighter*, Purnell's History of the Second World War, Weapons Book No. 9, 1969.

CALVOCORESSI, Peter and WINT, Guy. *Total War: Causes and Courses of the Second World War*, Allen Lane, 1972.

CANT, Gilbert, *American Navy in World War II*, Hutchinson.

CHURCHILL, Winston S. *The Second World War*, Vol IV, 'The Hinge of Fate', Cassell, 1951.

COLLIER, Basil. *The War in the Far East 1941–1945: A Military History*, William Morrow, 1969.

COLLINS, Vice Admiral Sir John. *As Luck Would Have It*, Angus & Robertson, 1965.

CONNELL, John. *Wavell: Scholar and Soldier*, Collins, 1964.

CONNELL, John. *Wavell: Supreme Commander*, Collins, 1969.

CRESWELL, Captain John. *Sea Warfare 1939–1945*, Longmans, Green & Co, 1950.

D'ALBAS, Andrieu. *Death of a Navy: Japanese Naval Action in World War II*, Robert Hale, 1957.

DULL, Paul S. See *International Military Tribunal for the Far East.*

EDMONDS, Walter D. *They Fought With What They Had*, Atlantic-Little Brown, 1951.

FARAGO, Ladislas. *The Broken Seal: The Story of Operation Magic and the Pearl Harbor Disaster*, Random House, 1967.

FELDT, E. A. *The Coast Watchers*, 1946.

FORRESTAL, Vice Admiral E. P. *Admiral Raymond A. Spruance USN: A Study in Command*, USGPO, Washington, 1966.

FRANK, P. and HARRINGTON, Joseph D. *Rendezvous at Midway*, John Day, 1967.

FUCHIDA, Mitsuo and OKUMIYA, M. *Midway: The Battle That Doomed Japan*, US Naval Institute, 1955.

FURER, Rear Admiral J. A. *Administration of the Navy Department in World War II*, Washington, 1969.

GILL, G. Hermon. *Australia in the War of 1939–1945*, Series 2 (Navy), Vol I, *Royal Australian Navy 1939–1942*, Australian War Memorial, 1957, and Vol II, *Royal Australian Navy 1942–1945*, Australian War Memorial, 1968.

GLINES, Carroll V. *Doolittle's Tokyo Raiders*, D. Van Nostrand, 1964.

GRENFELL, Captain Russell. *Main Fleet to Singapore*, Faber & Faber, 1951.

GREW, Joseph C. *Ten Years in Japan*, Hammond, Hammond & Co, 1944.

GREW, Joseph C. *Report From Tokio: A Message for the American People*, Simon & Schuster, 1944.

GRIFFITHS, Brigadier S. *The Battle for Guadalcanal*, 1963.

GWYER, J. M. A. and BUTLER, J. R. M. *Grand Strategy*, Vol III Part II June 1941–August 1942, *History of the Second World War: United Kingdom Military Series*, HMSO, 1964.

HALSEY, Fleet Admiral William F. and BRYAN, J. III. *Admiral Halsey's Story*, McGraw-Hill, 1947.

HARA, Captain Tameichi, SAITO, Fred and PINEAU, Roger. *Japanese Destroyer Captain*, Ballantine Books, 1961.

HASHIMOTO, Mochitsura. *Sunk: The Story of the Japanese Submarine Fleet 1942–1945*, Cassell, 1954.

HASLUCK, Paul. *Australia in the War of 1939–1945*, Vol I, *The Government and The People*, Australian War Memorial.

HATTORI, Colonel Takushiro. *Dai-Toa Senso Zenshi* 4 vols, Tokyo, 1953. English translation ('Complete History of the Greater South East Asia War') in the Office of the Chief of Military History, Washington.

Hitler's Table Talk 1941–1944: His Private Conversations, introduced by H. R. Trevor Roper, Weidenfeld & Nicolson, 1953.

HOPKINS, Captain H. *Nice to Have You Aboard*, Allen & Unwin, 1964.

HOYT, Edwin P. *How They Won The War in The Pacific: Nimitz And His Admirals*, Weybright & Talley, 1970.

HUMBLE, Richard. *Japanese High Seas Fleet*, Pan/Ballantine Illustrated History of World War II, 1974.

IKE, Nobutaka (Ed. and Trans.) *Japan's Decision For War: Records of the 1941 Policy Conference*, Stanford University Press, 1967.

ISHIMARU, Lieutenant-Commander Tota. *Japan Must Fight Britain*, The Paternoster Library, 1937.

ITO, Masanori with PINEAU, Roger. *The End of the Imperial Japanese Navy*, Weidenfeld & Nicolson, 1962.

Jane's All The World's Fighting Ships, 1941.

JOHNSON, Stanley. *Queen of the Flat Tops: The Story of The USS* Lexington *and the Coral Sea Battle*, Dutton, 1942.

JONES, K. *Destroyer Squadron 23*, Chilton & Co, 1959.

KARIG, Captain Walter *et al*, *Battle Report: Pearl Harbor To Coral Sea*, Vol I of Battle Report Series, Rinehart & Co, 1944.

KATO, Masuo. *The Lost War*, Knopf, New York.

KENNEDY, Paul. *Pacific Onslaught 7 December 1941–7 February 1943*, Pan/Ballantine Illustrated History of World War II, 1972.

KILLEN, John. *A History of Marine Aviation 1911–1968*, Frederick Muller, 1969.

KING, Fleet Admiral Ernest J. *The United States Navy at War: Official Reports to the Secretary of the Navy*. (The bound volume of Cominch's annual reports to the Secretary of the Navy.) USGPO, Washington.

KING, Fleet Admiral Ernest J. and WHITEHILL, W. M. *Fleet Admiral King: A Naval Record*, W. W. Norton & Co, 1952.

KIRBY, Major-General S. Woodburn, *et al, The War Against Japan*, Vol I, *History of the Second World War*, UK Military History Series, 1957 and Vol II, 1958, HMSO.

KONOYE, Fuminaro. *The Memoirs of Prince Fumınaro Konoye*, Okuyama Service, Tokyo, 1945.

KUSAKA, Ryunosuke. *The Combined Fleet*, Memoir of former Chief of Staff, Admiral Kusaka, Mainichi Shimbun, Tokyo, 1952.

LEASOR, James. *Singapore: The Battle That Changed The World*, Hodder & Stoughton, 1968.

LENTON, H. T. and COLLEDGE, J. J. *Warships of World War II*, Ian Allan, 1964.

LESLIE, Robert. *Challenge For the Pacific*, Doubleday, 1965.

LOCKWOOD, Douglas. *Australia's Pearl Harbour: Darwin 1942*, Cassell Australia, 1966.

LORD, Walter. *Incredible Victory*, New York, 1968.

MACDONALD, Scot. *Evolution of Aircraft Carriers*, 1964.

MACDONNELL, J. E. *Valiant Occasions*, Constable, 1956.

MACINTYRE, Captain Donald. *Fighting Admiral*, Evans Bros. 1961.

MACINTYRE, Captain Donald. *The Battle For The Pacific*, Batsford, 1966.

MERRILL, James M. *Target Tokyo: The Halsey-Doolittle Raid*, Rand McNally, 1964.

MILLOT, Bernard. *The Battle of the Coral Sea*, Ian Allan, 1974.

MORISON, Rear Admiral Samuel Eliot. *The Two-Ocean War: A Short History of the US Navy in The Second World War,* Little, Brown & Co, 1963.

MORISON, Rear Admiral Samuel Eliot, *History of United States Naval Operations in World War II*, Little, Brown & Co, Vol III *The Rising Sun in the Pacific 1931–April 1942* Vol IV *Coral Sea, Midway and Submarine Actions, May–August* 1942.

MORTON, Louis. *Strategy and Command: The First Two Years*, United States Army in World War II, *The War in the Pacific*, Vol 10, Office of the Chief of Military History, 1962.

MOSLEY, Leonard. *Hirohito: Emperor of Japan*, Weidenfeld & Nicolson, 1966.

POTTER, E. B. (Ed.) and NIMITZ, Chester W. *The Great Sea War,* Prentice-Hall, 1960.

POTTER, John Deane. *Admiral of the Pacific: The Life of Yamamoto*, Heinemann, 1965. The US edition by The Viking Press is sub-titled *The Man Who Menaced America*.

PRATT, Fletcher. *Fleet Against Japan*, Harper, 1946.

REYNOLDS, Clark G. *The Fast Carriers*, McGraw-Hill, 1968.

REYNOLDS, Quentin. *The Amazing Mr. Doolittle*, Cassell, 1954.

ROHWER, J. and HUMMELCHEN, G. *Chronology of the War at Sea*, 1939–1942, Vol I, Ian Allan.

ROSCOE, Theodore. *United States Destroyer Operations in* World War II, US Naval Institute, 1953.

ROSCOE, Theodore. *United States Submarine Operations in* World War II, US Naval Institute, 1948.

ROSKILL, Captain S. W. History of the Second World War Series. *The War At Sea 1939–1945*, Vols I and II, HMSO.

ROSKILL, Captain S. W. *A Merchant Fleet in War 1939–1945*, Collins, 1962.

SAUNDERS, H. St. G. *The Fight Avails: Royal Air Force 1939–1945*, HMSO, 1945.

SAUNDERS, H. St. G. *Valiant Voyaging*, 1948.

SHERMAN, Admiral Frederick C. *Combat Command: The American Aircraft Carriers in the Pacific War*, Dutton, 1950.

SHERROD, Robert. *History of Marine Corps Aviation in World War II*, USGPO, Washington, 1952.

SHIGEMITSU, Mamoru. *Japan and Her Destiny*, Hutchinson.

SMITH, S. E. (Compiler and Editor). *The United States Navy in World War II*, Morrow, 1966.

SMITH, William War. *Midway: Turning Point of the Pacific*, Crowell, 1966.

TAKAGI, Sokichi. *Taiheiyo Kaisen-shi* (History of Naval Battles in the Pacific). Iwanami Shinso, Tokyo, 1949.

TAYLER, Theodore. *The Magnificent Mitscher*, W. W. Norton & Co, 1954.

TERASAKI, Ryuji. *Navy Spirit: Life of Commander Jisaburo Ozawa*, Tokuma Shoten, Tokyo, 1967.

THOMAS, David A. *Battle of the Java Sea*, André Deutsch, 1968.

TOLAND, John. *But Not in Shame: The Six Months After Pearl Harbor*, Random House, 1961.

TOLAND, John. *The Rising Sun: The Decline and Fall of The Japanese Empire, 1936–1945*, Cassell, 1970.

UKAGI, Matome. *Record of Sea Battles*, Diary of the late Vice Admiral Matome Ukagi, 2 vols, compiled by Rear Admirals Kanji Ogawa and Toshiyuki Yokoi, Nippon Shuppen, Kyodo, Tokyo, 1952–3.

WATERS, Sydney D. *The New Zealand Navy*, Wellington, 1956.
WATTS, A. J. and GORDON, B. G. *The Imperial Japanese Navy*, Macdonald & Co, 1971.
WHEELER, Gerald E. *Prelude to Pearl Harbor: The US Navy and the Far East 1921–1931*, University of Missouri Press, 1965.
WIGMORE, Lionel. *Australia in the War of 1939–1945*, Series 1 (Army) Vol IV, *The Japanese Thrust*, Australian War Memorial, 1959.
WOODWARD, L. *British Foreign Policy in the Second World War*, HMSO, 1962.

REPORTS, DOCUMENTS, PAMPHLETS & ARTICLES

Action Report, Crudiv 6 (WDC 160997).
Action Report, USS *Lexington*, May 1942.
Action Report, Operations, Actions and Sinking of USS *Langley*, 22 February–5 March 1942.
Action Report, Task Force 17, Battle of the Coral Sea, 4–8 May 1942.
Action Report, USS *Chicago*, May 1942.
Action Stations! HMS Dorsetshire. Compiled and edited by John Creasey, John Lang Ltd, n.d.
Agar Papers: The papers of Captain A. W. S. Agar VC, Imperial War Museum, including reports of survivors from HMS *Dorsetshire*.
Air Group Report, USS *Lexington*, 11 May 1942.
Allied Translator & Interpreter Section (ATIS): Supreme Command of the Allied Powers, Far East: translations of captured Japanese documents etc:
—Enemy Publication No. 6: 27 March 1944, containing *inter alia Naval Operations in Hawaii and Malaya*, and *Sinking of* Prince of Wales.
—Research Report No. 132, December 1945: *Japan's Decision to Fight*.
—Document 1626 9A, April 1946, *Battle of the Coral Sea*.
—Document 18665F (WD 156) *MO Operation* (Tulagi, Port Moresby, Nauru-Ocean Invasion Operations).
—14 May 1948, *Invasion of the Dutch East Indies*.
Battle of the Coral Sea, 1 May to 11 May inclusive 1942, Strategical and tactical analysis, US Naval War College, made available to S. E. Morison: see his *History*, Vol IV, page 21.
Damage Report, USS William B. Preston, 1 May 1942.
Far Eastern Quarterly, Vol 9, May 1950: 'Check List of Seized Japanese Records in the National Archives' by James W. Morley.
International Military Tribunal for the Far East: The Tokyo Trials: A Functional Index to the Proceedings (IMTFE), University of Michigan Press, 1957, by Professor Paul S. Dull and Michael T. Umemura.
Japanese Aircraft and Armaments, Office of Chief of Air Staff, Intelligence, No. 44, March 1944.

Japanese Naval and Merchant Shipping Losses During World War II by all Causes, USGPO, Washington, February, 1947.

Letter, Rear Admiral Sir John Crace to Admiral Sir Guy Royle, 1st Naval Member, Australian Navy Board, 12 May, 1942.

Naval Operations off Ceylon, Battle Summary No. 15, Historical Section, Public Records Office, No. ADM/15694.

Officer Biography Sheets, Department of the Navy, Washington.

Operational Experience of Fast Carrier Task Forces in World War II, Weapons Systems Evaluations Group, WSEG Study No. 4, 15 August 1951.

Operations in the Eastern Theatre Based on India from March 1942 to December 1942, Despatch by Field Marshal Earl Wavell, *Supplement* to *The London Gazette*, 17 September 1947.

Operations in the North Coral Sea 5th–11th May 1942, Report by Rear Admiral John Crace to Australian Navy Board.

Proceedings by Admiral Sir James Somerville.

Profile Warship No. 12 – Kongo, Profile Publications Ltd, Windsor, and No. 37 – *Takao.*

Report by Paymaster Commander (S) E. F. McNeil-Smith, Imperial War Museum, on sinking of HMS *Hermes.*

Report and *Supplementary Report* by Captain A. W. S. Agar VC, 8.4.42 and 13.4.42 to C-in-C Eastern Fleet.

Supplemental Report of Certain Phases in the War Against Japan, derived from interrogation of Senior Naval Commanders at Truk, known as 'Truk Report'.

Tabular Record of Movements (TROM). I am indebted to Professor Paul S. Dull, Professor Emeritus of History, University of Oregon for the following information. The source of TROMS is the Operational Archives Branch, Navy Historical Center, Washington. TROMS for battleships, heavy and light cruisers (with some missing) are in English on microfilm reels AR 2–74–F–108. The reel for carriers is too poor for use. The reels for destroyers, JD 204–JD 205, with thirty-three destroyers missing, 'are written in execrable cursive Japanese'. The Japanese Defence Agency has officially published TROMS in Japanese: the Indian Ocean raid is in Boe Ken Shujo (BKS), *Kaigum Shinko Sakusen*, Vol 23, with a separate supplement and track charts: the Coral Sea is in BKS, *Kaigun Sakusa*, Vol 39 Pt 1, also with supplement. The microfilmed material 'will take a specialist in naval Japanese and cursive handwriting to read'.

United States Naval Administration in World War II, DCNO (Air): 'Air Task Organisation in the Pacific Ocean Areas, Ship-based Aircraft', 1945.

United States Naval Institute *Proceedings*, Annapolis, Maryland:

—*Japan's Heavy Cruisers in the War*, Warren S. Howard, May 1950.

—*The Navy's War Against Japan*, E. B. Potter, August 1950.

—*The* Shokaku's, Hajime Fukaku, June 1952.

—Akagi, *Famous Japanese Carrier*, Walter L. Robinson, May 1948.
—*Papua: A Lesson in Sea Power*, Commander James C. Shaw.
—*The Carrier Task Force in World War II*, Lieutenant W. H. Hessler, November 1945.
—*The* Pecos *Died Hard*, Rear Admiral E. P. Abernethy, December 1969.
United States Navy Office of Public Relations:
Communiqués 1–300 and Pertinent Press Releases December 10 1941–March 5 1943.
United States Strategic Bombing Survey (USSBS) (Pacific) Naval Analysis Division, *Interrogation of Japanese Officials*, Volumes I and II, Op Nav P–03–100.
—Nav No. 8 *Coral Sea Battle* 7–8 May, Commander H. Sekino, Staff 6th Cruiser Squadron, and Commander M. Okumiya, Staff 2nd Flying Squadron.
—Nav No. 10 *Solomon Island Operations & Battle of Coral Sea*, Captain M. Yamaoka, Operations Officer, Staff 5th Air Flotilla.
—Nav No. 19 *Operations of the Main Body of Second Fleet.*
—Nav No. 43 *Japanese Naval Planning*, Captain T. Ohmae, Bureau of Military Affairs.
—Nav No. 50 *Aircraft Availability and Loss Reports*, Commander J. Fukamizu. It was impossible to extract from these figures accurate losses incurred during engagements and battles described in this book.
—Nav No. 80 *Japanese Naval Plans*, Fleet Admiral O. Nagano, Chief of Naval General Staff Operations April '41 – February '44.
—Nav No. 90 *Observations of Japan at War*, Admiral K. Nomura, former Ambassador to America.
—Nav No. 95 *Japanese Naval Operations New Guinea Area*, Captain T. Ohmae.
—Nav No. 97 *Air Operations by Japanese Naval Air Forces Based at Rabaul*, Captain T. Miyazaki.
—Nav No. 106 *Cape Esperance & Coral Sea Battles*, Captain K. Kijima, Chief of Staff, 6th Cruiser Squadron.
—Nav No. 115 *The Naval War in the Pacific*, Vice Admiral S. Fukudome, Chief of Staff, Combined Fleet 1940–April 1941: Chief 1st Secretary Naval General Staff, April 1941–May 1943.
—Vol I p. 539: *Japanese Notes on Battles*, Captain Y. Watanabe, Gunnery Officer, IJN *Yamato*.
War Diary, Rear Admiral Sir John Crace, Imperial War Museum.
War Diary, IJN *Shoho* (WDC 160465) 7 May 1942.

APPENDIX B

Darwin Air Strike: Losses February 1942

The following compilation lists all the losses of shipping in the port of Darwin on 19 February 1942.

The casualties aboard ships totalled 172 killed with another nineteen dying of wounds aboard the hospital ship *Manunda*. Another 330 were wounded, 200 of them seriously.

Ironically, in 1959 – seventeen years after the strike – the Fujita Salvage Company of Osaka salvaged the following wrecks and towed them back to Japan for scrap: *British Motorist, Mauna Loa, Meigs, Neptuna* and USS *Peary*.

Ship	*Tons*	*Nationality*	*Fate*
British Motorist	6,891	UK tanker	Capsized and sank
Meigs	12,568	US transport	Bombed and sank
Mauna Loa	5,436	US transport	Bombed and sank
Neptuna	5,952	Australian	Exploded and sank
Zealandia	6,683	Australian	Bombed and sank
Peary	1,190	US destroyer	Bombed and sank
Mavie	14	RAN lugger	Sunk by near miss
Kelat		Coastal hulk	Gunned and sank
The following ships suffered varying degrees of damage:			
Manunda	9,115	Australian hospital ship	Severely damaged
Barossa	4,239	Australian	Bombed and burnt
Port Mar	5,551	US transport	Near missed & beached
Tulagi	2,300	Australian	Near missed & beached
Admiral Halstead	3,289	US freighter	Near missed & damaged
Platypus	3,455	RAN depot ship	Gunned and damaged
Swan	1,060	RAN sloop	Near missed & damaged
Gunbar	481	Minesweeper	Gunned and damaged
Benjamin Franklin	7,034	Norwegian	Near missed & damaged
William B. Preston	1,190	US tender	Bombed and damaged
Kara Kara	252	Boom vessel	Gunned and damaged
Kookaburra	730	Boom vessel	Gunned and damaged
Kangaroo	730	Boom vessel	Gunned and damaged
Coongoola	34	Motor boat	Gunned and damaged

The following ships were sunk outside Darwin:

Don Isidro	3,200	US supply ship	Bombed, burnt and beached
Florence D	2,638	US supply ship	Bombed and sank

APPENDIX C

Allied Shipping Losses South of Java

27.2.42	USS *Langley*	11,050 tons	USS *Stewart*	1,539 tons
1.3.42	*Toradja*	981 tons	*Enggano*	5,412 tons
	Modjokerto	8,806 tons	*Bintoehan*	1,021 tons
	Tomohon	983 tons	USS *Pecos*	14,800 tons
	USS *Edsall*	1,190 tons		
2.3.42	*Sigli*	1,579 tons	*Prominent*	2,232 tons
	HMS *Stronghold*	905 tons	USS *Pillsbury*	1,190 tons
3.3.42	HMS *Scott Harley*	620 tons	USS *Asheville*	1,270 tons
4.3.42	HMAS *Yarra*	1,060 tons	HMS *Anking*	3,472 tons
	HMS *Francol*	5,620 tons	HMS *MMS 51*	255 tons
7.3.42	*Poelau Bras*	9,278 tons		

Note 1: Four more vessels were sunk by submarines in this area during the period under review:

Parigi	1,172 tons	Submarine *I-2*	1.3.42
Siantar	8,667 tons	Submarine *I-1*	3.3.42
Merkus	865 tons	Submarine *I-62*	4.3.42
Le Maire	3,271 tons	Submarine *I-7*	4.3.42

Note 2: Another two vessels were captured by Japanese warships:

Tjisaroea	7,089 tons	4.3.42
Duymaer van Twist	1,030 tons	4.3.42

Total Losses = 95,357 tons

APPENDIX D

Shipping Losses at Tjilatjap 3–7 March 1942

4.3.42	*Manipi*	536 tons	Air attack
	Kidoel	775 tons	Air attack
	Tydeman	1,160 tons	Air attack
5.3.42	*Rokan*	563 tons	Air attack
	Pasir	1,187 tons	Air attack
	Tohiti	982 tons	Air attack
	Barentz	4,819 tons	Air attack
	Canopus	773 tons	Air attack
	Sipora	1,594 tons	Scuttled
6.3.42	*Mandar*	536 tons	Air attack
	Dajak	174 tons	Air attack
	Atjeh	495 tons	Air attack
	Sipirok	1,787 tons	Scuttled
	Reteh	513 tons	Scuttled
	Mampawa	468 tons	Scuttled
	Makian	537 tons	Scuttled
	Rengat	512 tons	Scuttled
	Nias	75 tons	Scuttled
	Kampar	574 tons	Scuttled
	Asahan	75 tons	Scuttled
	Valk	1,018 tons	Scuttled as blockship
	Poseidon	696 tons	Set on fire
7.3.42	*Alfoer*	473 tons	Scuttled

Note 1: The survey ship *Tydeman* was subsequently salvaged by the Japanese later in the month and she was re-named *Choyo*.

Note 2: The auxiliary minelayer *Ram* of 2,400 tons still under construction was also sunk.

Total Losses = 22,722 tons

APPENDIX E

Indian Ocean Naval Operations: Sinkings April 1942

(A) NAGUMO'S CARRIER STRIKING FORCE SINKINGS:

Heavy Cruiser	HMS *Cornwall*	9,750 tons
	HMS *Dorsetshire*	9,975 tons
Light Carrier	HMS *Hermes*	10,850 tons
Destroyer	HMAS *Vampire*	1,090 tons
	HMS *Tenedos*	905 tons
Corvette	HMS *Hollyhock*	925 tons
Armed Merchant Cruiser	HMS *Hector*	11,198 tons
Merchantship	*British Sergeant*	5,868 tons
	Athelstone	5,571 tons
		56,132 tons

(B) OZAWA'S MALAYA FORCE SINKINGS OF MERCHANT SHIPS IN THE BAY OF BENGAL

Van de Capellan	2,073 tons	*Gandara*	5,281 tons
Dardanus	7,726 tons	*Malda*	9,066 tons
Silksworth	4,921 tons	*Sinkiang*	2,646 tons
Dagfred	4,434 tons	*Harpasa*	5,082 tons
Bienville	5,491 tons	*Hermod*	1,515 tons
Banjoewangi	1,279 tons	*Batavia*	1,279 tons
Taksang	3,471 tons	*Exmoor*	4,999 tons
Autolycus	7,621 tons	*Indora*	6,622 tons
Shinkiang	2,441 tons	*Elsa*	5,381 tons

Total 93,260 tons

(C) SINKINGS BY JAPANESE SUBMARINES IN THE INDIAN OCEAN

Fultala	5,051 tons
Bahadur	5,424 tons
Washingtonian	6,617 tons
Clan Ross	5,897 tons
Glenshiel	9,415 tons

Total 32,404 tons

In addition three unidentified sailing ships and one other unknown ship all of undisclosed tonnages were sunk by submarines during this period.

APPENDIX F

Main Features of Principal Ships in Indian Ocean and Coral Sea

Class	*Ship*	*Tonnage*	*Completed/ Converted*	*Main Armaments*	*Fate*
US abbreviations have been adopted to distinguish ship types as follows: CV = Carrier CA = Heavy Cruiser BB = Battleship CL = Light cruiser					
IMPERIAL JAPANESE NAVY					
CV	*Akagi*	36,500	1927/38	91 planes	Sunk Midway 1942
	Kaga	38,200	1928/35	90 planes	Sunk Midway 1942
	Hiryu	17,300	1939	73 planes	Sunk Midway 1942
	Soryu	15,900	1937	71 planes	Sunk Midway 1942
	Shokaku }	25,675	1941	84 planes	Sunk June 1944
	Zuikaku }				Sunk October 1944
	Shoho	11,262	1939	30 planes	Sunk Coral Sea 1942
BB					
	Haruna	32,156	1915/34 }	8 14″ 14 6″	Sunk July 1945
	Hiei	32,350	1914/40 }		Sunk Nov. 1942
	Kirishima	31,980	1915/36 }		Scuttled Nov. 1942
	Kongo	31,720	1913/37 }		Sunk Nov. 1944

CA	*Atago*				Torpedoed 23.10.1944
	Chokai			10 8″	Torpedoed 25.10.1944
	Maya	13,400	1932	8 5″	Torpedoed 23.10.1944
	Takao				Surrendered 1945
	Haguro				Sunk 16.5.1945
	Myoko			10 8″	Surrendered 1945
	Nachi	13,380	1929/40	8 5″	Bombed 5.11.1944
	Ashigara				Torpedoed 8.6.1945
	Kinugasa			6 8″	Sunk 14.11.1942
	Aoba	9,380	1927	4 4·7″	Sunk 28.7.1945
	Kako	9,000	1926	6 8″	Sunk 11.10.1942
	Furutaka	9,150	1926	4 4·7″	Torpedoed 10.8.1942
	Chikuma		1939		Torpedoed 25.10.1944
	Tone	11,215	1938	8 8″ 8 5″	Sunk 24.7.1945
	Mogami		1935		Bombed 25.10.1944
	Mikuma		1935	10 8″	Bombed Midway 1942
	Kumano	12,400	1937	8 5″	Bombed 25.11.1944
	Suzuya		1937		Scuttled 25.10.1944
CL	*Yubari*	2,890	1923	6 5.5″	Torpedoed 27.4.1944

ROYAL NAVY & ROYAL AUSTRALIAN NAVY

CV	*Formidable*	23,000	1939	36 planes	Scrapped 1953
	Illustrious	23,000	1939	36 planes	Scrapped 1956
	Indomitable	23,000	1940	36 planes	Scrapped 1955
	Hermes	10,850	1919	15 planes	Sunk Indian Ocean 1942
BB	*Warspite*	30,600	1913/35	8 15″ 8 6″	Wrecked 1947
	Ramilles		1916	8 15″	Scrapped 1948/9
	Resolution	29,150	1915	12 6″	Scrapped 1948
	Revenge		1915	8 4″	Scrapped 1948
	Royal Sovereign		1915		Scrapped 1948

US abbreviations have been adopted to distinguish ship types as follows: CV = Carrier CA = Heavy Cruiser
BB = Battleship CL = Light cruiser

Class	Ship	Tonnage	Completed/ Converted	Main Armaments	Fate
CA	*Australia*	9,870	1927	8 8" 8 4"	Scrapped 1955
	Cornwall	9,750	1926		Sunk Indian Ocean 1942
	Dorsetshire	9,975	1929		Sunk Indian Ocean 1942
	Exeter	8,390	1929	6 8" 4 4"	Sunk 1.3.1942
CL	*Hobart*	7,105	1934	8 6" 8 4"	Scrapped 1962
	Perth	6,980	1934	8 6" 8 4"	Sunk 1.3.1942
UNITED STATES NAVY					
CV	*Lexington*	33,000	1925	91 planes	Sunk Coral Sea 1942
	Yorktown	19,900	1936	84 planes	Sunk Midway 1942
	Enterprise				Scrapped 1958
Tender	*Langley*	11,050	1912/37	4 5" 55 planes	Sunk South of Java 1942
CA	*New Orleans*	9,950	1933		Scrapped 1959
	Minneapolis				Scrapped 1960
	Astoria			9 8" 8 5"	Sunk Savo Is. 1942
	Chester	9,200	1929		Scrapped 1959
	Portland	9,800	1932		Scrapped 1959
	Houston	9,050	1929		Sunk Sunda St. 1942
	Chicago	9,300	1930		Sunk Coral Sea 1943
CL	*Marblehead*	7,050	1923	10 6" 8 3"	Scrapped 1946
ROYAL NETHERLANDS NAVY					
CL	*De Ruyter*	6,470	1935	7 5.9"	Sunk Java Sea 1942
	Java	6,670	1921	10 5.9"	Sunk Java Sea 1942

APPENDIX G

Carrier Aircraft in the Coral Sea 1942

(A) JAPANESE

Mitsubishi A6M-2 Type O Model 21 ZERO fighter

One of the world's most famous aircraft. In the same class as the European trio Hurricane, Spitfire and Messerschmitt Bf 109. More than 11,000 of all variants of the Zero were produced during the war. Everything, including protection, was sacrificed to performance. Constructed of an ultra-light alloy, it became an invincible interceptor carrier aircraft with a magnificent performance, establishing undoubted superiority over US adversaries in the early period of the Pacific war.

Wing Span	39′ 00″ (12.00 m)
Length	29′ 05″ (9.06 m)
Weight Unloaded	3696 lb (1680 kg)
Engine	Nakajime Sakae 12,940 HP
Maximum Speed	331 mph
Climbing	18,000 ft in 7 minutes
Range	1470 miles
Armaments	2 × 20 mm cannons
	2 × 7.7 mm machine guns
	250 lb bomb

Aichi 99 VAL D 3A.1 Dive Bomber

The design of this two-seater dive bomber was based mainly upon the famous Junkers Ju 87. In action against the Allies the Val earned a deservedly high reputation for the high number of direct hits, made possible by its ability to dive at a very acute angle, retain stability and adopt a low speed of descent. It was superior in range and bomb load to the Blackburn Skua and the Douglas Dauntless.

Wing Span	46′ 08″ (14.364 m)
Length	33′ 03″ (10.231 m)
Weight Unloaded	5 654 lb (2570 kg)
Engine	Mitsubishi Kinsei 54 1300 HP

Maximum Speed	267 mph
Climbing	9000 ft in 5 minutes
Range	930 miles
Armaments	3 × 7.7 mm machine guns 1 × 500 lb bomb and 2 × 120 lb or 4 × 120 lb bombs

Nakajima 97 B5N.1 Type 97 KATE Bomber

The Kate was the first low wing monoplane of its class constructed entirely of metal with a whole range of qualities superior to its rivals. Two types of the Kate were designed, the first as a straightforward medium- to high-level bomber with a 6 bomb pay load: the second as a low-level torpedo bomber designed to launch a 1600 lb self-propelled weapon. It takes its name from the year 1937, or 2597 in the Japanese calendar. It was in the same class as the Fairey Battle and showed the same vulnerability to fighter attack.

Wing Span	50′ 05″ (15.518 m)
Length	32′ 11″ (10.340 m)
Weight Unloaded	5013 lb (2,2,79 kg)
Engine	Nakajima Sakae II 1000 HP
Maximum Speed	235 mph
Range	634 miles
Crew	3
Armaments	1 × 7.7 mm machine gun 1600 lb torpedo or 1 × 1000 lb bomb or equivalent in smaller loads.

(B) AMERICAN

Grumman F4F.3 WILDCAT Fighter

In 1940 a large number of Wildcats were introduced as interceptor monoplanes into the US Navy and were believed to be the peak in aircraft design achievement – until they encountered the Zero. The Wildcat was solidly built with a good deal of protection detracting from its performance which was made to appear clumsy and slow. Given height advantage and an experienced pilot the Wildcat became a destructive weapon. It proved to be a useful workhorse and with its variants no less than 8000 were produced by the Eastern Aircraft Division of General Motors.

Wing Span	37′ 07″ (11 58 m)
Length	28′ 05″ (8.76 m)
Weight Unloaded	5335 lb (2425 kg)
Engine	Wright R.1830–76 1200 HP
Maximum Speed	329 mph
Range	1689 miles
Armaments	4 × 12.7 mm machine guns + bombs totalling 200 lb

Douglas SBD DAUNTLESS Dive Bomber

This splendid aircraft appeared in 1939 and became the standard US Navy dive bomber. It was solidly built; it served primarily as a dive bomber but secondarily as a reconnaissance aircraft, and once its bombs had been used, the Dauntless served adequately as a fighter. It was a manoeuvrable aircraft with excellent diving stability to ensure accuracy of bombing, but its horizontal speed was low.

Wing Span	41′ 01″ (12.652 m)
Length	31′ 09″ (9.785 m)
Weight Unloaded	4580 lb (2082 kg)
Engine	Wright R.1820–52 1000 HP
Maximum Speed	246 mph
Climbing	9000 ft in 6 m. 40 seconds
Range	1100 miles
Crew	2 men
Armaments	2 × 12.7 mm machine guns 2 × 7.7 mm machine guns 1 × 900 lb + 2 × 90 lb bombs

Douglas TBD.1 DEVASTATOR Torpedo Bomber

By 1941 the Devastator was an out-dated aircraft. It was designed in 1934 and came into service three years later as the first all metal monoplane of its class. It was too slow, it lacked protection and had none of the qualities demanded of the torpedo bomber in 1941. It was an easy prey to Zero fighters. It is sad that the torpedoes it carried were so often faulty: thus it was often doomed as an effective weapon even before it took off. The heavy losses of the Devastator in the Coral Sea and Midway Battles finally put paid to its career.

Wing Span	49′ 06″ (15.24 m)
Length	34′ 08″ (10.67 m)
Weight Unloaded	6168 lb (2,804 kg)

Engine	Pratt & Whitney R.1830–64
	900 HP
Maximum Speed	205 mph
Climbing	700 ft per minute
Range	652 miles
Crew	3 men
Armaments	2 × 7.7 mm machine guns
	1 torpedo or 900 lb bomb

Index

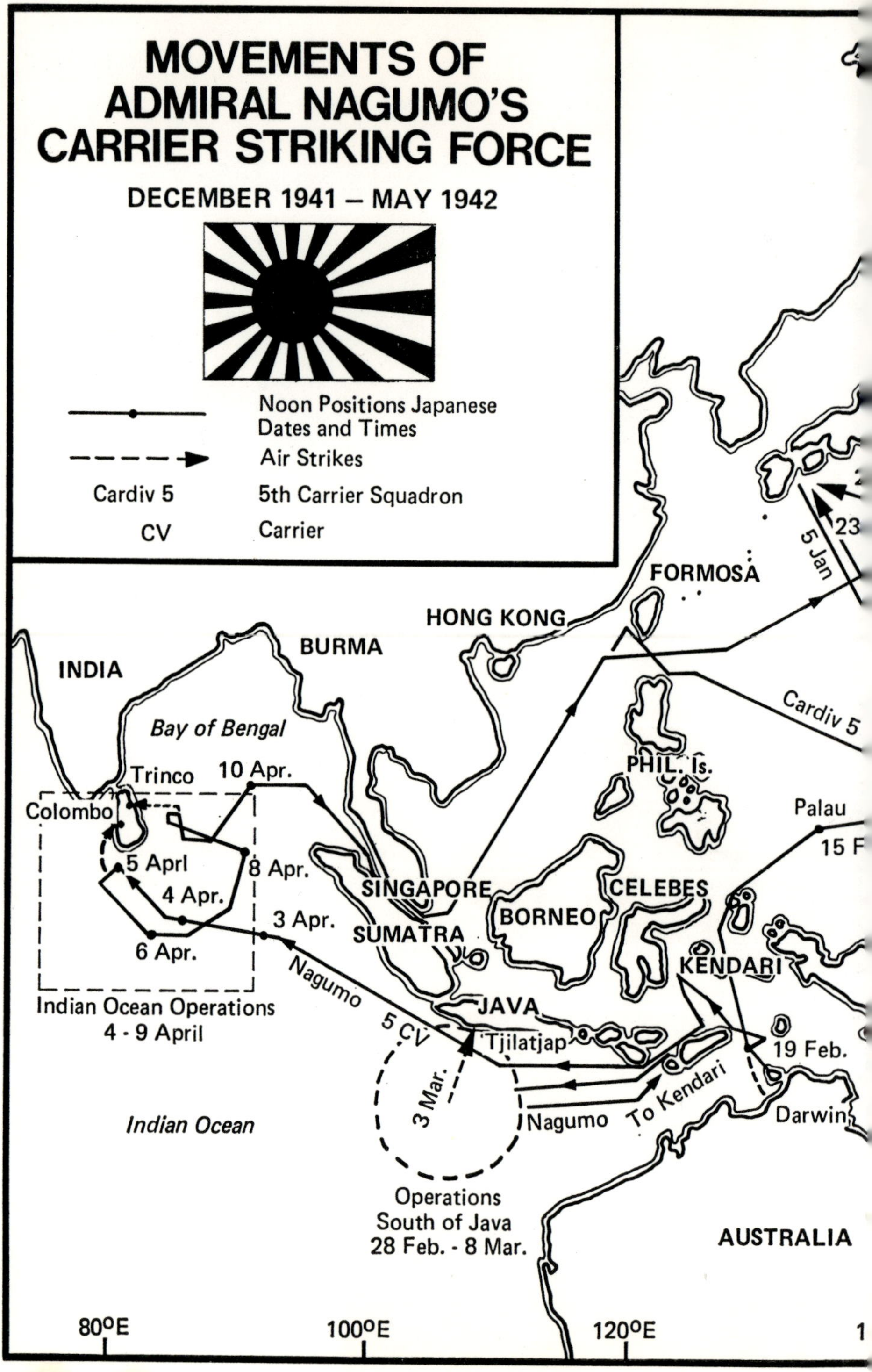
MOVEMENTS OF
ADMIRAL NAGUMO'S
CARRIER STRIKING FORCE
DECEMBER 1941 – MAY 1942
Noon Positions Japanese
Dates and Times
Air Strikes
Cardiv 5
5th Carrier Squadron
CV
Carrier
FORMOSA
HONG KONG
BURMA
INDIA
Bay of Bengal
Trinco
10 Apr.
Colombo
5 Aprl
8 Apr.
4 Apr.
3 Apr.
6 Apr.
Indian Ocean Operations
4 - 9 April
PHIL. Is.
Palau
SINGAPORE
SUMATRA
BORNEO
CELEBES
KENDARI
JAVA
Tjilatjap
Nagumo
5 CV
3 Mar.
Nagumo
To Kendari
19 Feb.
Darwin
Cardiv 5
5 Jan
23
Indian Ocean
Operations
South of Java
28 Feb. - 8 Mar.
AUSTRALIA
80°E
100°E
120°E